Real
Glasgow

This book is dedicated to my uncle
Jack Hart (1929-2014)
A Real Glasgow Man

Real
Glasgow

Ian Spring

SERIES EDITOR: PETER FINCH

Seren is the book imprint of
Poetry Wales Press Ltd
Nolton Street, Bridgend, Wales

www.serenbooks.com
facebook.com/SerenBooks
Twitter: @SerenBooks

ISBN 978-1-78172-311-1

A CIP record for this title is available from
the British Library

The publisher works with the financial assistance
of the Welsh Books Council

Printed by Short Run Press Ltd, Exeter

CONTENTS

CENTRAL

SOUTH

WEST

POEMS AND PROSE

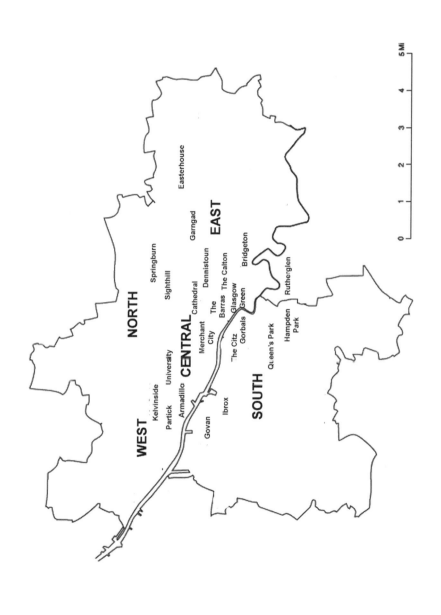

NORTH

WEST

CENTRAL

EAST

SOUTH

Easterhouse

Garngad

Springburn

Sighthill

Cathedral

Dennistoun

The Calton

Bridgeton

Merchant City

The Barras

Glasgow Green

Rutherglen

The Citz

Gorbals

Hampden Park

Queen's Park

Kelvinside

University

Partick

Armadillo

Govan

Ibrox

0 1 2 3 4 5 Mi

SERIES EDITOR'S INTRODUCTION

Glasgow is not Edinburgh and that's putting it mildly. Flying into the airport you can tell. Scotland's sister capital has a size and strength that the official government seat simply does not possess. Glasgow's urbanity begins miles out, high rise marking the periphery, the smoke silenced and the wrecked industry cleared. If you imagined this post-industrial place was a mere working-class suburb then you were wrong. This is the second city of Queen Victoria's reign and it's still going strong.

Glasgu, as this place was called in early Scots, or Glaschu as the Gaels had it, started life as a monastic village near the banks of the river Clyde. Here, in the sixth century, St Kentigern established a religious site. The name in the Gaelic means green place. It's still there in Glasgow Green by the Clyde river where a hidden tributary, the Molindinar Burn, discharges from its urban pipe. Kentigern was known colloquially as Mungo in the early Welsh they spoke in these lowlands back then. His bones are in a much venerated crypt right under Glasgow's ancient cathedral.

But it wasn't simply veneration that built this place. It was the slow creep of civilisation. This first made the town a bishopric and then established an early university. The navigable Clyde waters gave Glasgow trade. Initially sugar, then cotton, linen and tobacco. Eighteenth century merchants – the Tobacco Lords – dredged the Clyde to build the salt water port. At its height more than half of Britain's tobacco came through here.

The roar of the industrial revolution manifested itself in Glasgow like no other place. Grime, grit, unceasing noise, a bedlam of dust. Canals brought in coal and iron ore. Associated trades mushroomed. There were rolling mills, foundries and steam hammers everywhere. By the nineteenth century Glasgow was building half of Britain's ships and at least a quarter of the entire world's steam locomotives. On the back of this dirty, industrial activity came textiles, garments, carpets and chemicals. Population expanded to overtake royal Edinburgh as the conurbation of Glasgow inflated itself towards the grimy apogee of Victoria's Empire.

Walking the city you get an immediate sense of a dishevelled nineteenth century still present among the twenty-first's repairs, replacements, regrowths and restorations. Industrial decline, which started between the wars and accelerated towards almost complete collapse during the pre-Thatcher years has been cleaned up and painted over. What's left is a real city: a mix of determined modernism and revived fortune. The place is Scotland's powerhouse. It is still the third most economically successful municipality in Britain.

Heavy industry may no longer be writ large here but work certainly is. The Clyde shipyards may have reduced from twenty-two to two but the place still builds. At BAE Systems they make destroyers and large sections of Britain's new giant aircraft carriers. You can walk there, taking the footpath on the river's north side below the Castlebank apartments and stare right into the dry docks.

Elsewhere in the city biosciences, light manufacturing, financial and business services, and healthcare have blossomed. So too, and amazingly given the relative impenetrability to outsiders of the local speech, have call centres. Universities – Glasgow has three – seem to be building new lecture halls and accommodation blocks on every corner.

This city is enormous by British standards and with its own underground metro system, rocketing urban renewal programme and burgeoning cultural industry sector. It was created European Capital of Culture in 1990 and does not seem to have looked back. It was also one of only four places in Scotland to vote overwhelmingly for independence in the 2014 referendum. The Saltire flies everywhere. The sense on the streets is not of cloying nostalgic nationalism seeking the rebirth of a lost past but a genuine air of great distance from the London centre of government. Who needs them when we've got J.G. Ballard's future present in the new architecture of the west, the revitalised Merchant Quarter, the splendours of George Square and the wonders of the Barras.

The route here has not been easy. The council, Labour controlled for decades and during the past five years under the controversial leadership of marathon-running former priest Gordon Matheson, often finds itself at odds with the population. Tory Lite, it's been called. Plans for the eleven statues in George Square, Walter Scott on his column, Robbie Burns gazing into the distance, most of Scotland's heroes plus a young Queen Victoria seated on a horse and Prince Albert galloping, all to be removed and replaced with stalls, cafés and a water feature did not go down well. Given Glasgow's propensity for driving rain this is not surprising. A further proposal to launch the Commonwealth Games (which Glasgow mounted in 2014) with the sequenced demolition of five

60s tower blocks was abandoned after public outrage threatened to draw more attention than the audacity of the original proposal. The six north Glasgow Red Road flats would be reduced to one, all falling within 15 seconds of each other. The remaining tower, silhouetted against the dust, would continue as a residence for Glasgow's allocation of asylum seekers.

High on the concrete sides of one of the University of Strathclyde's towers at the back of George Street is a slogan writ large, writ giant in fact. People Make Glasgow. I walk past it on my way to see Ian Spring. 'That slogan is everywhere,' he tells me. It is. Bus stops, shop windows, leaflets, sides of buildings right across the city. This is a place that runs on words. Back in the eighties it was Glasgow's Miles Better, followed in the nineties by Glasgow, Scotland With Style. They do this in Scotland. Edinburgh is Incredinburgh. Local wits have suggested that Glasgow: Bonny with Clyde, or Glasgow – Still Riveting might have been improved choices.

Ian, true Scot, folk music scholar, author among many other things of *Phantom Village, Myth of the New Glasgow*, was born here – round the corner from Tennents Brewery. The city runs in his veins. To see the place in a day, he has advised a bus tour to get round including taking in the smooth and artistic West End, rich in galleries, the art college and enough Rennie Macintosh to sink a Clyde-built battleship. Glasgow's cultural importance (for the world and not just Scotland) rides near the surface. It's an artistic hub. BBC Scotland, Scottish Opera, Scottish Ballet and the National Theatre of Scotland are all based here. Follow that with a walk around Glasgow's atmosphere-rich Necropolis. This is the Victorian city of the dead built in what was once known as Fir Park atop the hill. Here John Knox, religious reformer, stands on his column, viewing both the Glasgow past and the Glasgow future.

Going back down towards the river, the roads wind through parts of the city as yet un touched by redevelopment. Calton, an area which houses the market known as The Barras, is a sort of lino shop and chippie city. It's home to Scotland's largest weekend street market. It would feel threatening late at night but it's easy mid-day when I get there. Barrowland Park, a scrub of grass with a technicolor-striped path down its centre displays the names of thirty-years' worth of bands who have played at the celebrated Barrowland Ballroom. It's a roster of rock music to die for. Gillian Welsh, Funeral For A Friend, Oasis, Elvis Costello, Placebo, Simple

Minds. The housing gives way to open space as Glasgow Green comes into view. An oxygenating lung in the heart of shantytown. The slums are vanishing although they haven't all gone yet. 'Not long ago this city has the highest incidence of knife crime anywhere in Europe,' Ian says. 'Things have improved but Glasgow has yet to solve all its problems.' There is still a sectarian divide. There are areas where nine out of ten adults are on benefits. Heart disease is through the roof. But in the green fields of the people's park, not here.

On the river is a weir marking the highest point reached by tides. You can throw a stone across easily. To the west the waters widen progressively. Several miles on, reached easily on the subway, is the Zaha Hadid designed Riverside Museum. This curved twenty-first century building is, like much else in this wonderful place, totally free to enter. Here are retired steam trains, automobiles and motorbikes, trams, vans and buses along with a mock-up of a turn of the nineteenth century Glasgow pub. Wooden. Polished. No seats, everyone stood. Two taps, beer and whisky, nothing else. Women not admitted.

Outside floats a tall ship, the *Glenlee*, a barque with towering masts. Beyond it operates a ferry crossing the short width of the Clyde River. To use it there's no charge. On the south bank lies Govan, a hard-faced working class district that once built all those ships but now sits halfway between slum and regeneration. More out of work than in. Betting shops, charity shops, Poundland. The streets are lined with red sandstone tenements, the four and five storey Victorian answer to rapidly expanding populations. In Govan Old Church, squashed in by the remains of now closed dry-docks, is strong evidence of the city's Celtic past. Carved Celtic crosses, slabs with interlaced sides, and five Viking hogback stones looking like Klingon arrivals from another dimension. Charge for entry: none. At the Fairfield Shipyards they've restored the offices to house a display of the place's history. The 85-year old volunteer attendant asks me if I ever worked in the Govan yards. My accent must be slipping.

Glasgow's resilience and willingness to change keeps it at the heart of the new Scotland. I haven't found yet the stumbling drunkenness of James Kelman's *How Late It Was, How Late* nor discovered the Unthank Hell as Alasdair Gray portrays this city in *Lanark*. I have, however, witnessed the speech Tom Leonard uses in his dialect verse. To work out what's happening stand there like a radio and tune yourself in. This Glaswegian I'm hearing is English, after all. It's just been on a journey. Quite a one.

Ian Spring's engaging and information-packed *Real Glasgow* stretches well beyond the limits of the Glasgow I've witnessed. From the outer high rise suburbs to the metropolitan centre, from the grit to the glamour, from the Clyde to the sea, quite a journey too.

Peter Finch

INTRODUCTION

Glasgow Citizenship Test

Whit
ginger's
made o
girders?

Whit
d'ye
pit
oan yir
chips?

Whit'll
ye
hiv wi a
hauf?

Whaur'll
ye
git a
dizzy?

Whaur'll
ye
hiv a
hingy?

We
arra
whit?[1]

If you can master the patter (Glasgow patois) and the west coast lore, you might pass the Glaswegian citizenship test. The citizens of Glasgow, a large, rude industrial (or now post-industrial) city, have their own particular ways. It was once a powerhouse – the second city of the Empire; an anthology of poems about Glasgow is titled *Noise and Smoky Breath*.[2] Today the clamour of the shipyards and the steelworks and the smoking lums of endless coal fires that blackened the tenements of old grey sandstone are gone, but Glasgow is still a loud, raucous city; not for the faint-hearted. It offers you not a polite Edinburgh handshake or a tacit Aberdeen nod but a giant bear hug of a welcome (not a Glasgow kiss, which is a different thing altogether!).

So here I am in Glasgow, *the* Glasgow – well, the biggest one (there are 24 Glasgows, including one on the moon). Glasgow, the largest city in Scotland, but not the capital of the country. Someone once said 'the idea of Glasgow is bigger than the nation it inhabits' but I can't remember who. This is preying on my mind as I try to make a start to describing this hydra-headed monster of a city – a big city and not an easy place to portray in a short book. However, that is the plan: and here I am – in the Scotia Bar in Stockwell Street, pretty much in the centre of the greater urban metropolis of Glasgow.

Ostensibly, there is not much to see in Stockwell Street: a few shops tapering off from the larger stores of Argyle Street, two rather deserted car parks and the butt-end of a large glass-roofed shopping centre, a few desultory red sandstone tenements above a shop that used to be called 'Brides of Glasgow' (for years, mischievous neds would steal the letter 'B'). At the bottom, a collection of three pubs and a fairly new hotel leading down to the bridge over the river Clyde to the Southside. Yet, like a lot of Glasgow, there is a hidden history; the street is named after the stock well, once halfway up the street on the east side, at which cattle heading into the old city for market would stop to water. So the street tracks the transition of the rural to the urban city. And, now practically unnoticed (but still marked with a street sign) is a small stretch of a lane opposite the Scotia called the Goosedubbs, which also marks a sort of journey. The geese belonging to Lord Provost John Aird, so the story goes, who would, at the beginning of the eighteenth century, waddle from the Provost's house to splash in the puddles, or 'dubbs'.

Sometimes you have to dig for your history in Glasgow. Not least because, in fact, for many years, the city fathers seem to have been intent on destroying the city. If you love architecture and have tears to weep, read Frank Worsdall's *The City that Disappeared*.[3] The book is a litany of buildings demolished in Glasgow over the last two hundred years or so: medieval castles, Georgian manor houses, Victorian civic buildings, schools, churches, theatres, art nouveau-style tenements, even the entire grounds of the old seventeenth-century university. Always in the name of 'progress'.

It is the second half of the twentieth century, however, that has radically shaped the Glasgow we have today. Faced with the decaying Glasgow tenements ravaged by the depression of the 1930s, the post-war consensus was that Glasgow had to be demolished and built anew. The first such visionary scheme was mooted by the Tory city corporation in 1949. The city centre was to be razed and replaced by a series of large rectangular monolithic blocks! This project was, however, largely conceptual. Ten years later, in 1959, several grey-suited men met in Glasgow City Chambers. Among them was David Gibson, a member of the old Independent Labour Party obsessed with his personal vision of a future Glasgow.[4]

Under Gibson's leadership, Glasgow was to undergo a major demolition of its housing stock and the construction of housing schemes and, notably, multi-storey blocks in excess of any other city in the Western world. Glasgow was to be a city in the sky. The folly of this concept is apparent today as the Modernist project has, in its turn, created its own slums and social problems, and Glasgow has embraced a new project – demolishing or 'blowing down' the multi-storeys themselves.

I could recount many other examples of corporate vandalism that have plagued Glasgow: the urban motorway (extravagantly planned for a city that had a car-ownership ration of only 1:11) that was only just averted from cutting right through the city centre, the day Glasgow's vast research library, the Mitchell, put antiquarian books in a skip on the road, the neglect of listed buildings in the city centre, etc.

Of course, the city has more sense nowadays? Well no, actually. Recently, a proposal to revamp the city's George Square at the cost of £1.5m (it had, already, to my mind, been vandalised a few years earlier with the removal of the old whitebeam trees on the north side) controversially included one councillor's determination to remove the famous statues in the square and add a water feature. In this case, people power prevailed and it was scrapped. The famous Glasgow resilience and humour will no doubt be tested again in the future.

So, never relax your vigilance in Glasgow, it could disappear from under your feet! Twice I've arranged to meet friends in pubs in Glasgow only to arrive to discover that they have been demolished! Years ago, the old Eagle Inn at the back of the now demolished St Enoch's station (the shopping centre mentioned above replaced it) and, not very long ago at all, the Bay Horse. I arrived and it just wasn't there any more. I went into the pub across the road – coincidentally also a 'horse', the Iron Horse. 'Burnt down. Insurance job,' the barman said.

Online, you can find an interesting book, *The Secret Geometry of Glasgow*, by Harry Bell, a Glasgow printer who died in 2001 and privately charted what he believed was a hidden ancient archaeology of Glasgow revealed by prehistoric communication lines. The title alone seems a good metaphor for what I'm trying to do. Secrets? Well, Glasgow has them and I hope I can unearth some of them. Geometries? Some pattern is what I hope to find and, perhaps, the rigid geographic structure of the book insists on it.

So, here we are, gathered in the Scotia Bar. Me, a few friends: an artist, a local historian. Just friends, punters. Glaswegians all.

'Well,' they say to me almost accusingly, 'It's over twenty-five years since you wrote a book about Glasgow and now you intend to write a new one. Is it going to be a miserable as the last?'

Fair enough, The last book I wrote, *Phantom Village: the Myth of the New Glasgow* (1990),[5] was a sustained criticism of fake nostalgia and hyperbolic triumphalism laced with images of death and destruction.

'No,' my voice seems very small. 'I thought it would be more, well… cheerful.'

'Hmmm. And you intend to start by walking several miles around some of Glasgow's most deprived housing schemes?'

'Well,' I feel a bit more spirited, "it is going to be called *Real Glasgow* and where people live is pretty real! And someone once said 'the history of Glasgow is the history of Glasgow housing".'

Unfortunately, I can't fire up a lot of enthusiasm for this idea, so I suggest a subway pub-crawl or a night at the Grand Ole Opry or dinner at the Rogano. My friends know more than me. They still live in Glasgow. I'm an exile with a failing memory – like Joyce in Italy visualizing all the shops in O'Connell Street. Willie Gallacher is here and he knows the Scotia well.

The Scotia is a cosy sort of pub. Old oak beams, panelled walls. In the seventies, it was called Ye Olde Scotia Inn – it was later un-anglicised to the Auld Scotia Bar. Nowadays it is just the Scotia and it has a website that promises 'cosiest pub in Glasgow; cheekiest face in Scotland; biggest welcome in the world'. From the late sixties it was a noted folk music pub. Billy Connolly used to drink here and Danny Kyle, Hamish Imlach and other noted folk performers. Willie Gallacher, along with the poets Freddy Anderson and Jimmy Blackburn – who used to write under the pen name Sheldon B Finkelstein III – some years ago edited a broadsheet called *Scotia Folk*, a mixture of pub gossip, some writing and news about the Glasgow folk music scene. That is defunct, but the Scotia is still a folk and a literary pub (they have their own poet laureate) and there are glazed cabinets on the walls containing records, memorabilia and books written by regulars. One of these is *The Speil Amang Us*,[6] an anthology of writing from the Scotia resulting from a competition launched by the proprietor.

The Scotia is an institution and a place that attracts real characters. I remember some of them from the time I first discovered it. Jimmy Connelly, with his cowboy hat, Peter Feeney 'a shan gadgy',[7] Mary Murray, Andy Stewart. The resident bard, Freddy Anderson immortalised them in a poem, 'Old Scotia':

> Years ahead, let's draw the scene: an aged
> man leaves Glasgow Green, and slowly then on
> weary feet, stops for a breath in Stockwell Street.
> Then from his eye there drops a tear, recalling
>   days o' folk spent here...
>
> And cam here upstarts o' the Clyde; we douced their
> zeal an' damped their pride, spared nor conceit nor
> follish fancies, but in the wake o' Poosie Nancy's,

the 'King or Country' raised nae cheer, we a' were
jolly beggars here.[8]

The history of the Scotia in the last thirty years is also interesting.
Predominently a folk pub, for a while it was partly taken over by
The Blue Angels, a Glasgow motorcycle gang. This prompted some
of the folk regulars to decamp across the road to the Victoria Bar, a
standard sort of Glasgow pub run by a man called Kenny Moffat
who always seemed to be between one crisis and another. The
increase in customers led to a few changes, the bar was moved back
a couple of feet and, eventually the tiny Gents toilet was extended
and the back room opened up, but Kenny was gone by this time,
and so were the ornate pub mirrors from the walls. Sometime in the
late seventies, Brendan McLaughlin, a folkie who was at university
with me, had moved from being a customer to the proprietor of the
Scotia and, a bit later, had his eye on another pub across the road,
The Wee Mann's. Pat Hughes was the landlord and named it after
the his wife's maiden name 'Mann'. It was once a popular lounge
called the Popinjay, an old name for a stuffed parrot used as an
archery target. For a while it was also called The Merchant but
Brendan decided to have a competition to rename the place which
was won by local pub historian John Gorevan[9] who suggested the
Clutha Vaults. 'Clutha' was the old name for the river Clyde, a few
yards away, and also for the little boats that used to sail up and
down the Clyde mostly conveying passengers from one side to the
other. Strangely, Gorevan, claims to have discovered that the pub
was called by the same name once before and used to sell a blended
whisky called Clutha. The old Popinjay stood under an impressive
five-storey tenement, but that is long gone and the Clutha became
one of many (fewer now) Glasgow pubs that stood alone or almost
alone, their tenement hosts having deserted them.

These three pubs – the Scotia, the Victoria and the Clutha – for
a while constituted what was called Glasgow's 'folk village'. Then
the Victoria came under new ownership and went through several
incarnations, a Bavarian Bakehouse, a 'Scotch Corner' whisky bar,
then a pizza place. The owner eventually bought the Clutha and the
space between the two pubs has been knocked through at the back.
Rumour has it they would like to purchase the shop in between – a
strange wee place that has, for years, sold old sinks and toilet fit-
tings. The owner, apparently, has resolutely refused to sell.

The Clutha Vaults became the Clutha Bar and the music

changed complexion, moving from traditional to more contemporary but still hosting local bands. Then there was a bizarre, tragic twist to its history. On 29 November 2013, I was watching television news when a newsflash came through of a tragedy at the Clutha Bar. At first I didn't twig – there must be another Clutha, surely, in Australia or somewhere – but then the truth dawned. A police helicopter, patrolling the Glasgow night skies, had crashed into the roof of the pub. All three passengers of the helicopter and seven customers of the pub died. Of the dead I remember meeting one, John McGarrigle, who was involved in the poetry sessions in the Scotia. For some time the pub was cordoned off; bunches of flowers appeared in quantity around the facade. A trust fund to aid the families of the dead and to support young musicians was set up.

Then the owner, Alan Crossan, thinking about the eventual re-opening of the pub, had a great idea. He engaged two artists, with the enigmatic names of RogueOne and EJEK,[10] to paint full length murals on the external walls celebrating musicians and customers of the pub. The eventual painting featured icons of the pub's history – a boat, the Clutha No. 9, a drayman's cart – and well-known local musicians such as Billy Connolly, Alex Harvey, Gerry Rafferty and Jon Martyn (and a couple of unlikely figures who apparently did visit the pub – Woody Guthrie and Frank Zappa). Local characters also feature, Benny Lynch, the flyweight boxer who died tragically at the age of 33, 'Gentleman' Johnny Ramensky, the safe-cracker, and Jimmy Reid, the socialist activist who led the Upper Clyde Shipbuilders work-in in the 1970s.

There is an alternative history to Stockwell Street that I have not yet mentioned – a theatrical history. The Scotia Bar once stood next

to the famous Scotia Music Hall, built in 1862 which, reportedly, housed up to four thousand customers. It changed its name to the Metropole Threate in 1897 and remained so until it burned down on 29 October 1961. One of its managers was Arthur Jefferson whose son appeared on stage in the early days of his career. And he too, best known by his stage name, Stan Laurel, appears on the Clutha walls, along with other thespians who visited the pub while performing – Rupert Everett, Spike Milligan and Glenda Jackson.

The Clutha has risen then, as best it can, from the ashes, and this wonderful work of art evokes a whole hidden history; a people's history, of those still with us or no longer with us who have supped a dram in Stockwell Street.

One final figure is featured in the mural. Mary Barbour, a councillor for Govan in the 1920s who organised rent strikes and promoted family planning. Mary, Alan admits, is unlikely to ever have visited the pub. However, she is included to emphasise the socialist credentials of the area. Mary Barbour has recently seen her kudos rise. There is an association to promote her and plans for a memorial funded by a gala concert.

It was in one of these pubs (the Victoria, I think), a wee while back, that I remember meeting Harry McShane, the last of the Red Clydesiders. A solid and polite man; he would usually only drink half a pint of heavy beer. Clean living and rigid morals were essential for anyone on the Left, he told me, as their enemies would accuse them of almost anything (would that latter-day politicians would heed his advice). Harry McShane knew John Maclean, 'the fighting dominie', an immense figure in the history of Glasgow, who was appointed Bolshevik Consul for Great Britain by Lenin. Three degrees of separation?

So that is another strand to the story of Glasgow: radical Glasgow. And radical left-wing socialism still pervades Glasgow today – just round the corner, overlooking the river Clyde, is a monument to the Glaswegians who volunteered to fight in the Spanish Civil War. It is inscribed 'Better to die on your feet than live forever on your knees'. Elsewhere there are monuments to John Maclean, the Calton Weavers and other revolutionaries.

Secret Glasgow, Literary Glasgow, Radical Glasgow, Sporting Glasgow. These and others are the sub-heads that run through this book. And this is *my* Glasgow because, you don't just come from Glasgow, you *belong* to it (as in the words of the well known song). And that is where, for better or worse, I belong.

Born in Glasgow

Baby fat forged from memory's desire,
That moment present and already gone
Will future me, foundry me
From a dry gasp of Glasgow words.
Hopes of a lost empire of stone,
The lead grey rod of a buried canal,
A ballad of books yet to be read,
The inconsequential friction
Of two opposing football teams.
Testaments of a golden city,
Blackened, battered and bled.

A perambulation in dust-soaked streets,
Starling screeching roost and scorching rain.
Bri-nyloned tribes of tattie-seeking women,
Blind, pay-packeted bunnets of men.
History windae-hinging in siren call,
Fossil full middens of memories lost.
Briquette burning breast of smoky pall.
Cuckoo corporeal nesty city,
Necropolitical in bluff municipality,
Corporation cold in streetwise livery,
City chambered In caulky caul

Baby fat forged from blood of iron,
Clyde carried to the littoral heart,
River rusted from the ferry's journey.
Dredged from depths unmeasured,
Drumlin rumbled from west to east.
Tenemented in sand-strand crumbling,
Rotten rowed raw from dusty womb,
Schooled in grey friary, churched wetly wise,
Branded rivet red, soused in mother's milky bru.
Fate-fucked, festered fool machine,
Once and future fledgling maybe me.

Notes

1. The answers are: Irn Bru; salt and vinegar (not sauce, an Edinburgh affectation); a hauf (a half pint of beer and a whisky); Boots Corner (or sometimes the Hielandman's Umbrella – the railway bridge at Central Station – was where you could be stood up on a date; out of the window (to gossip); peeple!
2. Hamish Whyte (ed.) *Noise and Smoky Breath: an Illustrated Anthology of Glasgow Poems 1900-1983* (Glasgow: Third Eye Centre, 1983).
3. Frank Worsdall, *The City That Disappeared* (Glasgow: Molendinar Press, 1981).
4. For an account of this period see Miles Glendinning & Stefan Muthesius, *Tower Block* (Yale University Press: New Haven, 1994). David Gibson's career has been fictionalised in Andrew O'Hagan's novel *Our Fathers* (Faber: London, 1999).
5. Ian Spring, *Phantom Village: the Myth of the New Glasgow* (Polygon: Edinburgh, 1990).
6. Brendan McLaughlin (ed), *The Speil Amang Us* (Mainstream: Edinburgh, 1990). The title is a reference to the Burns quotation 'There's a cheil amang us takin' notes' – ie, some nondescript but mischievous person is watching us! Two substantial prizes of £500 were awarded to the winners by Billy Connolly at a ceremony in the City Chambers in 1990. Modesty forbids me from mentioning the winners!
7. Cant or tinker slang for an undesirable.
8. See Freddy Anderson, *At Glasgow Cross and Other Poems* (Glasgow: Clydeside Press, 1987).
9. See John Gorevan, *Glasgow Pubs and Publicans* (Glasgow: Tempus, 2002).
10. Their alter egos are Bob McNamara and Danny McLaughlin.

NORTH

THE SECRET GEOMETRY OF GLASGOW

As I've mentioned, I like the idea and the title of Harry Bell's book, *The Secret Geometry of Glasgow*[1] even if I don't subscribe to its theories. Bell identified various lines – which he called prehistoric communication lines – that connected various sites in and around Glasgow. Bell was an amateur archaeologist whose passion was searching for prehistoric sites – ruins, mounds, burial places – that, he believed, could be linked to provide a sort of grid, a precursor, if you like, of the Glasgow grid – the parallel organisation of streets in the city which, actually, have a geological influence, running along and across the drumlins (ridges formed from glacial ice) on which Glasgow is situated.

In contrast to these organised structures and straight lines, there stands the concept of the dérive, developed by the Situationalist movement founded by the French philosopher Guy Debord. The dérive is a sort of unplanned wander round the city, tuning into a sort of psychic sense of place.

Both Bell's work and Situationalist theory have inspired a work by the Glasgow filmmaker May Miles Thomas. *The Devil's Plantation*[2] is a multimedia project including a film and a website containing an archive of photographs. Miles Thomas takes the wanderings of Bell and Mary Ross, a patient from Leverndale Psychiatric Hospital (once Hawkshead Asylum, built for the Govan District Lunacy Board) and weaves them into images of Glasgow that are off kilter, beautiful and disturbing at the same time. My approach to Glasgow is more straightforward but my intentions are somewhat the same, to show the familiar from a unusual perspective.

Glaswegians have their own word for the dérive. It is a *daunder* and it is a popular form of entertainment for Glaswegians. The Glasgow journalist Peter Ross has an affection for it and has titled his recent collection of acute amusing sketches of Scottish life *Daunderlust*.[3]

If you like, the very origins of Glasgow can be traced back to a line – the route by which St Kentigern arrived in Glasgow following the body of Fergus drawn by a bull cart. The story of St Kentigern, or Mungo, as he is better known, is that he was born to St Thenew. Thenew had the misfortune to be raped and thrown from a high place (possibly Trapain Law near Edinburgh). She survived and was set adrift on a coracle that took her to Culross in

Fife where she gave birth to Kentigern. Trained to be a holy man, Kentigern ministered at the death of a hermit, Fergus. He then set Fergus on a cart drawn by two wild oxen and let it go free. It ended up on the banks of the Molendinar which Mungo (his patronymic became the commonly used name) chose to set up his church and named Glaschui (possibly 'the dear green place'). Mungo eventually became the patron saint of Glasgow. Whether this was a preordained communication line is not clear. But it is entirely possible that Glasgow was the result of a dérive, if not a daunder.

Another artist inspired by both Glasgow and Situationalist theory Tom Butler, who is from the Midlands, but came to Scotland to study music and somehow ended up in Glasgow. I meet him in Café Hula opposite the Theatre Royal in central Glasgow. Café Hula describes itself as 'offbeat and rustic-like' serving 'mouth-watering combinations using pear salsa and lemon mayo [for example]'. It is a mix of odd chairs and tables and eclectic decor but seems quite busy on a weekday afternoon.

When Tom first came to Glasgow he lived in a flat in the Scottish Co-op Wholesale Society Building in Tradeston, a grandiose Victorian creation fairly recently developed into prestigious flats which are unfortunately dwarfed by the Clydeside Expressway only yards away. Tom's first impression was of the overwhelming noise from the urban motorway that sort of subsumes the building, encroaching on the west-facing windows. This fuelled his interest in the Modernist development of Glasgow and the films produced in the forties and the seventies about it: specifically *Glasgow Today and Tomorrow* (1949, directed by Erica Masters) and *Glasgow 1980* (1971, directed by Oscar Marzaroli).

Tom describes the Situationist approach as 'a sort of archeological approach that tries to dig out the dreams and ambitions of people'. He is a composer and has taken these archive films, added new footage and set them to music for a commissioned piece – *Elbow Room*, completed in 2014.[4] An approach that tries to 'dig out the dreams and ambitions of people'. He is clearly influenced by visual imagery: not only the films but the cityscape of Glasgow today. He refers to the 'dark urbanism of J.G. Ballard.'

Glasgow Today and Tomorrow was, in some ways, the progenitor of the massive slum clearance that resulted in the destruction of whole areas of Glasgow in the sixties and seventies. The project was a response to serious overcrowding in the slum area of the city. Even into the seventies families of 8-10 people could be found in tenement flats in some areas of the city. I know this personally as my school thought that a good way to occupy its six-formers was to get them to trod round tenement closes doing a demographic survey.

The first part of Tom's piece highlights the repeated captions 'ELBOW ROOM' and 'BREATHING SPACE', superimposed on the film – the music counterpointing the irony and contradictions of the film's message.[5]

The stentorian voice-over of *Glasgow 1980* (written by the Scottish filmmaker Douglas Eadie, partly in response to the reactionary Tory council's more pointed message) is countered by what Tom regards as an equally over-the-top hyper-eighties clichéd sound based on Kraftwerk and OMD. The more ominous aspect of the voice-over's impulse towards an imposed 'planned freedom' is emphasised by the exaggeration of the dust clouds that rise from the demolition of the tenements. The focus moves from above, literally looking down on the changes in the city and also, metaphorically, speaking down to the people, to the level, with personalised and grounded point-of-view shots of the demolitions. Tom's composition employs the film as a tool to make a homogenous statement – editing it or slowing it down or repeating bits. It is astonishing how the imagery combines with the music to provide a vivid yet disturbing vision of a city destroying itself. I am reminded of words from a book I am reading at the time: 'all cities are built with their ruin in mind'.[6]

Harry Bell, Tom Butler and May Miles Thomas have all identi-fied aspects of Glasgow and interpreted them in fresh forms that contribute to our deeper understanding of the city. All have experi-enced the city in different ways. As I come back to parts of the city after many years, I wonder how accurate are my memories of the many streets that have passed out of history into declining personal memory.

Going Back (Dunchattan Street)

Feet fall and fall and fall and fall,
Never-knowing trek and trawl of a grey
    unspoken street,
Swing parks dandelion-cracked,
Backs and breaks of midden-mud, smoky odorous pubs,
    Small stout, fag ash, Johnny Walker neat.

'Three pun o tatties, missus?
Yuir man's up the close' (toe to toe with the
    back-street bookie),
School weans sagely chalking walls,
And once again the street, living its day until day is done,
    (History forgot to call).

Feet fall and fall and fall and fall,
That unnamed day that ebbs and flows and softly
    calls in dreams,
The gaunt authority of the lost,
Within the land mapped in memory unstitched,
    The man returning yet a boy.

EASTERHOUSE

It is time to take a daunder myself and, to do so, I intend to follow a sort of communication line – the route from, roughly, Provan Hall in the east of the city through Springburn towards the city centre and the Necropolis. No doubt this is also some sort of prehistoric communication line but, more simply, it is the line I followed, in the late sixties, on the bus to school from the housing scheme to which my parents and I had been decanted after our tenement in Dennistoun was demolished.

Accompanying me on this journey is my friend Chris who was born in Easterhouse, where we are headed. As we sit on the bus to Baillieston, ominous sheets of rain sweep against the windscreen wipers of the bus, but fortunately – as we intend to walk about six miles – it is a dry but dull day when we disembark.

Easterhouse was once western Europe's largest social housing scheme with a population of 40,000 at its height, as many as a small city like Perth. It has declined in size and some of the blocks built in the fifties and sixties have been demolished.

At this point it may be relevant to outline a little more of the genesis of the housing schemes we are visiting. The move towards eradicating Glasgow tenements and replacing them with housing schemes and tower blocks had been mooted earlier than most realise. In February 1936, James Gray, leader of the Conservatives in Glasgow Corporation proposed in the *Glasgow Herald* the adoption of the continental style of mass housing in Glasgow city centre. In 1945, Robert Bruce, the City Engineer, produced a plan for radically rebuilding the city. However, it is reasonable to date Glasgow's project of mass rehousing to 1949 and to the film, *Glasgow Today and Tomorrow*. The film is partly based on a Glasgow Corporation exhibition of the time – *Your Glasgow, Its Future* – and features lingering panning shots of a model of an imagined Modernist Glasgow. Beyond the inner ring road, represented by translucent tubes, to the north of the city are tower blocks, perhaps a hundred of them, fifteen storeys plus in height, in long lines. The vista, in its startling bleakness, could compete with Fritz Lang's *Metropolis*. It cuts to a caption, 'The Future of Glasgow is in your hands', followed by shots of a small boy playing with toy bricks.

The 1949 Glasgow project was largely conceptual. However, ten years later several grey-suited men met in Glasgow City Chambers. Among them, David Gibson, was the most striking. Thin, pale with dark-rimmed eyes, he was something of a rebel. A rambler and a community activist in his youth, he became a gaunt chain-smoking workaholic, simple in his ways (he lived in an east end council house next to a bone-boilers) and obsessed with his vision of a future Glasgow. He is fictionalised in Andrew O'Hagan's *Our Fathers*[7] as Hugh Bawn, (Mr Housing), who is sentenced to old age in a decaying tower block. His career is summarised: '…lost himself in a welter of ambition; unsafe buildings, cheaper materials; he cooked the books to make more blocks.'

Chris guides me through the scheme, pointing out where he used to live (his block has been demolished now). There were always green(ish) spaces in the schemes and he shows me one field he used as a shortcut when he was with other boys. One day, in the dark, they were walking across when one of them almost fell down a large hole that had appeared due to a collapsed mine working.

There were mines and quarries here and nearby Gartcosh was the site of a firebrick and iron works. Bedlay Colliery was the last to exist, ceasing mining at the end of 1981. I remember about that time the trial of members of the Scottish National Liberation Army, sometimes known as the Tartan Terrorists, who, apparently, plotted to steal explosives from here. There are still fanciful stories about the SNLA hoarding anthrax or ricin ready to strike at the heart of English-dominated society, but they have been one of the least well-known and least effective terrorist organisations of all time! Amazingly, however, they still seem to exist, as they have a page on Facebook.

What is often forgotten about the peripheral housing schemes is that their very location merged with the countryside. There is greenery in Easterhouse – parks, nature trails – and also, on the west side of the scheme, in Auchinlea Park, a well-preserved fifteenth century fortified house, Provan Hall, now owned and preserved by the National Trust. It is reportedly occasionally open to the public, but when we visit, the house and gardens are locked. I always found it strange to contemplate that the Modernist housing schemes were built in areas that had a pre-history, even if it was one the local authorities would prefer forgotten. I have a distinct memory, as a child, visiting my aunt in Drumchapel and, playing in an area of trees, finding the remains of an old villa with garden walls and orna-mental ponds.

Back in the sixties and seventies Easterhouse was known for its problematic youth gang culture. Chris remembers this. Parts of the scheme were clearly demarcated for gangs – there was the Torran Toi, the Drummy Pack, the West Rebels. If you belonged to a certain school or area you knew you weren't welcome in another area. There was violence but it wasn't commonplace.

Cemented in Glasgow lore is the occasion when Frankie Vaughan, the entertainer, came to Easterhouse in an initiative to sort out the gang culture. He invited youngsters to his dressing room at the Alhambra Theatre and came to the scheme itself. Chris recalls that youths were encouraged to demonstrate their change of heart by throwing their knives and razors into an oil drum. Housewives across the scheme, Chris tells me, were furious the next day when they opened their kitchen drawers.

Easterhouse was once totally corporation (or latterly council) housing, but there is an increasing amount of private housing. Glasgow Housing Association have, through a process of demolition, some building and renovation of existing properties, improved the look of the place, although, many would argue, at the cost of affordable social housing. Walking through the scheme there are quite a few gardens that have been maintained and landscaped, although often their neighbours are still basically maintained or left to nature. I remember the 'gardens' that were tacked on these housing blocks as generally just dirt. No-one would take the responsibility of maintaining them and, if they did, they would stand a fair chance of being vandalised. Years ago, walking through nearby Garthamlock I noticed one of the blocks had just one fenced, well-maintained garden. I wondered how it escaped damage until it was explained to me that that apartment belonged to the scheme's most prominent gangster.

There have been improvements in Easterhouse. It has been celebrated for its mosaics, although the oldest and most substantial was destroyed in 2004. There is John Wheatley College (now, due to merger called Glasgow Kelvin College) and, along with the college, The Bridge, a combination of a swimming pool, a library and Platform, an arts centre which features concerts, plays and exhibitions. The most important new development, however, is probably The Fort, an enormous shopping centre on the edge of the M8 but shut off from the road by a vast shiny silver wall. The advantage of its location is that it now provides employment for a substantial portion of Easterhouse people.

Old Easterhouse, however, is still to be found in the old shopping centre, known as the Township Centre. The signs here are of urban decay and poverty. The shops are not designer outlets, they include Cheque Centre, various pawnbrokers, and BrightHouse, a store specialising in what used to be called hire purchase. Products include 'health cigs' and union jack handbags. A convenience store is called Fresh n Less, which one internet review says is known locally as the 'Eat n Die'. Of the two pubs that were once here, one seems permanently shut, the other was closed when we were there.

My overall impression of Easterhouse is of an emptiness. Once these streets would be buzzing with gangs of boys, women out for shopping, men gathered round the bookies. Now, presumably people sit at home. *Bowling Alone*, by Robert Putnam, is a well-known study of the decline of community life in the United States.[8] I sometimes use his term 'desert island society' to describe the forms of isolation induced by new technology and social mores.

Things to do in Easterhouse

Sit in bedroom in the dark
on Playstation for a lark.
Snuggle on sofa, get your kicks
watching Netflix

No dominoes (club closed down),
no need to go to town;
just wait for BrightHouse to deliver
new white goods on the never-never.

The shopping centre was called the Township Centre for a reason. All Glasgow's housing schemes were originally to be called townships, although the term was dropped because of negative connotations. However, it reveals a hope that was never realised – that they would become integrated communities in themselves, independent but linked to the greater city by the urban motorway and ring roads.

Strangely, the Modernist dream has actually, in a perverse way, been delivered. But at what cost? The conclusion is stark and strangely puzzling, the inhabitants of these massive schemes are, perhaps, content in their own way but they have, largely, abandoned the streets.

In 1957, *Glasgow Our City*,[9] based on the 1949 exhibition, fictionalised the typically Glasgow family as the Macdonald family who sit around their tenement fire – father smoking his pipe, mother knitting and Johnny wearing his Boy's Brigade cap at a jaunty angle, whilst engaging in their favourite pastime, fulminating over the immense virtues of Glasgow and, especially, the City Corporation. The book ends with them in a fit of ecstasy after listening to a radio broadcast by the Lord Provost about the utopian future for Glasgow's citizens which ends with a quotation from an American planner: 'Make big plans… Remember that your sons and grandsons are going to do things that will stagger us. *Let our watchword be order, our beacon be beauty.*' How long did it take for that to sound as ludicrous as it does today?

Let Our Watchword be Order

Let our watchword be order,
Our beacon be beauty.

Let our witch words be augured,
Our banter be bitchy.

Let us watch what we ponder,
Our bounty is broken.

What words have we murdered,
Our beanfeast is busted.

Let us be conned by booty,
Our wisdom is withered.[10]

COMFORT AND JOY

Walking down through Garthamlock there is only one person that comes to mind round this neck of the woods. Freddy Anderson, once resident bard of the Scotia Bar and Glasgow's premier folk poet, lived here, and I frequently came to visit him and his family. Freddy was often short of a bawbee or two and would hawk broadsheets of his poems in the local pubs with a famous line of patter: for example, 'the only thing that exceeds your generosity is your good looks!'. In 2001 I was living in England and hadn't seen Freddy for some time but had heard that his wife, Isabel, had died. Then I met him in the Clutha Bar. I didn't at first recognise him. He looked very frail and was staring into a bowl of soup which had been delivered with only a knife and fork. But after a moment he greeted me with a smile. 'Ah, Ian, it's yourself. Can you get me a spoon?'

The funeral service at Daldowie Crematorium was quite an occasion. Writers – Alasdair Gray, Jim Kelman – and folksingers were there (Arthur Johnstone concluded the service with a rousing singing of *The John Maclean March*) and a great many old lefties. If the ghost of Lenin had turned up himself it would have surprised no one. Afterwards, upstairs at Lynch's, one of Freddy's haunts in the Calton, a traditional funeral meal of steak pie and tatties was served (no pastries or curled-up sandwiches – at a Glasgow funeral you get properly fed). The family bought a round of drinks then, one by one, the landlords of all the pubs that Freddy drank in and had sometimes been barred from – as Brendan McLaughlan, of the Scotia, pointed out: 'if you hadn't fallen out with Freddy, you didn't really know him.' Several people gave informal tributes and Freddy's son Paul sang Joe Hill's gospel parody 'Pie in the sky when you die'.

As Brendan had noted, Freddy had a fierce tongue, especially when in his cups. Many moons ago, local residents, including Freddy, had worked hard to ensure the construction of a social club in Garthamlock. Within no time at all it was reckoned that it had been taken over by the local hard men. One night, Freddy, with little concern for his own safety, stood up and harangued them one by one.

This was a risky business as they were, around here, hard enough. This area was the centre of what was called, in the mid-80s, the ice cream wars. Ice cream vans were an important lifeline for the tenants of housing schemes, delivering basic necessities. However, they also became involved in the selling of drugs. Competing families in the trade started a turf war which culminated in 1984 in an

arson attack on a house in Ruchazie in which six members of one family died. Unfortunately, this occurred roughly at the same time as the release of a film directed by Bill Forsyth, *Comfort and Joy*[11], a comedy that featured a mock war between two families of Glasgow ice cream van owners which was, naturally, accused of trivialising the crime in Glasgow.

We walk on, past Garthamlock into Craigend where Freddy moved in his later years. Pubs were uncommon in the housing schemes, but several years ago one opened in Craigend, between Garthamlock and Ruchazie. The one and only time I was there, I went to the Gents and the urinal was dripping with blood. Someone had been glassed, I heard. The police came, but it turned out that no-one had seen anything much. Later, I wrote a short prose piece about it employing an urban legend from another Scottish city.

The Day It Never Got Dark In Dundee

Ah wis doon the Johnny Come Lately on the skite an ah wis tellin the punters aboot

THE DAY IT NEVER GOT DARK IN DUNDEE

Ma mither wis fae Dundee an she minded it, like. Honest as God's ma witness. She tellt me. Aw night it wis jist like day. Only in Dundee, mind.

There wis this punter caed Big Eck, an he wisnae hivin it. Ah've heard it aw noo, he ses. Fuckin couthy tales fae Aiberdeen.

HOOTS MON

an aw that. Ah sed fuckin Dundee no fuckin Aiberdeen, he ses, aw the fuckin same. Cheuchter land as far as ah'm concerned. Fuckin Dundee, he ses, no even in the fuckin first division, are they?

Aye mebbe no, ah ses, but whit aboot the fuckin tangerine terrors, eh. Mind o Jerry Kerr, Jim Maclean an aw that. Eh, big man, I ses. Never mind yir fuckin teddy bears an yir fuckin flute an whistle, y'cunt.

He took a big glug o his pint and made a sort o snortin noise.

Well, fuck the lot o yous east coast cunts, onyway, he ses. Ah've heard mair sense fae King Billy's fuckin cuddie's fuckin airsehole, ya bastard. Fuck Jim Maclean an the fuckin tangerine terriers an yir fuckin maw.

Haud on noo, I thought. This is gettin right oot o order. Fuck this fir

A GEMME O FUCKIN SODGERS

So, next time he's up ah follies him intae the lavvie. An ah've picked up a hauf pint tumbler on the way. As soon as ah wis in the door ah gies it tae the bastard in the mooch. There wis blood aw ower the place. Ya rotten bastard, ya heidcase, ya fucking psychotic bampot, he ses, you've done in ma face.

So ah washed the mess off o ma hands an ah turned the cuffs o ma shirt up under ma jaicket. He wis greetin like a wean an shoutin ah cannae see, ah cannae see. Ah hid a pee. Ah went over tae were he wis sittin in the corner. Ah liftit him up wi his lapels. He jist fell ower agin but.

Hey, chum, Hoy, big man, ah ses. He wis still greetin. The blood seemed tae be turnin black between his fingers. Ah hiv tae tender an apology, ah ses. Ah wis jist a wee bit confused wi aw the bevvy. It wisnae The Day It Never Got Dark in Dundee, it wis

THE DAY THE FUCKIN SUN NEVER CAME UP IN DUNDEE

Black as a bunker o coal, it wis. Aw day. My maw wis there but.

HOGGANFIELD LOCH

From Garthamlock Chris and I descend into Ruchazie, the name once of a rural village but latterly a housing scheme smaller than, but similar in character to, Easterhouse. Here I spent the later part of my childhood years. Again the streets are curiously deserted. Once gangs of boys would hang around outside the few shops. I remember a street of larger houses for large families. I tried to avoid it as there were always wild children who would shout, swear or throw stones at you if they were in that mood. Today, however, it is eerily quiet. There are cars parked here (I don't remember any in the old days) and there are also, for a reason that defies comprehension, three boats on trailers.

We've ascended again, to Bigton Street, a later addition to the scheme – semi-detached houses built to the highest standard in 1965, and I recognise my childhood home, returning after 35 years. Rehoused from an inner city tenement scheduled for demolition, we got to play what was facetiously nicknamed 'housey-housey', a sort of Corporation lottery whereby you were offered three choices of housing – tough if you didn't take the third. Our first offer was in a rough scheme, the second was a high rise south of the city – Bigton Street was our third.

This is the end of the scheme and there is grassland to the north leading up to what once was Avenue End Farm (one of my schoolmates was the son of the farmer). Beyond lies Millerston and, I discovered one day out for a walk, a well dedicated to William Wallace. Some of this area has now been built on, but we still find the grassy incline that leads down to the area's main – well – *tourist* attraction, Hogganfield Loch. There is a golf course here and once there was a pitch-and-putt and rowing boats for hire and ice cream cones on sale in a pavilion. And you could come fishing here, for pike and perch. Today there are a few people and a burger van. Ahead of us is, of course, a body of water. The loch is one of several

'kettle ponds' formed through glaciation. It is often mistakenly referred to as the source of the Molendinar but that is further east in Frankfield Loch, the burn flowing *through* Hogganfield Loch.

Today, it is still dull but windless and the water is dark and flat as a slate. As we approach it is punctured by a few drips of rain. But it is a pleasant spot populated by a variety of semi-urban wildlife: ducks, geese, mergansers, moorhens, swans – especially swans. This brings back a memory of my early childhood in Dennistoun. We often saw swans in the pond at Alexandra Park. These fascinated me and I asked my father one of the few questions he couldn't answer – where do they sleep at night?

Questions for Swans

Where do you hide your whiteness
in the night? In a stone grey wrap
of rain about the loch? Lost
in snuggle tight? Wafted by
a wire of wind? Or in the snap
midst dark and light? Where do you
hide your whiteness in the dark?

Where do you hide your whiteness
in the dark? In the skin
of still water? In the hidden quarter
of an empty park? Shielded
by a secret wish? Or in the touch
twixt light and dark? Where do you
hide your whiteness in the night?

BLACKHILL AND THE BAR-L

From the rural idyll of Hogganfield Loch, skirting Lethamhill golf course, in a couple of shakes the sun is making a brief appearance. Chris and I pass some fields that, I remember from my youth, were known as the rhubarb fields, and next we're walking past the Ponderosa, a thirties council house with some extensions in a rather undistinguished street. Who knows who lives there now, but this suburban landmark was notorious in my time as the headquarters of a crime dynasty led by Arthur Thompson, who ran a protection racket and was, reputedly, an occasional hit-man for the Kray Brothers. At his funeral in 1993 (he died of a heart attack) hundreds congregated outside here. We are now entering Blackhill and, there is no doubt about it, this is gangland Glasgow.

Blackhill, a housing scheme constructed in the fifties was always infamous as Glasgow's roughest area due, in some part, to Glasgow Corporation's rather unenlightened policy of housing all their least undesirable tenants in the same area. I know it well enough. I used to get the bus through here to school. Like most of the housing schemes it has been 'improved' – some houses demolished, some done up – but it is still gloomy. As if on cue, the sun disappears behind some clouds as we stop at a dreich junction. Nothing much is happening. A youth in a stained anorak is entering a low building which seems to be a community health centre. Below and to the left is a deserted children's playground and a little stream running a few yards into a concrete culvert. This is, in fact, the Molendinar – popping up for while before continuing its underground journey to the Clyde. Shortly after we reach the area which is to be landscaped and called Molendinar Park.

To the right stands the burnt out and boarded up hulk of an old roadhouse pub; the Provanmill Inn closed in 2004 after a fire and, it seems, no-one wants to do anything much with it now. But once it was not, by all accounts, a place for the faint-hearted. This is where the infamous Thompson and Ferris families did deals, fought battles and generally terrorised their neighbours. The characters of the time had evocative names: Bananas Hanlon, Fatboy, Speccy Boyd, The Blackhill Butcher, Blind F*****g Jonah, but there is nothing very glamorous about the mayhem they caused here in the sixties and seventies. Paul Ferris, the one-time enforcer for the Thompson crime dynasty, is out of jail now, and a film, *The Wee Man*, has been made about his career, directed by Ray Burdis. But the Glasgow polis[12] weren't having any of it! They refused permission for the movie to be filmed in Glasgow and it was all shot in London.

Another of Ferris's occasional residences in the vicinity lies just up the road – the bulky black colossus of Barlinnie prison with its three heavily chimneyed blocks, known in Glasgow as the Bar-L. There is a story that Ferris took a book into the prison that is still being passed around. Punted by Ferris as the best book ever written, it comes as a surprise to its new owners that it tells them so little about their own predicament. It is, in fact, *The Brothers Karamazov* by Dostoevsky.

Barlinnie is part of Glasgow folklore and there is more than one song about it:

> There's bars on the windows, and bells on the door,
> Dirty big hard beds, attached to the floor.
> I know cause I've been there, and sure I can tell,
> There's no place on earth, like the Barlinnie Hotel.

Paul Ferris is, however, small fry compared to the most famous ex-inhabitant of Barlinnie. Jimmy Boyle was infamous as the hard man and loan shark from the Gorbals who was labelled Scotland's most violent criminal but subsequently rehabilitated in the Barlinnie Special Unit which sought new ways of treating violent criminals, including creative activities such as art and writing. Boyle now lives between the south of France and Marrakesh and has become a wealthy man through, he says, selling his sculptures.

Crime, drug-addiction, poverty are all part of the make-up of the poorer parts of Glasgow, as in any big city, and they come with their concomitant problems. But Glasgow has become known for something else. Let's tell it straight – people are dying in Glasgow: dying earlier than anywhere else, especially men. In some parts of the city, the average male expectancy is as low as 55. This, of course, can be explained by contextual factors: poor diet, drink, drug addiction, murder, suicide. No it can't. Compare Glasgow with similarly deprived communities elsewhere and we still die sooner. And it isn't just the poor, the whole demography is affected. This is called the Glasgow Effect and much has been written on it but, although there theories as to its causes – the psychological effect of post-industrialisation, toxins in the water supply – no-one really knows why.

BABBITY BOWSTER AND THE GLAD CAFÉ

So, it is time to take a diversion as part of my attempt to come to terms with the Glasgow Effect. On a pleasant early summer evening I am at an event organised by Carol Craig in Babbity Bowster, a renovated old banana warehouse in the Merchant City just off the High Street. Carol is the author of some important books about Scottish cultural history including *The Tears That Built the Clyde*[13] which deals with the Glasgow Effect. On this occasion, Carol is reeling from a personal attack in a Scottish journal from a well-known Glaswegian academic. A review of her latest book has called it 'pernicious mince'. 'Pernicious' is bad enough, but 'mince'? Apart from the personal invective there seems to be two main strands to his argument: that searching for other reasons for the Glasgow Effect is absolving capitalism of its responsibility for the plight of the people; secondly that classifying the working class is a sort or pejorative labelling in itself. This is the sort of Catch 22 situation that I find commonly arises when discussing aspects of Glasgow.

Tonight, I immediately feel a little uncomfortable. Firstly, I am late, even though I thought I was on time. There is barely a seat left in the crowded space. Secondly, I suddenly suspect I may be the youngest and the only working-class Glaswegian there (although I am wrong about this). Certainly, everyone seems confident and well-dressed and of a certain age – *not* victims of the aforementioned Glasgow Effect.

The topic for the evening concerns the 'baby-boom' generation of which, I suppose, I am one, and the consequences of social change for them. The discussion ranges widely: the meritocracy, vocationalism, social mobility, the democratic intellect and liberal education, and there is an occasional newspeak buzz of customer care philosophy, risk management, citizenship, political correctness.

Most of the contributors are, it seems, articulate and successful, but the tone of the argument is, largely, one of pessimism. Our parents, high on post-war euphoria and the grand narratives of Modernism, were the optimists and maybe they were right. Their children have certainly seen an increase in their subjective well-being. Yet the conclusion seems to be that the hegemony that we are healthier, wealthier, happier disguises the fact that we have largely lost a sense of community and, in fact, have seen neo-liberalism elide a society that is less egalitarian, more unequal and more apathetic about the future than ever before.

Someone says 'we have narcissisised our intolerance' which sounds so good that I write it down. Later, I contemplate what it might mean, but find myself at a loss. The meeting begins and ends with me feeling uncomfortable. I feel I could sit here all night and accumulate a reference library of emotions. Perhaps that is the legacy of baby boom, working-class Glasgow

Later, I am sitting with Carol in the beer garden in the sun. Carol's thesis is quite simple but undeniable confirmed by statistical evidence. The Glasgow Effect undoubtedly exists, but cannot be easily explained. It seems we Glaswegians have some sort of collective psychological death wish. I am worried. According to the postcode of the east end Glasgow tenement in which I was born, I should be ready for popping my proverbial clogs. Men invariably predecease women by a fair number of years in Glasgow. It's tough for Glasgow men, especially young men, thrust into a dominantly macho culture that can encourage them to live up to a hard man image without the substance or education to do so, they also find themselves in a minority in a gender unbalance. Glasgow men don't just die, Carol tells me, they also leave. Like me too.

Glaswegians are also lonely. And they are not too hot on relationships. There are higher than average levels of domestic abuse in the city but, more importantly, there are many failed relationships. The average length of a marriage or cohabitation for any gender mix is low. There is a high percentage of single person households.

Carol amasses a great many possible reasons for the Glasgow Effect in *The Tears That Built the Clyde*, but today she is tenuously mooting a more contentious explanation. We are dying for lack of love! In Alasdair Gray's great fantastical novel set in a dystopian version of Glasgow, *Lanark*,[14] the inhabitants develop various pathological conditions, including one called dragonhide, from lack of love. Carol has constructed a thesis about the novel based on Alasdair's own childhood experience to develop this metaphor.

It sounds temptingly correct. Glaswegians, especially males, deprived of proper mature relationships have a sort of death wish and neglect their health and well-being, turning to the easy alternatives of drink and drugs, and perhaps crime and violence, and even self-harm. Carol runs the Glasgow Centre for Confidence and Well-being and offers events, publications and classes. But there is no easy fix for Glasgow's problem.

The concept of well-being is not really my cup of tea so my mind wanders. I have recently been to the cinema to see *Under the Skin*,[15] a movie set in Glasgow. In it Scarlet Johanson is doing her level best to further reduce male life expectancy in Glasgow. She plays an alien 'dressed' in a human figure who cruises the streets of Glasgow in a van speaking with an English accent (well, she is an alien) searching for lonely single men (played by real Glaswegians, not actors, I believe) to lure them to a deserted symbolic space where, in various stages of tumescence, they are absorbed into a strange black pool. The story follows a common piece of mythologizing:

looking at her beautiful reflection in the mirror seems to humanise the alien character. Unfortunately, when she attempts to have a real sexual encounter (in Oban, for some reason) she discovers that she doesn't have the necessary equipment!

The impossibility of sex in Glasgow

I met
Glasgow
between
the sixth and
seventh jar
in the Aragon
Bar.

She took me
to her bed.
I'd cracked it,
I thought, but
turned out
I'd not.
She said:

'You made me
from old bones,
tenement stones,
housing schemes,
wet dreams.
But, know what,
there's something
you forgot!'

I kissed
her smoky
mouth, hard
and hot.
And then
I thought;
the heart
might be
the part.

'No.' She rose
from the bed.
'Something more
fundamental,
I'm afraid!'

I am just about to put this book to bed when the Glasgow Effect again rears its head. There develops, in the popular press and on the internet what we describe in Glasgow as a stooshie, which I will forthwith explain – and, no, it is not the first of April (although you could be forgiven for thinking that that occasion occurs more than once a year in Glasgow).

Creative Scotland (the arts agency for public funding) have awarded a young artist, Ellie Harrison, £15,000 project funding. She has called the project *The Glasgow Effect* and provocatively topped it on her web page with a graphic of some greasy chips and a photo of her looking glaikit and pointing to the sky: 'The Glasgow Effect is a year long "action research" project/ durational perform-ance, for which artist Ellie Harrison will not travel outside Greater Glasgow for a whole year... By setting this one simple restriction to her current lifestyle, she intends to test the limits of a "sustainable practice" and to challenge the demand-to-travel placed upon the "successful artist/ academic".'

So, to be clear, the essence of the project is that she will stay in Strathclyde (not just Glasgow) for a whole year, eschewing the sup-posedly globe-trotting lifestyle of the successful artist to engage with the local community in ways that are unclear.

It is also not clear whether remaining in greater Strathclyde will hasten her demise but it is certainly a dubious hardship. In the region she could, for example, take the train up to Oban and go seal watching in the harbour, get the ferry over to the Isle of Arran, stay at the prestigious Auchrannie Resort Hotel and go climbing on Goat Fell, take a daunder down to the Burns Museum at Alloway, etc. Oh, one problem. It will mean she can't go to work for a year as she works in Dundee. Her intention is to pay for a sabbatical from the grant, but it doesn't seem that that is allowed in the conditions.

If it is an attempt to see how much one artist can take the piss and deliberately create controversy, it is NOT regarded as funny by most of Glasgow. Wasting £15,000 of public money that could be spent elsewhere is one thing but it isn't the heart of the matter –

ridiculing the Glasgow working class is.

However, what most likely started as a sort of student prank or spoof has escalated to a major controversy. Creative Scotland have defended their decision exactly in the ludicrous terms in which it was couched. The newspapers have latched on to it, coining the term 'poverty safari'. In short, just about everyone who can be offended has been: those too poor or disinclined to venture outside the city, people who like chips, artists who have unsuccessfully applied for grants for more worthwhile causes. Deliberately offending thousands of people who really need to be on the side of art doesn't seem to be a good idea. Surely, artists, writers, creators need to be responsible to the public?

Anyway, I go along to the Glad Café on the Southside to join a discussion session hosted by the writer Gerry Hassan. The Glad Café is a popular place that hosts music and various events and produces a literary newspaper – the *Glad Rag* – but I don't take to it. It is an odd shape, crowded and dark, there are queues at the bar and they serve you beer in plastic glasses, for goodness sake. Gerry and I study most of the same stuff but differ completely on our perspective on it. He takes politics seriously, which I do not, and he believes there may be practical solutions to problems, which I am unsure of.

Gerry makes some good points about our perceptions of Glasgow and he is joined by Darren McGarvey, best known as Loki, the rapper. Loki comes from Pollock and he is interested in social problems such as domestic violence which he raps about and talks to prisoners in an attempt to get them to come to terms with their crimes. He is a stimulating talker, although it comes out of the top of his head and is pronounced in a colourful and blunt Glaswegian. One point he makes is that '[charitable institutions] are there to maintain poverty, not to eradicate it!'

Ellie Harrison is the star turn though. She tries to be engaging, She laughs, she jokes ingenuously, she is confiding – but what she has to say is mince, pure unadulterated brown stodgy stir it in your tatties mince. She dodges why she has, rather randomly, but certainly courageously, linked the project to the Glasgow Effect. Asked if she was surprised to receive attention she answers no, having previously answered yes. She didn't apply for the grant because she wanted to, she says, but because it is a condition of her probation as a lecturer at Duncan of Jordanstone College of Art and Design. She doesn't really know what she is going to do for a year, but a 'durational' project takes time. However, what she *might* think about is revolutionising the whole practice of art schools and producing a new funding model for the arts based on renewable energy (eh?). Oh, and she is going to sort out the First buses, too. As for the Glasgow Effect, the company are generally flabbergasted at the staggering effrontery when she announces that there too many academics engaging with it who are paid far too much for doing nothing. Perhaps this is all a spoof. We have all been duped and will have to hold our hands up and share a nervous laugh. I certainly hope so as anything else is too awful to contemplate.

Of course, there is a whole debate to be had here about contemporary art practice in Scotland, but this is not the place to have it. The discussion revolves mostly around the perception of Glasgow. Glaswegians are notoriously touchy about the representation of their home and, perhaps surprisingly, on this occasion, tend to side against the press who have exposed the whole farrago.

All this tells us a lot about popular images of Glasgow but not a lot about the Glasgow Effect. I am of the mind that it is of little avail to overly concern ourselves with, something that we can't understand and about which we can do nothing. There are more immediate issues to be addressed in Glasgow today.

RED ROAD

I am back in Blackhill, and my next port of call is the famous, or infamous, collection of tower blocks named Red Road. These steel-framed giants, completed in 1968, were the tallest, at 31 storeys, of all the high rise developments in Glasgow and, for a time, the tallest flats in Europe.

A little history of Glasgow's obsession with high-rise housing is in order. In the fifties, representatives of the Corporation housing committee were, famously, shipped to Marseilles to examine Le Corbusier's Unite d'Habitation and Glasgow became the *sine qua non* of progressivist planning. Subsequently, Glasgow was to embrace high-rise more enthusiastically than any other city in the Western world and, within a few years, a mass of Glaswegians – equivalent to a town the size of Luton – were to be re-housed in the towers in the sky.

The flagships of high-rise building in Glasgow were the tower blocks designated Queen Elizabeth Square. Designed by the most prominent British architect of the time, Basil Spence, famous for the radical Coventry Cathedral, they were lauded as the culmination of the Modernist project. However, they were not popular with their tenants. The A, B and C blocks at Queen Elizabeth Square (named the 'Lizzie' by its tenants) were nicknamed Alcatraz, Barlinnie, and Sing Sing. Spence's allusion to the sails of a ship evident in the giant concrete cantilevers was replaced with the siege mentality of the 'battleship' as they became stained and grey. The new tenants found the 'village in the sky' baffling compared to their previous more grounded existence.

And then things began to deteriorate badly. The fabric of some of the buildings fell in disrepair and vandalism took its toll of the communal areas. The lifts had small windows which were smashed and a terrible accident took place when a teenager put his head through a window and was decapitated.

In time, the lift windows were sealed and other innovations came about. Questa, a tenants association was set up. At the height of the Thatcher era, a bizarre scheme to 'yuppify' the blocks at the cost of £75m was devised by Piers Gough of CZWG architects. All that came of it were some fanciful drawings. In the early nineties, the Corporation ordered a survey of the building and teams of abseilers came from England and Wales to complete it. Some additional building work was undertaken including the bizarre 'hatting' of the flats with coloured pitched roofs. However, although clawback would have made it unprofitable to cancel this work, by the time it was completed the decision had been, to all intents and purposes, made. The flats were uninhabitable and would follow their near neighbours, the Hutcheston E Blocks, deck access blocks disparagingly described as 'Tunisian holiday homes moved 1000 miles too far north', to the ground. The tenants were called to a meeting and were given various reasons why they had to be moved – the stairs were unsafe, the windows didn't fit – and eventually all accepted rehousing. They were given £2000 plus £750 'discomfort' money

The infamous 'blowdown' of the Queen Elizabeth Square flats took place on 12 September 1993. Thousands turned out for the spectacle. A pensioner, Mrs Helen Tinney, returning from shopping, was safely outside the perimeter when a concrete block, part of the debris from the explosion, hit her. She died instantly from 'blunt force trauma'. Tragic as this accident was, the fault was compounded by the comments of the demolishers who publicly stated that, because the 'fly' had been contained within 359 degrees of the circle, they regarded the operation as a success! The high-rise project, heralded by Gray in 1936, Kernohan and Armour in 1949 and Gibson in 1959 had ended in a sad spectacle of tragedy and farce.

Miles Glendinning, author of *Tower Blocks*[16], noted in 1994: 'Only thirty years ago the cry was that 'all Victorian private housing is bad – pull it down and build Modern public housing!' Now we hear that 'all Modern public housing is bad – pull it down and preserve Victorian private housing!' In 2016 we are still no wiser as to the overall strategy for Glasgow's housing. Has anyone seriously debated what to do with Glasgow's high-rise blocks? Several have been demolished but many remain.

You cannot eradicate the past, but sometimes you can re-evaluate it with a degree of understanding and sensitivity. The Red Road Flats Cultural Project was set up in 2008 as a joint project between Glasgow Housing Association and Glasgow Life. It later resulted in an illuminating exhibition. Iseult Timmermans's photographs that were exhibited at Street Level Photoworks, Mitch Miller's[17] fascinating drawings of the Red Road flats and their inhabitants (a mixture of diagrams, drawings and spoken testimony which he calls dialectograms). Alison Irvine's fictional account of the lives of the people who lived there (based on actual testimony) and the accompanying People's Palace exhibition, have provided a new and more positive narrative about the high rise experience that personalises the houses and lauds the experiences of real life working people over three decades. As Alison Irvine states in her blurb to her novel *This Road is Red*:

> It is 1964, Red Road is rising out of the fields. To the families who move in, it is a dream and a shining future… It is 2010, the Red Road flats are scheduled for demolition. Inhabited only by intrepid asylum seekers and a few stubborn locals, the once vibrant scheme is now tired and out of time… Between these dates are the people who filled the flats with laughter, life and drama. Their stories are linked by the buildings; the sway and buffet of the tower blocks in the wind, the creaky lifts, and the vertigo.[18]

And here we are, Chris and I, at the Red Road. And we are gobsmacked. Nothing could prepare you for the stark poignant beauty of the sight. Red Road has genuinely become red, for that is the colour of the gauze that holds the crumbling features of the towers together awaiting demolition. Some of the flesh has been torn from the structures and the rusty red steel frame is exposed. The whole site is cordoned off with fencing proclaiming the forthcoming demolition but, amazingly, there is still some life in the very centre of the blocks. A fenced pathway has been created into the very centre of the brooding beast, to an infant nursery, dwarfed by the other blocks, and, as we watch, some little children are being led through, gazing skywards.

We are considering another issue. Yes, it's that first of April feeling again. However, on 4 April 2014, the announcement that the iconic Red Road flats in Glasgow were to be demolished as part of the opening ceremony for the Commonwealth Games simply beggared belief. This wacky plan was a complete slap in the face to all the good work that had been done. The bizarre suggestion of Eileen Gallacher, chair of the Glasgow 2014 board, and David Zolkwer, artistic director, that the ceremony would be a 'respectful recognition and celebration of... city families' and 'a rebirth of urban Glasgow' come from an all too familiar wish-fulfilment rhetoric that has plagued Glasgow for some time. In 1988, a local newspaper announced that 'the old Glasgow – perceived for so long as a place of drunks and tenements has been transformed into a vibrant and confident city with a glittering future'.[19] There are still drunks and tenements. There are still high rise blocks and there will be no rebirth of the Red Road. What will remain is another patch of

wasteland to add to the acres of such all over the east end of Glasgow. This is not a renaissance, it is a funeral; it is not a ceremony, it is a dirge.

Thousands of Glaswegians once again got on the case. 'What will those who lived and died in the Red Road, those who still live in inadequate tenements and high rise blocks throughout Glasgow, think when they watch this act of gross (and expensive) destruction along with a billion others (apparently) on live television', they asked. And, thankfully, people power and common sense did prevail and Red Road got to live a little longer.

Three Thousand Windows

This window washed its face in a decade of rain,
This window loved to shine,
This window buckled and bled,
This window executed a one-eyed bird,
This window absorbed a thousand screams,
This window leant against a lazy cat,
This window grew black with smoke,
This window believed it was a ghost,
This window was frosted for Christmas,
This window dreamed of lipsticked breath,
This window wished it could bray at the moon,
This window missed the weans,
This window showed an old woman the dawn,
This window thought it was a door,
This window smelled the camphor of a coffin,
This window wanted to live longer,
This window whispered but no one heard.

    The rest of the windows are saying nothing,
      For now . . .

The Red Road flats were finally demolished in October 2015, although sixteen of the top storeys hung around for a bit longer, settling on the ground without toppling. No-one died, and now the Red Road is just dust dispersing in the Glasgow air.

DOON IN THE WEE ROOM

From near the Red Road flats, Royston Road winds its way towards
the city centre. I remember as a boy coming here to watch St Roch's
junior football team with my father and their stadium still stands,
although rather dilapidated. This was traditionally a poor working
class, mainly Irish Catholic area, although Jim Forrest, the Rangers
footballer, came from here. I remember meeting him in one of these
streets (I think my parents knew his cousin). It is still a relatively
poor area but recently a publicly funded renovation project has
contributed to building two parks, introducing artists and poets to
the area and promoting local businesses. This also involved two
interesting, if slightly unusual, creative strands. Jenny Brownrigg, of
Glasgow School of Art, launched a project – *Romantic Vanguard* –
which introduced 'the spirit of romanticism' to the community
through workshops with authors and artists. The resulting book, is
a concoction of both fictional and real characters based around a
workshop by Jessica Hart, a Mills and Boon author. It is described
as 'Seeking romance and the spirit of romanticism in an urban environment'. The romantic setting is, perversely since I have recently
found it so uninspiring, around the waterfall in Molendinar Park
and is a strange mixture of social comment and melodrama. It is a
sound reminder, however, that many things are to be found in
urban environments, inspired by the people who live there. The
introduction begins: 'The Romantic Soul: Dwelling on love...
insanity and death... emotionalism emphasis on individuality...
rejection of drab reality... glimpses of transcendent loves... the
need to escape from ourselves... a fabulous dream world.'[20]

At the same time Molendinar Park designer and artist Graham
Fagen commissioned a new rose from a nursery and named it
through consultation with the community; a pupil from St Roch's
Primary School submitted the winning entry 'Where The Heart Is'.
I am contemplating this wee injection of romance into the inner city
and passing the primary school when I come across a rather sadder
sight. On the railings of the school a little shrine has been created
with some mementoes and a Celtic strip, presumable in memoriam
of a child who has died.

St Roch, I should mention, is the patron saint of falsely accused
people. He is also known as St Rollox in Glasgow, which could be
a corruption of 'St Roch's Loch'. This area has always been called

Garngad, although in order to, supposedly, improve its image, the city renamed it Royston in the thirties. From the mid-eighteenth to the mid-twentieth century it was the site of the fearsome St Rollox Chemical Works which employed most of the locals. Chimney stacks here rose more than four hundred feet in the air, but they didn't prevent the pollution and Garngad was said to be a dark hole even on a sunny day. The reason for the location of this industry here was the proximity of the Monklands canal, which brought coal and steel from Lanarkshire.

Anyway, it is a mild and sunny late February day and I'm walking from the foot of Royston Road up towards Springburn with Stuart Murray. Stuart knows the east end of Glasgow: he was born here, his family were all from here and he lives here, in the centre of the Calton. He is also a postman and delivers all around the area, but more than that, Stuart is an artist, with a studio in Dennistoun in a

converted part of the old Wills cigarette factory. Here he constructs drawings and screenprints of Glasgow and the east end especially. However, his main focus is not on the buildings of Glasgow but its people. He makes books of drawings of characters he meets in pubs, at work or just on the street and he accompanies them with their words, which can be humorous, poignant or just revealing. Some examples: 'Ah like it when ye get the shakes, cos ye know ye've had a right good fuckin booze'; 'scarf's a fuckin beauty eh? Eh? Oh aye, whin ye steal something that's worth a hunner quid ye fuckin wear it!'; 'It's… It's the maist terrible… maist horrible word in the English language… cancer.'

But Stuart is no impartial observer, no flâneur or 'chiel amang us'. He knows everybody – the barmaids, the shop owners, the dossers. And they know him. He cuts a notable figure with his sleeked back hair and his winkle-picker shoes. A time traveller from the fifties.

We are here with a purpose, not so much to see what is here, but more to see what is no longer here. Springburn was once an important part of the city – and Victorian industrial Glasgow was a city with a purpose. Coal from the Lanarkshire coalfields would feed the forges and steelworks that would send their produce here to make locomotives which, in turn, would be trundled down to the Clyde docks and loaded by giant cranes onto Clyde-built ships and transported to the far corners of the Empire. Springburn manufactured one quarter of all the locomotives in the world at one time. Once, places like Springburn and Govan, full of dirt and noise, had a stated purpose, to serve the locomotive works and docks. But now here, in Springburn today, there is nothing much – most of the tenements gone and the people decanted to high-rise blocks. The main site of the St Rollox Locomotive Works has been razed (replaced partly by a Tesco supermarket) but the façade and part of a building remains – now offices. The only clear indication of its original purpose is indicated by an iron gate leading to a courtyard with the large steel letters BREL[TD] (British Rail Engineering Ltd). Stuart tells me that his uncle used to work here.

There is little sign of anyone around today except for cars going into the supermarket car park. People still live here, in some modernist maisonettes and high rise flats, but, apart from a couple of remaining red sandstone blocks, the tenements, the shops, the pubs, the community that once existed here and fed off the heavy industry of a busy industrial city, are all gone.

In the eighties, public art reflected part of this industrial heritage. The Vincent Butler sculpture, *Heritage and Hope*, still stands in a reconstructed square in Springburn. It features a railwayman and a young girl holding out her hands. Past and Future. More poignantly, to reflect the demise of heavy industry and the Clyde, the sculptor George Wylie created a straw locomotive which he suspended from the Finnieston crane, one of Glasgow's most iconic landmarks and the most striking of several cranes on the Clydeside constructed to load heavy exports, such as locomotives, on to ships.

That is now history, but there *are* memorials of life in the old Springburn. A website creates a virtual Springburn: reminiscences of pubs that are gone: Bauldy Bain's, the Locomotive Bar, Sherry's, the Eureka Bar, and some that are still there: the Spring Inn (sometimes, unfortunately, known as the Stab Inn), the Highland Fling. And there is a song that you may hear in folk clubs or bars that celebrates one of them, the old Quin's Bar that stood on a gushet in Balgrayhill Road:

When you're tired and weary and you're feeling blue
Don't give way tae sorrow, we'll tell you what to do
Just tak' a trip tae Springburn and find the Quin's Bar there
And go doon tae the wee room underneath the stair
Doon in the wee room underneath the stair
  Everybody's happy and everybody's there
  We're a' makin' merry, each in his chair
  Doon in the wee room underneath the stair

It was written by Daniel McLaughlin, grandfather of Brendan McLaughlin, erstwhile landlord of the Scotia. It is still well known in folk song circles and its distinctive tune (stolen from a Laurel and Hardy movie!) is easily recognisable. Why has it proved so popular? It is a simple song; an evocation of conviviality and simple pleasure. Can those still be found in Glasgow today? The answer is hopefully yes, but there isn't much to be found in Springburn today. Everyone, presumably, is at their Sunday dinner or watching football on the television. Besides, we are turning south again, towards the city centre on a more exacting quest.

SIGHTHILL

Springburn, perhaps surprisingly, was once a Roman settlement (the Antonine Wall was only a few miles south of here) and Springburn, like Rome, was built on seven hills, extensions of the drumlins that formed glacial Glasgow: Stobhill, Springburnhill, Balgrayhill, Petershill, Keppochhill, Barnhill and Sighthill. Six of them can wait. Today we are on a mission to rediscover what might be forgotten or lost or just hard to find, and we are starting at Sighthill Cemetery.

Not as grandiose nor, in some way, as eerie, as the Necropolis, Glasgow's oldest burial place by the cathedral, Sighthill Cemetery, nevertheless, is the second oldest such burial place in Glasgow, opened in 1840, and a pleasant stroll on a settled day, with views across the city to the south. The most notable memorial here is to two of the leaders of the Scottish Insurrection of 1820[21], a radical rising of artisans and weavers against the Government. Both John Baird and Andrew Hardie were hanged and beheaded for their part in the short-lived revolution. They are remembered here:

> Here lie the slain and mutilated forms,
> Of those who fell and fell like martyrs true,
> Faithful to freedom through a time of storms,
> They met their fate as Patriots always do,
> Despising death which ne'er can noble souls subdue.

Down from the cemetery, however, on the site of the soda waste – the residue of the old chemical works that originally occupied this area, is the remains of the Sighthill housing scheme. During the Modernist-stimulated advance of the mid-sixties, ten enormous twenty-storey tower blocks were built here, five designated the Pinkston Heights and five the Fountainwell Heights. Each had its own name, evocative of history or its skyscraper structure: Barony, St Rollox, Eagle, Phoenix. In 2008, the Pinkston scheme was demolished and, of the five remaining blocks, three are now scheduled for future demolition. These blocks are neither the tallest nor the largest in Glasgow, but for me they are emblematic of the Glasgow high rise – vast stern monoliths with stained concrete faces punctuated by hundreds of identical windows. The Glasgow poet, Edwin Morgan, once wrote:

A multi is a sonnet stretched to ode
And some say that's no joke. The gentle load
Of souls in clouds, vertiginously stayed
Above the windy courts, is probed and weighed.[22]

A less fêted poet, a resident of the tower blocks himself, Bill Sutherland, is more blunt in his *High Flat Sonnets*:[23]

So in some high-flats nicknamed 'Babel Towers'
Anne sits and drinks, her kids at school that day;
flicking through magazines to pass the hours
She comes across the name Corbusier.
'He dreamed of fine, tall cities in the sky,'
she reads, and almost chokes upon her drink.
She laughs and laughs and laughs (so not to cry)
then groans, 'For dreams like that you need a shrink!'

There is also a song, released in 1999 by The Lanterns (Sylvia Rae Tracy, Gina Rae and Jim Sutherland) entitled *Highrise Town*: 'You live in highrise town, the lift's no working and the stairs are getting you down'.[24]

In fact, on top of the popular tradition of 'stairheid nostalgia', there was to develop a humorous, and sometimes ironic, popular tradition around high-rise living exemplified, for example, in Adam McNaughtan's *Jeely Piece Song* – 'Ye cannae fling pieces oot a twenty-storey flat/ seven thousand hungry weans will testify tae that.' There was even, for a time, a television soap opera about the high flats – Scottish Television's *High Living*.

Today, in the wintry sun, a peculiar effect can be seen – some of the windows seem to be black and empty. But this is just an effect of the light. Some have been opened or tilted and are not reflecting the afternoon sunshine. Below and before these vast blocks, however, our destination is Huntingdon Square where once stood some of the blocks of maisonettes that accompanied the high-rise, and a selection of community shops and a pub.

While I'm looking at this, my walking companion Stuart has wandered off on a quest of his own. Some paving stones still mark the boundaries of the square and the pavements on either side. Stuart has found the road he once walked down and is standing where he remembers the entrance to his granny's house. Secret Geometries. As a child, he tells me, he was happy here. What does he remember. The play parks, walking in the cemetery? Yes, and the noise! The noise of the seagulls attracted to the wasteland, the rubbish tips.

There is not much here these days. Only the ghost of Huntingdon Square, although there still stands one pub on the corner and there are shops along one side of the old square (closed today). The end premises is a community advice centre: 'One-Stop Shop: serving the Sighthill community'. And the Sighthill community – what is left of it – is nowadays a different type of community. Notably ethnically diverse since the high-rise flats began to be employed to house asylum seekers a few years ago, it presents new challenges to those involved in social housing.

Although many people are housed in the sky above and to the left of us, however, the place is almost eerily quiet today and we won't be visiting the tower blocks themselves – we have a more esoteric quest! Heading down towards the city centre we pass a children's playground and find ourselves in a sort of parkland with a few knots of trees. Stuart knows where we are going. I don't. So, surprisingly, he leads us up a muddy bank to the side of some trees and suddenly here it is: the Sighthill Stone Circle (humorously known by the locals, I'm told, as Sighthenge).

No matter how random and old it looks, the Sighthill Stone Circle is not neolithic. In fact, it dates from the 1970s. Duncan Lunan is a well-known and kenspeckle Glasgow figure. Astronomer, journalist, folk singer and science fiction author and truly prolific writer and lecturer on all things to do with, well, the universe. The stone circle was initiated by him and was constructed as part of the local council scheme to sponsor local environmental projects. It was built by unemployed youngsters and the stones themselves, whinstone from the Kilsyth quarry, carefully astronomically aligned, were delivered by Royal Navy helicopters in an operation apparently called the Megalithic Lift. It is incomplete, but it is impressive. The seventeen stones are solid and cold, some unfortunately grafittied. Three of four sides are arranged around a central stone. Strangely, leaning against the centre stone, placed by someone unknown, is a little homemade cardboard cross and some wilted flowers. The cross is wrapped in plastic against the rain and is personally inscribed in handwriting with a religious inscription – 'thy will be done' – and, in memoriam, to the name of someone who has passed away. I won't relate the full name, but the middle name of this lost, but not forgotten, lady is Rose.

This site is still treasured by some Glaswegians including city druids who celebrate the solstice here. It is not signposted, something you have to find for yourself – no-one tells you to come here or what it's for. It is just there. So people come here for various purposes and have creatively appropriated the site for their own use, but, as it always seems to be Glasgow, celebration is matched by tragedy. In 2001 an asylum seeker, a Turkish Kurd named Firsat Yildiz, fleeing from political oppression in his own land, was stabbed to death here on his way home by a young Glaswegian who had apparently also attacked another asylum seeker for no reason other than a wilful prejudice.

The Sighthill Stone Circle is incomplete because, in the late seventies, the newly elected Tory Glasgow councillors, flushed with the success of the asset-stripping Thatcherite national government, pulled the plug on the funding before it was finished. Presumably they thought that a project conceived by an eccentric amateur astronomer (who believed that we are receiving messages via a space probe from a planet near the twin star Epsilon Boötis) and built by unemployed youths on a pile of toxic waste underneath an array of giant tower blocks was a waste of public money and time.

Common sense? Well no, let's just call it just reactionary cant and bloody-mindedness. The fact of the matter is that, to stand here in the quiet of a Sunday afternoon and view the smallish ancient stones against a background of enormous concrete tower blocks, touches the heart in some way despite of, or maybe because of, the craziness of it all. Bankers and politicians may build giant monuments to greed, but artists and visionaries create little things like this. And the whole thing is once again under threat. Glasgow City Council have suggested that it needs to be moved to facilitate regeneration – or more specifically to allow tests for chemical contamination as part of the city's preparations for a bid for the 2018 Youth Olympics (isn't there a whole athletes' village being built some two miles away on another empty site even bigger than this as I write these words?) Not surprisingly, a support group, the Friends of the Sighthill Stone Circle, has been formed to protest against this and is supported by many notable Glaswegians including Alasdair Gray, Scotland's most eminent writer.

The Sighthill Stone Circle should be preserved and be finished. Why? Because unfinished things need to be finished. Because if the axis of the earth pokes its way through every bit of the planet then it might as well be here. Because someone came here specially one day to remember their friend Rose. Because the youths who worked on it remember the experience. Because the locals remember the day of its erection. Even because teenagers gather sometimes and spray paint on the rocks. But mostly, mostly because it serves to remind us that, even if we are in the gutter, we can still look at the stars.

Life on Earth

> If Mars and Earth were close enough,
> That ours and Martian's heads
>   Could, almost, touch,
> Would we spare the time of day
> To turn towards the sky our eyes,
> To say hello or wave goodbye,
> To raise a hand or shake a fist,
> To sing the song that calls to us,
> And lifts us from the earthy dust?
>   Would we care as much,
> Stony-voiced in muddy bed,
> If Earth and Mars were close enough?

THE STATION BAR

Stuart and I are a wee bit weary. We've walked about seven miles in one day on our quest for the real Glasgow. However, we are now close to the city centre. So we can cut through the nondescript car salerooms and Chinese wholesalers of Dobbie's Loan, once a drover's road into the city, but now a minor artery of the urban motorway, to the Station Bar which is close to Cowcaddens subway station and whereby, shortly, I intend to hang a tale.

The Station Bar is not, however, named after the subway station. There used to be a railway station here, Buchanan Street Station. This was once of four major railway terminals in Glasgow along with St Enoch's, Queen Street and Central. Now only the last two survive, Buchanan Street, which once served Perth, Aberdeen and the north succumbed to the Beeching proposals in 1966 and the grandiose Victorian St Enoch Station was demolished in 1977 to be replaced (eventually) by a glass-topped monstrosity, the St Enoch Shopping Centre. The original four would have been ideal for the Glasgow Monopoly board but the lost two are now replaced by Buchanan Street bus station and Glasgow airport. Most of the tenements that surrounded this area are now gone, including the Variety Bar, sometimes called Taylor's Variety Bar and Jock Mill's Variety Bar after John Mullen (Jock Mills) a Scottish comedian who, with his kilt and glengarry, was a less famous version of Harry Lauder. Apparently, in the days of the recording studio, he would refuse to sing unless in full costume and make-up. This pub, with its marvellous art deco exterior and interior was a shrine to the Scottish music hall and theatre tradition. But it is long gone and so are the numerous shops of the Cowcaddens,

However, the Station Bar and the red sandstone tenement block that houses it still survive on the corner of Port Dundas Road (the port was named after the dock of a branch of the Forth and Clyde canal that once came here). A shelf behind the bar features a model of the pub in miniature alongside a stained glass feature of a railway train and other nods to the pub's origin. The walls host a variety of paintings and drawings by a local artist Mary Tyson, of Glasgow tenement life with nostalgic street scenes featuring old trams and little vignettes – children playing peevers, a couple winching up a close, the tin bath in front of the kitchen fire.

The current Station Bar dates to late Victorian times, but an

earlier version dated from 1850, and whch annexed to stables and also sold hay and grain. Now, unusually, it is a family-run pub, owned by three generations of the McHugh's. The current landlord is Michael Meque who is also president of the Scottish Licensed Trade Association, and it is still a worthy watering hole.

In fact, this is one of my favourite pubs in Glasgow. A certificate on the wall indicates that (again) it has won the Scottish Thistle title of Glasgow's friendliest pub and the award is well deserved. It is clean, bright, comfortable. The service is fast, efficient and friendly. The beer well-kept and the unpretentious food good value and tasty. It displays in an unfussy way everything that a local pub should offer and it is popular with the local office workers and journalists.

METAL PETALS AND PHOENIX PARK

Not far from here, despite its rather random features, is an area designated by some as Glasgow's Cultural Quarter. It is blocked off from the north of the city by the giant rumblings of the urban motorway – except at one point, that is, the Garscube underpass. It is from there that I am about to take a short digression with Neil Gray of the University of Glasgow, who studies and writes about the urban environment.

Neil's interests lead him to interrogate the plans and motives of Glasgow City Council and its various substrata. Unlike Glasgow Corporation, however, whose total immersion in the master narratives of Modernism and paternalistic strategy for the citizens of Glasgow led them to display, if not flaunt, their grand plans for the city, the current City Council are far more slippery customers. Their hydra-headed 'frameworks' for city developments, such as the Clyde Gateway, come and go as they angle for private invest-ment in different areas of the city. Part of one of these tacit strategies is a desire to expand the Cultural Quarter to the north and, to that end, they have spruced up this little underpass. Well, to an extent. In fact, today it is half flooded, the red composite surface is cracking and the landscaping is rather tatty.

The most impressive things here are the giant metal flowers – known locally as the metal petals. There are about thirty of them, silhouetted against the grey sky. They are, apparently, phoenix flowers. The phoenix is a symbol that the powers-that-be have taken as their own as it sums up the concept of regeneration which is dear to their hearts. Otherwise, you could argue that it is an appropriate emblem as Glasgow is a city endlessly destroying and recreating itself. Johnny Rodger, the cultural historian, notes that, since the beginning of the nineties, regeneration has been embraced and its opponents have become frenzied and touchy, deriding its oppo-nents as 'professional whingers, anarchists, cynics, misfits and crypto-communists'.[25] However, the various naysayers of regenera-tion have not gone away and there is still a feeling prevalent amongst the people of Glasgow that 'regeneration' is a disguise for 'gentrification' – to whit, the neo-liberal disposition of the city's assets from working-class citizens towards big business and private investment.

In terms of housing this is evidently so. Glasgow, which once, mistakenly or otherwise, prided itself on its Corporation housing no longer has any council houses. In 2003 all its stock was effec-tively privatised on transfer to Glasgow Housing Association, a commercial organisation that has since branched out into commer-cial letting. What remains of social housing in Glasgow is also decreasing rapidly through demolition and there is a suspicion that it is being deliberately allowed to run down. In short, municipal housing for which Glasgow was once renowned is in serious decline. In 1979, when Margaret Thatcher promoted the 'right-to-buy' policy, around 35% of the population of Glasgow lived in some form of municipal housing. Since then, the ideological shift towards market forces has eroded that provision – and whilst the housing stock decreases, waiting lists for social housing rocket. The only conclusion is that many working-class people are being forced against their will into the private sector.

Anyway, to return to the symbol of the phoenix. It is anchored in the fact that this was once the site of Phoenix Park, one of Glasgow's finer Victorian parks, with a bandstand and water fountain. It rose, well, like a *phoenix* from the ruins of the old Phoenix Iron Works. Anyway, enough of that. The fact is that Glasgow City Council have this shape-shifting area of Glasgow in mind as an extension of their demarcated cultural quarter and to that purpose have purloined Phoenix Park as an indicator of an older tradition in a rather empty area. Therefore, it is commemorated by a large illustrated hoarding with some historical facts. Yet, they have been only partly successful in their attempts to attract people here. One development is that Scottish Opera have moved their workshops here and opened a rather pleasant café called Octavia. A little further up there a sort of post-industrial site that has, for a while, housed artists studios. Through a rusting gate you can in fact see a peculiarly shaped piece of metal, a sort of sculpture that has been left behind. There are steps here that should rise up to Spiers Wharf, but which have been cordoned off for safety reasons.

Spiers Wharf itself stands at the top of the hill. This is the terminus of a canal and some of these erstwhile useful features have been preserved and repurposed – there is canoeing here, for example. An old warehouse has been converted to flats and a newer block has been built. In general, the attempt has been to find uses as housing or offices for the industrial buildings around here.

Neil points out that it is a mantra of Glasgow City Council that the community must be involved in regeneration, but that they seldom are in any real way. It is not, in fact, totally clear who the 'community' around here are – a few original residents, incomers, workers?

Some critics have coined the term 'housing monster' to describe an obsession with housing, the trauma of finding and living in a home. There has been a call to 'de-fetishise' housing. As we move farther on Neil talks about the rent gap, another American concept that moots an economic model for gentrification. Basically, if an area can claim a higher rent than it currently does, this allows developers to move in and *improve* that area, making, of course, a profit for themselves.

Passing behind the Spiers Wharf development we can examine a practical example of housing development, but we are heading further north, to Cowlairs. Cowlairs is an area adjacent to

Springburn known for its association with the railways; although there is no longer an engineering works here, there is a signalling centre. You pass it on the train from Edinburgh – and a massive bonded warehouse. This is a brownfield site that the City Council would love to develop, but no-one much has come forward yet. What is actually here is a decaying remnant of old Glasgow. Passing a single block of old tenements with a pub and a roadside café opposite, we come to Cowlairs Park. At one time, this was one of Glasgow's prime recreational parks, but it hasn't been maintained for some time. Ascending from overgrown steps to the top of a rounded hill, we pass a rusty abandoned car. A flat area boasts the metal stumps of some goalposts in an area of decreasing red blaize that once was a football pitch. Amazingly, a major football club once played around here. Cowlairs FC was founded in 1876, its players mostly workers at the railway works. It played, at one time, in the Scottish League and the FA Cup. Its short existence came to an end in 1896.

From this aspect we can trace a sort of history of housing on the north side of the city. To the north east the remaining traditional tenements of Springburn, to the east the tower blocks of Sighthill – and there, an example of 'rent gap' development; a little scheme of private housing adjacent to Sighthill.

We are alone in an area that has gone to seed, yet the park itself has found alternative uses since its demise. It has become a sort of urban/ rural wilderness area. Teenagers use it for motorbike scrambling. And, as we are gazing out over Glasgow, a deer emerges, bounding from some trees. Even in the centre of the city there is wildlife – urban foxes and some deer. Ironically, we have just passed, at a little shopping development down the road, Glasgow Field Sports Centre, with the figurative head of a stag as its logo. It is ironic, also, that this leisure area, once among a crowd of tenements and industry, should have found its way to these new uses.

My intention is to walk back to the city centre but it is not as easy as I anticipated. The only feasible way seems to take me back past Spiers Wharf where I can see, almost touch, the city centre, but the massive roaring swathe of the urban motorway is in my way. Zigzagging past the wharf, a remnant of the old Monklands canal where I used to walk as a boy, the only escape takes me back to the underpass and the metal petals. There are historic lines of communication here, the canal usurped by the motorway and the motorway traversed by the underpass, that Harry Bell never dreamt of.

However, now to Cowcaddens subway station, just around the corner but not so easy to find as it once was due to the redevelopment of the area which has left it sunk amongst some high-rise flats. Glasgow's underground railway, known as the subway and, more recently, as the clockwork orange (after the bright coloured carriages) is a circular route with fourteen stations and trains regularly in both directions – an inner and an outer circle. It is cemented into Glasgow lore. The journalist Cliff Hanley even wrote a song about it:

> There's Partick Cross and Cessnock,
> Hillheid and Merkland Street
> George's Cross and Govan Cross
> Where a' the people meet
> West Street, Shields Road
> The train goes round and round
> Oh, it's lovely going your holidays
> On the Glasgow underground.[26]

When we were students, some years ago, it was customary to do a 'sub-crawl', stopping at the nearest pub to every station for a drink. There were various rules and regulations, I'm told, although I don't really remember them all: a different drink in each pub (yes, I think I recall that), surfing the subway – that is, refusing to sit or hang on to the handrails (no, I don't recall that). I did the whole thing in the seventies as a student. Of course, that was many years ago, my more mature self wouldn't be daft enough to try it again, would I?

CLOCKWORK ORANGE

Right, so a few of us are assembled in the Station Bar, in Cowcaddens. The Author, Doonhamer, Munki, The Viscount, Kylun, Mr Yes, And Token Woman. Token Woman is objecting to being called Token Woman. She says that there is no place in this century for atavistic sexual stereotypes to be perpetuated. Well, she says something like that, only shorter, so we agree that she can be called Ciona. 'After all,' she says, 'that is my name.'

We may be daft, but we didn't come up the Clyde in a banana boat, as they say. So no fancy rules, just drink what you want and not *all* of the stations. This is our itinerary:

Cowcaddens: Station Bar
Kelvinbridge: Inn Deep
Hillhead: Tennent's Bar
Partick: Velvet Elvis
Govan The Brechin Bar
Bridge Street: The Laurieston
St Enoch: The Imperial Bar
Buchanan Street: The Vale[27]

And soon we are in the belly of the clockwork orange itself. The peculiar smell of the old subway was so familiar to Glaswegians that, when the whole thing was renovated, its chemical constituents were analysed so that it could be exactly replicated. Within a couple of minutes the train arrives with a sunburst of orange and an onrush of air than has been called the 'subway sook'. There are a few tourists in the queue and a visiting Irishman remarks to a friend 'wow, it's like easyJet without the wings!'

There are various urban legends about the subway. One – surely apocryphal – is that there were once 'subway runners'. Armed with a pair of running shoes and a miner's headlamp, they would wait until a train had pulled out of the station and run along the track behind it, hoping that they would reach the next station before the next train! I do, however, have a true story about the subway that I tell everyone, although I don't think they believe me. Once, years ago, I was heading to Partick for an appointment when I nodded off and found myself at Govan. Govan is one of the larger stations and has an entrance at either end of each platform – that is, four sets of steps in all. As the train pulled into the station, I noted a train also pulling into the opposite platform. I jumped off, ran up and down the stairs and just caught the closing doors of the train. When I looked round, something seemed wrong. I had run up and down the stairs and got back on the same train. God knows what the other passengers must have thought. Later, I used this incident as the basis for a comic novella which (probably thankfully) I have subsequently lost.

Our first stop is a fairly new addition to the landscape. Inn Deep (another rather sad Glasgow pun) is a bar constructed under the arched vaults along the river Kelvin and accessed one way by a long set of stairs from an entrance in Great Western Road. It faces Kelvinbridge subway and, on that side of the river, under a set of steps there is a competently executed but slightly disturbing mural

featuring a giant skull and a rat.

The bar also features something of a menagerie: an upright stag in a kilt drinking a bottle of beer, a skunk, a bison, an adder, a fox and some undefinable creature. It specialises in real ale: beers from Williams Bros. Brewing Co of Alloa, which include Fraoch Heather Ale and Profanity Stout.

It is a pleasant enough place, although I wouldn't fancy it too much in mid-winter. We sit at a long trestle bench while Mr Yes engages the company in some discussion of the forthcoming referendum on Scottish independence.

One more stop on, we are at Hillhead subway station. A major feature attraction of this refurbished station is a large tiled mural by the artist and author Alasdair Gray. This features a sort of diagrammatic panorama of the West End and a series of paired images: workers, scorpions, babies, dragons. What I have to reveal to the company with ill-concealed satisfaction, is that the dragons were actually drawn for *me* – as the logo for a writing broadsheet I was producing for Cardiff University.

There could be a choice of pubs at Hillhead. The closest is the Curlers, which takes its name the erstwhile local curling pond, fancifully claims to be 600 years old. It is certainly old enough, and still occupies a squat eighteenth-century building. We are, however, headed across the road, to Tennent's Bar. Tennent's was one of two pubs of the same name (the other in Rutherglen) set up in the 1880s by Hugh Tennent, of the Tennents brewery family. Ever popular, this is possibly the busiest pub in Glasgow *pace* the

Horseshoe Bar. A period interior, excellent service and good cheap food probably have something to do with it.

Our next two stops are iconic bars in Dumbarton Road: the Lismore and Velvet Elvis. We are interrupted only by a request to eat at a MacDonalds. It is a split vote decision. Someone protests that Ronald MacDonald has no place in our cultural experience as he is an American. However, I point out that he is actually 'a chieftain of high degree' so we stop for short while.

Anyway, to cut to the chase, everyone loves the Lismore, with its island references, creative decor and toilets labelled 'Fir' and 'Mna'. (The toilets in Velvet Elvis are labelled 'Ghandi' and 'Mother Teresa'). This is a more recent edition to the area, and probably the westernmost outpost of the trendy West End. It is a old butcher's shop with the butcher's bike hanging from the ceiling. The tiled walls bear the inscription 'Keep Partick Weird'. The fact is that, rather surprisingly, none of us much likes the place at all. It is crowded, the seats are uncomfortable and the prices too steep. So we soon head back to the subway and under the river to Govan, to Brechin's Bar.

William Brechin's family, from the late nineteenth century onwards ran up to twelve pubs in central Glasgow. This is the only surviving pub to bear his name. Sometimes called the Black Man's after the black bronze statue of Sir William Pearce, the erstwhile chairman of the Fairfield Shipyard, that stands outside. Standing on a gushet, with a turret on the corner, Brechin's has a baronial grandeur, but, like Govan in general, it has seen better times. Two plaques of local dignitaries (R. Napier and J. Elder) remain on the wall but they are faded and worn. Traditional plasterwork has now been replaced with acoustic tiles for, I guess, the karaoke that is advertised on the noticeboard. That it was once more prosperous is signified by the island bar and the partitioned smug at one end, but tonight it is strangely empty for a Saturday. We have to imagine it in its heyday, thronged with customers.

We are feeling more mellow by now and Doonhamer and the Viscount Walsingham encourage group hugs and photographs. Kylun, the mutant superhero, has returned to his alter ego, Colin McKay, and is lamenting the loss of all his flame-coloured hair. But, reluctantly we move on. This is our longest subway stage and it takes us to the Southside of the city centre, to Bridge Street and the Laurieston Bar.

The Laurieston has a fine thirties facade and the interior doesn't disappoint with its art deco bar shaped like the prow of a ship. The pub is busy. It is evident immediately that this is a place that caters for its locals. There are shelves of books, old photos, paintings by one of the regulars, Danny Fitzpatrick (a Tibetan girl and a portrait of John Hurt), various posters and signs – one is something that was commonly seen in Glasgow pubs in the old days – 'No ladies supplied in the bar' with its triple pun. Someone has added on this occasion 'bring your own'. There are sporting photos, pictures of trams, old press cuttings about the area and an advert for contributions to a forthcoming book about Glasgow pub dogs.[28] Conveniently, for its subcrawling customers, it has a map of the subway featuring its attendant hostelries.

This convivial hostelry has featured in a song by the Fratellis and in a Ewan McGregor movie, *Young Adam*.[29] John Clancy, the amiable landlord of the Laurieston, is happy to give us more gen and a potted history of pubs round about the Gorbals. He has run several of them – notably the Elizabethan beside the ill-fated Queen Elizabeth Court. There is a natty photograph of him with his brother outside another shop. One of my more discreet companions, Munki, is impressed: 'they look like the Kray brothers!' Most of his pubs occupied traditional areas of Glasgow that no longer exist. John is succinct about this: 'I've never sold a pub; I've been bulldozed oot o' them!'

We are nearing the end now. Two more stops: first the Imperial just off St Enoch Square. This is an old-fashioned sort of place that hasn't changed much over the years. Stained glass panels that once

featured in the front window have been shifted to the back of the bar. They have a medieval theme with rather cryptic inscriptions: 'Diet cures mair than doctors', 'Gladnesse without available no treasure', 'Beseech he sits be merrie for to be Blythe methinks tis best'. Slightly befuddled, methinks that Falstaff himself could tope on a pint of porter herein!

Finally, opposite Queen Street Station – The Vale. This is a rough and ready sort of place that I know best from waiting for a train but tonight it is busy and there is a function on upstairs. There are bouncers at the door. The pub in general bears its history on its walls: there are references to sporting events: 'Clay Wins', 'Busby Babes Air Crash', and, rather injudiciously, 'Lock Up Your Daughters – Mike Tyson Live at the Vale.' Other framed memorabilia figures: 60s football programmes (Scotland v Hungary, Belgium, England), caricatures of locals, a collection of beer bottle labels and photographs of the bar being renovated and (not obviously relevant) George Washington Wilson's famous photos of the construction of the Forth Road Bridge. There is a list of seventy malt whiskies that, presumably, were once on offer and, rather incongruously, a large vintage poster of a sinking ship with a lifeboat leaving it promoting temperance: 'Wrecked at the Bar VOTE NO LICENCE.'

Our little adventure has been an aid to getting a feel for the city. However, although popular pubs like Tennent's may go on for ever, many are under threat. At one time, the police and local authorities bore down on public houses. Strict licensing hours were imposed. In my student days pubs shut between 2.30 and 5.00pm and again at 10.00pm (not too long before that it was 9.00pm) and didn't open on Sundays. So keen were publicans to get punters out of the door before the police intervened that they would ring the fire alarm for the entire ten minutes of drinking up time. Nowadays, licensing hours are liberal but pubs are in decline perhaps because of a general decline in drinking, perhaps because of cheap supermarket drink, but, I fear, mostly because of the general move away from convivial and communal activities. Doon in the wee room? Bowling alone?

Notes

1. Harry Bell, *Glasgow's Secret Geometry* (Glasgow: Leyline, 1993). Much of Bell's work is available online.
2. See http://www.devilsplantation.co.uk/blog.
3. Peter Ross, *Daunderlust* (Dingwall: Sandstone Press, 2014).
4. See http://www.thomas-butler.co.uk/elbowroom.
5. Documentary films regarding Glasgow are preserved in the Scottish Film Archive and some are available online.
6. See Darran Anderson, *Imaginary Cities* (London: Influx Press, 2015).
7. Andrew O'Hagan, *Our Fathers* (London: Faber, 1999).
8. Robert D Putnam, *Bowling Alone: the Collapse and Revival of American Community* (New York and London: Touchstone, 2001)
9. W.G. Beaton, *Glasgow Our City: Yesterday, Today and Tomorrow* (Glasgow: Corporation of Glasgow Education Department, 1957).
10. The idea for this poem comes from a similar fest of linguistic virtuosity by Edwin Morgan. See Edwin Morgan, *Collected Poems* (Manchester: Carcanet, 1990).
11. *Comfort and Joy* (1984), directed by Bill Forsyth.
12. In Glasgow 'polis' (pronounced to rhyme with 'hiss') is always preferred to 'police' (pronounced to rhyme with 'fleece').
13. Carol Craig, *The Tears that Built the Clyde* (Glendaruel: Argyll, 2010).
14. Alasdair Gray, *Lanark* (Edinburgh: Canongate, 1981).
15. *Under the Skin* (2013), directed by Jonathan Glazer and based on the novel of the same name by Michael Faber.
16. Miles Glendinning, *Tower block: Modern Public Housing in England, Scotland, Wales and Northern Ireland* (New Haven: Yale University Press, 1994).
17. See http://www.dialectograms.com.
18. Alison Irvine, *This Road is Red* (Edinburgh: Luath, 2013).
19. See Ian Spring, *Phantom Village: the Myth of the New Glasgow* (Edinburgh: Polygon, 1990).
20. Jenny Browinigg, *Romantic Vanguard* (Glasgow: Royston Road Project, 2002).
21. See Peter Berresford Ellis & Seumas Mac a'Ghobhainn, *The Scottish Insurrection of 1820* (Edinburgh: John Donald, 2000).
22. See Edwin Morgan, *Collected Poems* (Manchester: Carcanet, 1990).
23. Bill Sutherland, *High Flat Sonnets* (Glasgow: Clydeside Press, 1990).
24. Released as a single and recorded on the album *Illuminate Yer Heid* (1999).
25. See Johnny Rodger, *Contemporary Glasgow: the Architecture of the 1990s* (Edinburgh: The Rutland Press, 1999).
26. Cliff Hanley was a noted Glasgow journalist and writer. He is also credited with writing *Scotland the Brave*.
27. The subway stops are Cowcaddens, St George's Cross, Kelvinbridge, Hillhead, Kelvinhall, Partick, Govan, Ibrox, Cessnock, Kinning Park, Shields Road, West Street, Bridge Street, St Enoch's, Buchanan Street.
28. Reuben Paris & Graham Fulton, *Pub Dogs of Glasgow* (Glasgow: Freight Books, 2014).
29. *Young Adam* (2003), directed by David Mackenzie.

EAST

MUNGO'S SEE

Victorian Glasgow was built round the broad waters of the Clyde, on which giant ships were built and locomotives forged at the steelworks were shipped to the far reaches of the Empire. But medieval, Glasgow was built on the banks of a gentler stream, the Molendinar, which flowed from Hogganfield Loch down past the cathedral and into the Clyde. It is still there, but now flows underground. You could imagine it or trace it, perhaps, with dousing sticks. When I was a boy, my father took me walks in Alexandra Park and pointed out a grating or drain under which, he told me, the Molendinar flowed.

I am playing fast and loose with the cardinal points here as the cathedral precinct was, in medieval times, the centre of Glasgow, indeed it was Glasgow, but here it serves as my starting point for a journey through the east end of the city (where I was born) going down Duke Street to Dennistoun, Parkhead then back to the Calton.

Anyway, I'll return to the story of St Mungo and the origins of the city – and I will be brief as the story is well documented and it is also, probably, all blarney invented centuries after the saint's death.

Mungo set up his church in Glasgow and had a small sparse cell on the banks of the Molendinar. And in Glasgow he remained except for, possibly, going to Rome to meet the Pope and, probably, meeting St David in Wales, where he may have been exiled for a time. He hobnobbed with various other saints – St Columba and St Asaph and probably St Constantine of Strathclyde and Govan who was as well known as Mungo in the early centuries of Christianity (Govan was, after all, once as big as Glasgow) but who has been seen off in the saintly stakes in more recent times.

Like all good saints, Mungo was noted for miracles, and the coat of arms of Glasgow, which as the civic symbol can be found all over the city, famously records four of these commemorated in the short rhyme:

> This is the tree that never grew,
> This is the bird that never flew,
> This is the fish that never swam,
> This is the bell that never rang.

Briefly, two of these relate to Mungo starting a fire from the branch of a frozen tree and Mungo bringing a dead robin to life. The third relates to a more complex story. Apparently the local queen, Langeoreth, had been accused of adultery although her jealous husband had actually taken her ring and thrown it into the river. Mungo commanded that a fish be caught and the ring was found in its stomach, thus proving her innocence. The origin of the fourth is obscure, although it may relate to a bell given to Mungo by the Pope.

The coat of arms dates only to the mid-nineteenth century although the symbols employed are clearly older. There is a perfectly plausible, if heretical, view that they have nothing to do with Mungo at all and relate to legends of Noah and his ark and dove and the fall of Adam. Looked at this way, the fish could well be a serpent winding around the tree and the bell actually an apple hanging from it.

St Mungo died 500 years before Glasgow Cathedral was built in the twelfth century, but it is reputedly situated over his burial place and a shrine to the saint dominates the lower part of the cathedral. Many other Glaswegians are honoured here also. The walls speak to you in their own words, commemorating the great, the good, the forgotten, the remembered: '74TH HIGHLANDERS • EGYPT 1882 • TEL-EL-KEBIR', 'HEIR AR BVREIT • KNICHIS OF THE HOVS OF MYNTO • WT THAIR WYFFIS • BAIRNS AND BRETHEREIN', 'DAIDIS ALLISON • SCHOLAE GRAMMATICAE • GLASGUENSIS'.

It is, strictly, no longer a cathedral, as there is no associated bishop, but it still a place of worship, noted for its organ music and choral performances. Apart from that it is generally busy with tourists and visitors. Although of no religious persuasion, I find it a

pleasant place to visit and wander reading the various inscriptions that trace a long history of worship in the city. It's situation is at the foot of a hill now known as the Necropolis, Glasgow's historic burial ground, from the top of which you can look down on the cathedral and its grounds. It must have seemed huge in its time although it is now dwarfed by the Victorian Royal Infirmary immediately to the north.

PROVAND'S LORDSHIP AND THE MUSEUM OF RELIGIOUS LIFE

Legend has it that the cathedral is linked by an underground tunnel to another building just across the road. Provand's Lordship, the oldest house in Glasgow, has survived while the buildings around it have been demolished time and time again. As a child it was presented to me as a kind of keystone, a link that demonstrated that this modern city, pulling itself by its bootstraps into the future, was also ancient, older than a child could imagine. The house was built by Andrew Muirhead, Bishop of Glasgow, in 1471 and once housed a clergyman known as 'Lord of Provan', thus the title. There were other medieval tenements around here, but many were demolished in the nineteenth century. Right up to the beginning of the twentieth it was still occupied as a house by various families, but now it is simply a museum maintained with period furniture. Quite recently, a garden has been created at the back of the property on the erstwhile site of St Nicholas Hospital. The most interesting and extraordinary feature here is the collection of what are called the Tontine Heads. These enigmatic heads or masks, sometimes called grotesques, formed part of the old town hall in the Trongate which became the Tontine Hotel. They only date from the eighteenth century although they appear much older. They may have a theatrical or mythological meaning but no-one is quite sure. When the hotel was demolished, the heads were dispersed around Glasgow. James Cowan,[1] the Glasgow journalist, began to search for them in the thirties and eventually they found their way here (all but one that has been lost) where they are happily reunited.

Provand's Lordship is genuinely old, but the building that has been erected immediately opposite only pretends to be. It is the latest addition to Glasgow museums, the Museum of Religious Life and Art, also called St Mungo's Museum, built in 1989.

Here, I am struck by a bout of political incorrectness. To my mind, coming across the symbols of ancient Glasgow in my youth, the triumvirate of Provand's Lordship, the Necropolis and the Cathedral formed a sort of perfect whole: they demonstrated that Glasgow was very old and that people lived here, died here and worshipped here.

Today, I see St Nicholas's Garden as a clever and welcome extension of that tradition, renewing and recuperating old symbols that relate to Glasgow and its past. St Mungo's Museum also has a garden, the Zen Garden, but that is just a courtyard with some stones loosely arranged and doesn't mean very much to me.

The Museum of Religious Life, in fact, doesn't fit in at all. It is a hideous imposition between the Cathedral and Provand's Lordship interrupting the sight line between the two. I recognised the progenitor of this building the first time I saw it. It was designed by Ian Begg (who also produced a notable eyesore in the heart of old Edinburgh, the Scandic Crown Hotel). It is supposedly of a traditional style but is actually nothing of the sort. It is a pastiche of different elements of Scottish baronial and vernacular architecture in that type of rough stone that reminds me of resin fireplaces that shops once sold.[2] A low level, inconspicuous modern building would have fitted better. Historically, it is given credence by supposedly being designed in the style of the old Bishop's Castle which, arguably stood on this spot (coincidentally, the foundations of the castle were found during the excavation for the creation of the building).

OK, it is not a bad thing to have a museum about religion, nor to celebrate multiculturalism, and it has a great view of the Necropolis, and some really interesting contents. Only one item, however, really offers me a connection with the religious tradition of this site – a bell that reputedly once belonged to Saint Lolan, a nephew of Saint Serf. I wonder what St Mungo would have made of it all.

St Mungo in Saint Mungo's Museum

Is this the bird on which rode Bodhisattvas Ghan-yin
    carrying souls to Nirvana?
Is this the fish called Matsya that was the first avatar of Vishnu?
Is this the tree that made the magical fan of Zhongli Quan?
Is this the bell that makes the sound of the letter OM?

THE NECROPOLIS

After the comparative bustle of St Mungo's Museum, it is a relief to cross over the Bridge of Sighs, constructed in 1836 for the convenient conveyance of funeral processions to the Necropolis. This little hill was originally the Fir Park, covered with fir trees, but a giant monolithic statue of John Knox, the Protestant reformer, was constructed there in 1825, presumably to keep a stern eye on the doings of the post-Reformation cathedral. In 1831, Glasgow Merchant's House sanctioned the construction of a burial ground here. Not long after the first corpses were interred, the Necropolis was a local attraction, with guides to walking there produced by Peter Buchan and John Strang.[3]

I have already commented on the uses of such a location and landscape for what has been called the celebration of death:

> ... The Necropolis was born out of the urgent need for more hygienic burial grounds, the frantic quest of the middle classes for monumental immortality in an age of uncertainty, and the peculiar Victorian fascination with the trappings of death. And, thus, the clear association, from the beginnings of the Necropolis, of remembrance with pleasure. Vicariously, amongst the last remains of strangers, we can turn our thoughts to the sentimental or the morbid, remembering, and indulging in a form of personal mortification while flirting with the wider mythology of community.[4]

John Knox is the übermeister here, a towering reminder of Calvinist orthodoxy. He presides over a collection of departed souls – merchants, businessmen, landowners – who are largely unknown now but whose wealth afforded them this tranquil spot for eternity. There are some better known figures too – William Motherwell, the poet and song collector; William Miller, who wrote *Wee Willie Winkie* and resided just over the cemetery wall in Ark Lane. Many of the memorials were constructed by the local family firm of J.G. Mossman and a few were designed by prominent architects – Charles Rennie Mackintosh, Alexander Thomson and John Rochead.

The Necropolis is both historically impressive and visually attractive, silhouetted against the skyline. Before I leave, I make a visit to a section at the very top (the areas are designated by Greek letters) to see a reminder that this place isn't completely lost in

distant history – the memorial to the firefighters who lost their lives in the fire in Cheapside Street in 1960, within my living memory.

DUKE STREET

Take the bottom exit from the Necropolis and turn left and you come to the Lady Well. It is a very old artesian well that has been capped long ago but is still preserved through a niche in the wall and a Victorian sculpted wellhead. It is still, to some extent, a place of pilgrimage, as can be seen by the little devotions gathered here – coins and twigs formed into a cross.

Ladywell Street is now a dead end and the well is maintained by the owners of the massive complex straight ahead. You can't miss it as it is marked by a giant red 'T' – a symbol ubiquitous across Scotland on adverts, posters, pubs and beer cans and as the symbol of an annual pop festival, T in the Park.

The Wellpark Brewery has been run by the Tennent family since 1740 as J. & R. Tennent, although brewing, due to the ready supply of water, probably took place here even earlier. Part of the family also made bleach and I like to tell devoted fans of Tennent's lager, probably spuriously, that Tennent's found out that they could use the same machinery for making bleach to make lager.

Certainly in Glasgow, but also in Scotland generally, Tennent's has exercised a hegemony over home-grown lager over the years, having seen off McEwan's, Harp, etc. I know their product well as my mother worked in the accounts department of Tennent's for years and I worked there too temporarily as a student. For years, even after my mother's retirement, we were entitled to 24 free cans of beer each month. These famously featured pictures of female models on the back, known as the lager lovelies.

Nowadays the brewery has expanded and, as well as a place of production, it looks a little like a theme park. There is a giant television screen promoting all things Tennent's, and the walls of the brewery are vividly painted with evocation of Scotland in the natural paradigm – Ben Venue, waterfalls and lochs. There is a giant T formed from beer barrels. There are also various amusing slogans relating to Glasgow or Scotland: 'land of the square sausage where corned beef is a skin tone', 'the only country made more beautiful by rain', 'two positives make one negative: aye right'. To continue the illusion, the brewing vats are painted like lager cans, there are red Tennent's phone boxes and a mock pub called the Molendinar. Across the road from the brewery most of the tenements which once stood have been demolished, but one remains and on the red sandstone wall at 202-204 Hunter Street is a memory of the craft of the brewer – carved tools and sheaves.

Just by the brewery, in the area bounded by High Street to the west and John Knox Street to the east is the Ladywell housing scheme, a large Modernist congregation of flats constructed in the sixties, but from 1798 to 1955 this was Duke Street Jail which housed a variety of prisoners and where hangings took place until 1928. Latterly, most of the prisoners were women and the last female to be hanged in Scotland, Susan Newell, who strangled a newspaper boy, was executed here. There is a street song about the jail which contains the puzzling words:

> There is a happy land,
> Doon in Duke Street Jail,
> Where a' the prisoners stand,
> Tied tae a nail.

I take this to refer to the practice of standing handcuffs which was once widely used in prisons and consisted of handcuffing a prisoner to a hook so that they had to remain standing for long periods.

Also in this section of Duke Street is what was the Great Eastern Hotel, now converted to flats. Despite its grandiose title, this was for years a model lodging house for the less prosperous of Glasgow's citizens. Right beside it you can peek down through a railing with some rusting barbed wire and a few strands of old cloth and see some dark gurgling water, which is a small remaining stretch of the Molendinar.

DENNISTOUN

Duke Street is the longest street in Glasgow and at its junction with Bellgrove Street, just past the site of Duke Street Hospital and where once stood the old meat market, starts the commercial stretch of Duke Street. There remains the shell of the meat market. I remember my father taking me here to see the pigs and sheep before they were slaughtered. Equally interesting, at the back, was a scrapyard for old cars and buses.

The area to the north of here is called Dennistoun and it is where I was born. The posher parts are to the west, but the more basic tenement are nearly all gone now, although my old school still stands, derelict, at Golfhill. I remember my blazer badge – a gold laurel tied by a red ribbon.

Dennistoun has her favourite sons and daughters: Charles Mackintosh who invented, well, the mackintosh, Charles Rennie Mackintosh, Lulu, the pop singer, the author of this book. But the only monument in place seems to be to Charles Rennie Mackintosh and here it is, lumpish in the shape of a bomb with a hint to Glasgow style in the form of thirty square holes. It was designed by the artist Jim Buckley for Glasgow's 'year of culture' and it is called the Dennistoun Milestone .

Today, my companion on a tour of Dennistoun is Mitch Miller, who lives here and was brought up in nearby Parkhead. To some extent, Dennistoun has been gentrified but the process is faltering. An art gallery prospered for a while but has now shut down. There are some reasonably fashionable cafés – Tibo, which is fairly new, and Coia's, featuring Italian ice cream which has been here a good while as the facade proclaims, but not on the same spot.

There is still a good deal of the old Dennistoun. I recognise the church where I went to the Boy's Brigade, the post office, the library. One little street I remember is Hillfoot Street, known as 'make-and-mend' street. There are still a couple of tailors here.

Just up the road once stood a famous dance hall, the Dennistoun Palais that features in a well-known Glasgow song, *Cod Liver Oil and the Orange Juice* that is worth quoting in abbreviated form:

> Oot o' the East there came a hard man,
> Oh oh, a' the way frae Brigton,
>   *Aw haw, glory hallelujah*
>   *Cod liver oil and the orange juice…*
>
> Does this bus go tae the Dennistoun Palais,
> Oh oh, I'm looking for a lumber…
>
> In the dancin' he met Hairy Mary,
> Oh oh, the floo'er o' the Gorbals…

Then Hairy Mary had a little baby,
Oh oh, its faither's in the Army...

As it happens, Duke Street is in demand today. A little further up I meet a film crew who are filming a piece about Duke Street for a series called *The Secret History of the Street*.[5] I speak to the producer and director and they tell me that part of the focus will be on someone I have never heard of, John Butterly, who formed the Reidvale Housing Association and fought for the renovation, rather than the demolition, of Dennistoun tenements.

Further up, Duke Street has recently developed something of an Afro-Caribbean flavour, with some ethnic shops and restaurants. Two pubs, the Loudon Tavern and the Bristol Bar mark the end of this stretch. Opposite is the old site of Haghill, the ground of Dennistoun Waverley, a junior football team long since defunct. Dennistoun Waverley was founded in 1939 and wound up in 1968. I used to come here as a boy with my father and climbed up rickety steps to the elevated pitch above the railway line. Waverley didn't win very much but it is recorded that they did beat Glasgow Rangers 2-1 in a friendly in 1960 – the Rangers team including a young Jim Forrest. Their most notable player was John McHugh, who went on the make 527 senior appearances for Clyde and Forfar and was included in the Scotland squad three times, although never capped.

These are serious sectarian pubs, dedicated to Glasgow Rangers, Protestantism and unionism. The Bristol, I'm told, is the more staunch, but the Loudon is certainly the most ostentatious, encircled by union jacks and painted royal blue. It smacks you right in the face and, just in case you weren't sure, it buttonholes you with slogans in large letters: above the door; 'WE ARE THE PEOPLE' and 'the greatest pub in the world' and 'the most famous pub in Scotland'.

I have a pint in the more subdued and traditional Alexandra Bar with a nice circular bar, an ornate ceiling, polished brass and globe lights in the old style. This too is a Rangers pub and a notice proclaims it is home to the William McAdam Loyal Rangers Supporters Club

I managed to grow up, somehow, largely unaware of the sectarian divide around me, but, roughly, north of Duke Street was Protestant and south of Duke Street, down towards the Calton, was Catholic. Not far from me, but on the south side, was where Lulu –

Marie McDonald McLaughlin Lawrie – was born. Strangely, I hardly ever came here but today there is a sight to be seen. Two giant monoliths, the Whitevale flats, are being demolished. They will soon be gone, but their image will remain as some graffiti artist has painted a crude representation of them on the metal parapet of a bridge opposite.

I have, unfortunately, missed out a major part of Dennistoun, the part that lies to the north along Alexandra Parade. The most notable feature in the Parade is the old Wills cigarette factory that now houses artist's studios – both Mitch Miller and Stuart Murray work here. There isn't all that much to see here but I'm on a mission to visit Alexandra Park, best known as Ally Park. I came here as a boy. It was a great escape from the surrounding tenements. There was a fountain, a boating pond where you could catch sticklebacks, a little lake with paddle boats and a giant draughts set. Not so much remains now, but it is still a pleasant walk. As I leave, on a nearby street there is a little sign of the recession. A car has been abandoned. It is pulling a trailer that gives a whole new meaning to the term portable loo (or, in Glasgow, cludgie) as it has its own toilet along with various signs indicating that the owner runs a plumbing business. I think this is a one-off, but a little later I come across a van with a bath which contains an inflatable man and a giant toy duck on the top.

The western end of Dennistoun is fancier and once, in estate agent speak, had a small pretence to the title of the new Merchant City. Part of it is known as 'the Drives' with villas crisscrossed by lanes of which Onslow Drive is the one I remember best. In a

strange way, it represented to me, as a boy in a fairly decrepit tenement, the pinnacle of luxury housing. I remember venturing into it when I was a boy looking for fallen apples from the trees. Down one of these lanes Mitch points out a stencilled figure that looks like a women with a machine gun. It is known as the Dennistoun 'Banksy', although no-one is sure whether it is genuine or not. The names of the drives, apparently, relate to the family and mistresses of Lord Dennistoun. They have a sort of faded splendour and the Victorian villas are sometimes very grand with Glasgow style features and stained glass. A substantial residence can be purchased here at a more reasonable price than similar in the West End or Southside.

A slight detour from the top end of Duke Street reveals a doocot built in a patch of waste ground. These were once a common sight around Glasgow, usually built on the site of demolished tenements. Although these makeshift, but often elaborate buildings technically had no owner, they were fiercely contested territorially by the practitioners of the rather arcane art of the homing pigeon.

It is possibly that one of the owners of this particular doocot has died as, among the graffiti slogans on the black tarred walls there is sort of memorial, a photo, a festoon of flowers in the shape of a name, more flowers and cuddly toys.

This little oasis, in a leafy little corner, however, marks just about the end of residential Dennistoun as further on, up towards Parkhead and the site of the old Parkhead Forge, long since demolished, there are few residents, or are there?

BEN HUR, BUFFALO BILL AND SHORT BULL

Amazingly, guided by Mitch Miller, I'm now entering a whole constituent part of Glasgow that I didn't even know existed: the hidden yards that are home to Edinburgh's travelling people, families who work largely at putting on shows and fairs. The families include the Garricks, the Marshalls, the Erskines and Mitch's own family, the Millers. The yards used to be their winter quarters as they travelled most of the summer, but they are largely permanent now. Some consist of new houses, but many are collections of caravans and temporary buildings, interspersed with roundabouts and rides. The yards are dotted largely around the east end of Dennistoun, Parkhead, Dalmarnock and Bridgeton. Mitch takes me to his family's yard, in Parkhead. It is comparatively small (the largest has about 100 dwellings) and inconspicuous behind high walls. It stands almost alone. The tenements that once graced this area having largely been demolished. Show people in Glasgow have a long pedigree. At the end of Gallowgate, towards Parkhead, Vinegarhill was the site of an all-year-round carnival from the 1870s.

Mitch also shows me somewhere in Dennistoun looking over to Dalmarnock where there isn't very much now but which once was the scene of a great epic. This was the patch of the first six families. That is, the families that set up the showgrounds. The Green family started Green's Playhouse and the Matchett family set up boxing stalls here. These families were also responsible, among other things, for the very earliest screenings of film. The Biddal family were one such and George Biddal was Mitch's great-great-grandfather. Apparently, a film of George Biddal's funeral in 1909 paid for his headstone, but he was also responsible for a more substantial production. The very first film of *Ben Hur* was made here. Some time later it was discovered and Mitch's grandfather remembers sees a scene of someone falling out of a chariot. Unfortunately, like many early films, it was lost in a puff of smoke in 1970.

If the thought of chariots racing through Dennistoun is exciting enough, another event is equally extraordinary. The East End Exhibition had been held in Dennistoun (it raised funds for the construction the People's Palace) and, for much of 1891-92 it hosted Buffalo Bill's Wild West Show. William Cody brought many Western legends to Glasgow including Annie Oakley. Today there is a monument to him roughly on the site of the show. There was also, for this time, an Indian reservation situated in Dennistoun. Cody had brought about 75 Indians, many of them Sioux and Lakota warriors who had fought at the Battle of the Little Bighorn. Among them were Kicking Bull, No Neck and Short Bull – described by the *Evening Times* as having a face like a chamber of horrors – who had been released from custody in Fort Sheridan. The visitors, it seems, became accustomed to Glasgow ways and one, Charging Thunder, was remanded on Hogmanay 1892 as being drunk and disorderly. Shorty afterwards, Neosreleata, the wife of Running Wolf, gave birth to a baby girl – the first and maybe the only Apache to be born in Glasgow. This whole fascinating period is detailed in a book by Tom Cunningham.[6]

THE BARRAS

When I was a boy, on a Sunday my father would often take me about half a mile down the road to the Barras. The Barras is an extended market place based on a few streets only a few hundred yards east of Glasgow Cross. The name comes from the original practice of selling odd items from barrows in the street (when I was a boy you could still some traders pushing their barrows through streets in the city centre, selling books or small items). But the Barras of recent times was the creation of Margaret McIvor, and the McIvor family still own the large green barns where much of it is situated, although they apparently now live abroad.

Gary Barton, who has a shop here called GEAR – Glasgow East Area Removals, a play on the old Glasgow East Area Renewal Scheme – has been here for a while, and his father before him. Their slogan used to be 'We buy junk, we sell antiques'. I ask him if that is still the case. 'Naw,' he says, 'we don't have to buy it anymore. People give it away.'

Gary is a man of many parts. He has a website called Mr Glasgow dedicated to east end lore. Another website called *realcaltontongs* features interesting photos of the Calton area but also a section of photos of Calton 'fighting men' ('knockout merchants and chib-men': Snarler Jimmy Lynn, The Fighting McCues of Anderston, 'Cathlic Hauns' Keatings) with a disclaimer: 'To put you in the picture ...the title of this website realcaltontongs is basically a romantic title for anyone wanting to know what's happening in and around the Calton area... So please don't bother complaining about any of the contents or you might become acquainted with a couple of the Romantic Tongs... one fine night...'

I'm here at his place to get a copy of a new book (or series of books in a box, to be precise) which features prose, photographs and drawings of the area.[7] It also has a substantial piece on Gary by Alison Irvine. Gary invites me into his small office, a space with a kettle and teacups and pictures of locals on the wall. He calls it the Calton Conservatoire. In fact, Gary's manor isn't just a trading post, it serves as a sort of social hub too, and there is sofa conveniently parked outside if you need a rest. A variety of east end characters turn up here and Gary films them (he is studying filmmaking part-time) and puts them on the web. He has ambitions for more substantial things – a heist movie shot in the Calton. Another possible topic could be John Walkinshaw, a Jacobite who owned this area in the seventeenth century. The youngest of his ten daughters, Clementina, had a liaison with the young pretender, it is said, so Bonnie Prince Charlie could have been winching on this very spot! Walkinshaw also built a house in nearby Camlachie which was occupied by General James Wolfe, famous for the capture of Quebec. In a letter from that period, he refers to the women of the Calton as 'cold, coarse and cunning', so it is not altogether clear whether he enjoyed his short sojourn there. A pub called the General Wolfe existed on the site of his house and later moved to the Gallowgate,

Willie Gallacher is not well-known, but to some he is a legend. Not a writer or a speaker himself, he is an authority on Glasgow lore and has spent years trawling for memorabilia, notably to do with the music hall, the circus and other entertainments, which he generally passes on to other folk. There are many collections and publications that owe a lot to Willie.

I'm meeting him at the east end of the Barras, beneath the old clay pipe factory and opposite St Luke's church which has recently been converted to a bar and concert space, the 'T' in St being replaced by, guess what, a large red T. There are a couple of businesses here that haven't changed much in years – Bill's Tool Store and Pearson's, which sells electrical supplies, buttressing an unreconstructed Celtic pub called the Squirrel. It has promotions for the Lurgan No. 1 Supporters Club and the Yes campaign (stuck to the loo), and a sign saying 'sectarian chanting: escorted from premises'. There are various byways of the Barras here and you can find almost anything. I note a life-sized plastic figure of ghoul with a skull under its arm, an armchair with two plastic arms sticking out behind the cushions and a mannequin with a horse's head. Willie and I go to a little café for tea. This is run by Rebecca, a local woman who lives in a caravan in Bridgeton. Her brother has a book-stall outside which consists of thousands of paperbacks piled higgledy-piggledy on straining shelves.

Willie has something interesting to show – a twenty pound note that isn't a twenty pound note. This is one of the few surviving pro-ductions of a noted Glasgow character, Thomas McAnea, aka Hologram Tam, who was once denounced as a threat to the security of the country for producing counterfeit currency from a little printing shop in Maryhill Road. The story goes that, after he was released from prison he went to the Imperial Bar for a pint. When the landlord held up his note to the light, he did the same with the beer.

Willie is much less mobile now than he used to be, but still comes here regularly. He takes me on a walk with his zimmer; he says that he sees a lot more at a reduced speed. Although many of the stalls appear to be piled with junk, there are still things to see: cheap Stenlake books of postcard scenes of Scottish places, a collection from a lawyer's office and, under a whole load of stuff, one of the

original barrows that were pushed through the streets of the city.

As a boy, I would come to a stall at the Barras every week to buy comics, mostly Superman and Batman, and one of my favourite superheroes was Bizarro, a sort of distorted Superman. And the Barras of today reminds me of a sort of distorted version of what it used to be, having declined for various reasons including the popularity of car boot sales and internet trading. And it might not be with us at all in the near future. The City Council has recently announced a thirty million pound 'investment' in the area which might result in it not being a market any more. So it is likely earmarked to make money for someone, but probably not its current residents.

Willie laments this too. There isn't the same interest and variety as there was in the old days, and new products, notably bootleg DVDs, abound. Willie says one trader sells cheap cigarettes and Viagra ('Have a fag and a shag'). The old Barras on the other hand had stalls selling just about everything. One I remember sold budgies and other pets and there was a place for fishing tackle with buckets of squirming maggots.

Before leaving the Barras, it is worth stating that it was definitely an *upmarket* market in comparison to Paddy's Market off the Briggait which was, to fierce opposition, closed down by Glasgow City Council in 2009. This was a compendium of junk or hidden treasure, depending on your point of view, sprawled along a few old stone arches. It is described in a poem by Freddy Anderson:

> I'll sing you a song of the Market,
> old Paddy's way down by the Green,
> where Watt got his Newcommen engine
> and the Wrights their grand flying machine;
> there's Kilmarnock editions, old masters,
> Noah's Ark and a pileful of junk,
> pieces of eight and an anchor
> from the year the Armada was sunk.[8]

With Paddy's Market gone and the Barras in decline, a vestige of what they were can be found in Glasgow's car boot sales. The biggest are at Jessie Street, Polmadie, on the site of an old locomotive factory, and Blochairn at the site of the Fruitmarket. There is a diversity of stuff flogged here when I visit – well beyond the capacity of the average car boot. One trader is selling full sized beds out of a lorry. A crowd are gathered around Stevie Broon's Meat Auction, where the proprietor is entertaining the crowd whilst dispensing walloping spare ribs – 'today's pork promotion'.

THE SARRY HEID

Two narrow streets head uphill on the north side of the Gallowgate opposite the Barras, Little Dovehill and Great Dovehill. Little Dovehill features some flats, a carpark and, unusually, a few trees. They were possibly originally called Dowhill or Doohill and named after the pigeons or 'doos' (or doves) who lived in the trees here. Although it is possible the name is just a corruption of 'dubh' or black hill.

What is beyond dispute is that Great Dovehill is a little higher than Little Dovehill. The reason for this is that, centuries ago, St Mungo was preaching to an assembled crowd and, finding that his congregation strained to see him above the heads, he commanded the hillock to rise underneath his feet. St Mungo's little chapel was built here in commemoration of the miracle. There is a lodging house here and a warehouse converted into a WASPS artist studio. I usually pop in here to see my old friend Douglas Bennie who makes frames for the local artists. He has some interesting stories to tell of the comings and goings around the area. Some of the artists here, he tells me, are very much in vogue with certain Glasgow gangsters.

Until recently, the remains of a well around here could be seen in the backyard of one of Glasgow's most venerable pubs which once welcomed a variety of customers including Robert Burns, John Wesley, William Wordsworth, Dr Johnston and Adam Smith.

Reputedly built with stones from the Bishop's Palace, the Saracen Head opened in 1755 as a coaching inn to receive the mail coach from Edinburgh. The name of the inn was not uncommon and supposedly refers to stopping points for knights returning from the holy wars. In its heyday, apparently, one hundred passengers could dine there and were received by waiters with embroidered coats, red plush breeches and powdered hair. Today the reality is somewhat different and the pub is a fairly modest space hosting local customers and Celtic fans on match days. It is known in Glasgow as the Sarry Heid. This is a pun by itself as it can be read as 'sair heid' or ('sorry head', I suppose) which is what you get when you've been there if you indulge in the local speciality which I remember as 'champagne cider', a particularly strong and cheap cider.

The pub is old school, but clearly has a community. People have lived here and they seem an eclectic mix. There is a notification of the funeral of a regular ('thanks for the memory, Francis'), a sign saying 'no dancing on the bar', various bits of Celtic memorabilia and old-fashioned slotted seats. The Saracen Head, interestingly, has a little museum, which contains a poem in the handwriting of Burns and the skull of the last witch to be executed in Scotland, Maggie Wall.

Naturally, being of its age, the pub is haunted by several spirits including the ghost of its ex-landlord, Angus Ross. On 9 May, 2005, a fine day in the full moon, a team of television reporters equipped with laser thermometers, parabolic microphones, infra-red motion sensor kits, dowsing rods, etc, etc attempted to find the ghost of Angus Ross. You can see the results, which looks very like a video of an empty pub, on the internet.

I am not very impressed by this, but, in search of the dead, I decide to take a little excursion outside of Glasgow. Near Dunning in Perthshire you can find the rough and ready monument to Maggie Wall on the site where she was burnt at the stake in 1657. When I visit it it is the day after Halloween and a pumpkin has been placed there along with other little devotions including flowers and a little doll. Nothing much is known about poor Maggie but she may have been persecuted for having an affair with a local landowner. Whatever, she is remembered and someone periodically renews her name on the monument in white paint. She was not alone in her unfortunate fate – Scotland executing several times the number of witches per head of population than England, and was trumped only by Germany.

PEOPLE'S PALACE

The little bits of Glasgow history I can relate on these pages are dwarfed by the exemplary collection of Glasgow history in the People's Palace, a museum just down the road from the Barras on the edge of Glasgow Green. I have a personal connection with the People's Palace. Years ago I donated some socialist pamphlets that were on display for a while and, more recently, a short quotation from my book, *Phantom Village*, was inscribed on the wall. Strangely, I only found this out when some friends from New York saw it when visiting.

The Doulton Fountain, the largest terracotta fountain in the world, constructed for the 1888 Glasgow Exhibition stands outside the People's Palace and before you enter there is a memorial to Sister Smudge, the museum's cat and the only cat, apparently, to have been a member of a union, and a little poem inscribed in the pavement:

> Ghostly workers sleep below,
> They hear no rain or heel or tow,
> Think of them where the forges glow,
> In the Glasgow of long ago.[9]

An adjunct of the People's Palace is a large glasshouse known as the Winter Gardens. This has been renovated and now serves as a café. I remember being at a conference here a few years ago at which the whole event was more or less drowned out by roosting pigeons. Ken Currie's series of paintings displayed here marks the 100th anniversary of the Calton Weavers Massacre, and that is the site I am visiting next.

THE CALTON

The area I've been looking at is Calton, or, to be correct, *the* Calton, It is not the most prosperous part of Glasgow and is often trotted out as the epicentre of the Glasgow Effect, with high mortality rates. It is, however, one of the oldest and most interesting parts of the city. The motto of the Calton was 'By Industry We Prosper' and it was a centre of industry in the old days, mostly weaving. Calton weavers were a progenitor of the modern trade union movement and have been renowned in song:

> I am a weaver, a Calton weaver,
> I am a rash and a roving blade,
> I hae siller in my pocket,
> I'll gang and I'll follow the rovin' trade

On the east edge of the Calton, two reminders of its earlier history

remain: Calton Jail and the Old Calton Burial Ground. In 1819, to
control the increasing unruly populace of the Calton, permission
was given for a 'Court House, Gaol and Bridewell or Workhouse
therein'. The old Court House still stands, its status marked by the
almost obligatory city crest above the door. It seems empty and
unused now – although it has quite recently employed (yet again!)
as artists' studios and a gallery, during the more prosperous eighties and nineties. Next to it stands the remains of an old pub, now
superbly derelict. It belonged to someone called John, as the faded
titles of 'John's Bar' can be detected on two sides. I want to take a
picture of it, but a small knot of children are gathered outside –
mostly young girls dressed in pink contrasting vividly with the ram-
shackle ruin of the bar. Oscar Marzaroli, Harry McKenzie and Joan
Eardsley may have made a reputation portraying Glasgow street
children, but I fear that in these changed times and on this occasion
I would be arrested, so I forego the opportunity.

Around the corner is the Old Calton Burial Ground. You enter its
confined space through one of two sturdy iron gates. It is quite
gloomy, but today it is brightened up by a pretty teenage girl
playing with a friendly wee dog. The two most notable monuments
are stones dedicated to the martyred workers of the weavers' rebel-
lion. In the eighteenth century, a group of Calton weavers went on
strike in protest at the threat to their livelihood caused by decreasing wages and the development of power loom factories. On 3
September 1787 the military were called to a disturbance and a
detachment of the 39th Regiment of Foot, from the nearby barracks
just off London Road near the Barras, opened fire on the demon-
strators with six fatalities. Two stones in memory of them were
erected here about a hundred years after the event. The inscription
on one says:

> THEY THOUGH DEAD STILL LIVETH
> EMULATE THEM
>
> WE'LL NEVER SWERVE,
> WE'LL STEADFAST BE,
> WE'LL HAVE OUR LIVES,
> WE WILL BE FREE.

I know this, however, because I have in front of me a drawing by
Alasdair Gray of Harry McShane standing in front of these stones

in 1977. In the twenty odd years since this was executed, erosion of the brittle sandstone has all but destroyed the inscription. Recently, however, some attempts have been made to preserve the old burial ground. And, at the entrance, part of the inscription is engraved on a pavement stone. So the memory of stone still persists.

MILE END AND DALMARNOCK

It is now time, however, to head southeast. I am leaving the fringes of the Calton and then walking east and south to Mile End and Dalmarnock. I should take a water bottle and some provisions: there won't be any amenities for a while!

The community, or what once was a community, I am now entering is, or was, Mile End. Mile End was originally a village (about one mile from Glasgow Cross) formed on the banks of the Camlachie Burn which flowed into the Molendinar. You can see a bit of the burn still – behind a shoulder-height stone wall and some twisted railings, the only section where it is still above ground, directed by a uniform concrete channel for about fifty feet. The water is a colour of rust and, among a little vegetation growing at the side, there is a large collection of empty Buckfast bottles. Mile End grew from being a village to a busy area of tenements and factories in the nineteenth century. There is little here now but a few warehouses and derelict buildings, but the pattern of the streets still remains. Sections are now tarmac, but there are also areas of stone setts and older cobbles. Stone traces. In one street, the cobbles are split by flat setts of granite an interval apart. This was to accommodate the wheels of carts going in and out of the original factories or warehouses.

Mile End has more recently been clearly demarcated. Eight boundary stones have been erected inscribed 'Mile End Quarter', perhaps to differentiate it from its better known neighbours, Bridgeton and the Calton. Ostensibly, there isn't a lot to see here, but the buildings that remain testify to the industry that prevailed in its heyday. Most are now warehouses – one houses a private museum of buses and transport vehicles. There is a substantial radiator factory in a more thirties kind of style with a hedge of tall conifers, looking conspicuously out of place. The only trees of any age in the area, in the grounds of a demolished primary school have, unfortunately, recently been cut down.

Moving further south to the fringe of Glasgow Green and Dalmarnock, there is further dereliction – yet there is the promise of a resurrection here; for this is to be the site of the 2014 Commonwealth Games. Dalmarnock station, so inconspicuous that you might not notice it if it wasn't for the large sign outside announcing its renovation, is being revamped. This is rather ironic as, for many years, it has been a railway station without much of a purpose – the tenements it once served having been demolished.

Hoardings along the road promise social and private housing, business facilities and, behind some boards, are new makings of an Athlete's Village for the Games. Hopefully, it will provide all the amenities needed for the visitors, as this is an area of Glasgow bereft of fashionable coffee shops or, indeed, just about anything else – although there still seems a long way to go since the Games are scheduled for summer 2014.[10]

However, just up from the Athlete's Village, one formidable vast structure has arisen. Large, uniformly grey and largely featureless, this is the Emirates Arena and Sir Chris Hoy Velodrome which faces an older and more renowned arena in the sporting world – Celtic Park, also known as Parkhead or 'Paradise', home of the world-famous Celtic football club.

This walk is planned to continue heading eastwards towards both these venues and, beyond them, Parkhead Cross, and it will. Temporarily, however, I am taking a detour to the south, through the area now named The Clyde Gateway.

THE CLYDE GATEWAY

What is the Clyde Gateway? Well, a bit like the Mile End Quarter, it isn't really anything! It is the name for the regeneration project aimed at developing the section of Glasgow centred around the Clyde that leads from the Gorbals to Rutherglen and further towards Lanarkshire.[11]

Today I am heading for the Clyde Gateway Stadium, aka New Southcroft Park, the home of Rutherglen Glencairn Football Club. The old Southcroft Park which I remember well, was built on a heap of waste from a defunct chemical factory, and was demolished to make way for an extension of the A74 a few years ago.

The route takes me down Rutherglen Road, past Richmond Park, a little oasis with a duck pond surrounded by waste ground (although a rather intimidating sign warns of toxins from blue-green algae in the water), some warehouses and businesses and Shawfield Stadium. Shawfield was once the home of Clyde Football Club, a venerable Glasgow football club nicknamed the Bully Wee. The suggested unlikely origin of this name is that it is comes from the exhortation 'Come on, the bully wee Clyde' ('Forward, you small but brave boys') or, even more ridiculously, that it comes from a French supporter who asked 'But il'y, oui?' ('Their goal, is it?').

What is certain is that Clyde haven't been here for several years (although the supporters club is still just down the road) having decamped to Cumbernauld, outside Glasgow. The stadium, however, is still in use. It is a popular venue for greyhound racing, known in Glasgow as 'the dugs'. This sport could once attract crowds of over 10,000, notably at the White City stadium at the other side of the city.

Further down the road – outside a unit that advertises sheds, fencing, etc – is one of these increasing common memorials to some local person who has died. They originally marked the site of road accidents but now can be found in various different circumstances. The display of football jerseys, slogans, etc is strange but poignant. Something much more direct and public than an intimation in the local newspaper. A few yards further on, however, and a rather decayed mural of football players on a wall near the site of the older Southcroft Park indicates that we are near our destination – the footballing home of Rutherglen Glencairn Football Club.

Junior football in Scotland is very old, nearly as old as its senior counterpart. The Scottish Junior Football Association was founded in 1886. 'Junior', of course, refers only to the level of the football. The players are of any age and they are not amateurs – they get paid.

Today's match is the Scottish Junior Cup semi-final, between Rutherglen Glencairn and Auchinleck Talbot. Auchinleck, named, perhaps surprisingly, not after a motor car but one Lord Talbot de Malahide who funded their formation, are one of junior football's premier teams having once won the Scottish Junior Cup three times in a row. They weren't even founded, however, when Rutherglen Glencairn first won it in 1902. Today Talbot are overwhelming favourites. The Glens haven't been in a semi for nearly forty years and haven't won the cup since 1939.

Once upon a time, a Junior Cup semi-final would have commanded a crowd equal to a senior match, but today about 1100 have turned up. Nevertheless, there is an enthusiastic and friendly atmosphere. You can buy tea and a roll and sausage, and a black and white Glencairn scarf. The mingled crowd shouts both for the 'Bots' and the Chookies': Glencairn equals the Glens equals the Chookie Hens! Strangely, there is more swearing on the pitch than in the crowd with both goalkeepers telling their defenders where they should be in no uncertain terms. Small boys play on the fringes of the pitch, their ball sometimes straying onto the playing surface, although nobody seems to mind. One has a strip with the name 'Messi' on the back. Any resemblance between this match and *el*

classico, however, is very limited. One fan laments 'It's no the way we used to play. We used to play on the carpet!' Indeed, the ball does occasionally touch the carpet – but it doesn't stay there very long, the hoof up the park being the preferred option.

Was it always like this? When I first saw the Glens play, Chic Charnley was in their team. Charnley is a Scottish football legend having played for several clubs in the west of Scotland including Celtic (for one game) and, notably, Partick Thistle. Maverick, volatile wayward genius, eccentric, hot-head; the only player to have engaged in a sword fight outside the ground after a game.

But the Chic Charnley spark is notably absent today. The Glens give away a first half own goal and don't look like getting back in the game. And that's it. Rutherglen may have to wait another seventy-four years for a Junior Cup triumph.

Junior football is professional football but without, mostly, the heated fan aesthetics of Celtic, Rangers or even Partick Thistle. It is local. Maybe the players are your pals from school. Sometimes you can travel to away games on the same bus as the players. It's not far removed from pub football, from skint knees on red baize pitches, from kicking a tennis ball in playground shelters.

Also, junior football is community football. Rutherglen Glencairn very much belongs to Rutherglen, once a proud independent burgh on its own, before it became integrated into the greater Glasgow city. The club's motto is the motto of Rutherglen itself: 'Ex Fumo Fama' ('Out of smoke comes fame'). A motto which (maybe) spawned a famous tongue-twister – 'Ru'glen's wee red lums reek briskly' – a reminder of the industrial heritage of the area. So football evokes community and it evokes local history too.

Years ago, when I actually lived in Rutherglen, each Saturday evening we would keenly await Jimmy Sanderson's radio show. Sanderson was a notable Glasgow eccentric, his encyclopedic knowledge of all things to do with Scottish football matched, to a fair extent, by his own conceit! Every Saturday, as well as refereeing chat-ins between enraged Old Firm fans, he would announce, with almost splenetic enthusiasm, some 'world exclusive' which would usually consist of a new signing for a minor local team or something equally earth-shattering. Nowadays, even the most diehard local fan will probably also watch wall-to-wall Premier and Champions League football on television, but the football tradition in Glasgow lives on and it thrives on a glorious mixture of nostalgia and story-telling.

Whatever Happened To The Foul Shy?

Whatever happened to the foul shy?
That indiscretion of unanchored foot and jugged palms,
To threepenny heads and flailing arms,
To Billy Bluenose and Tam the Bam,
To row-boat benders and big toe-enders?
Whatever happened to the foul shy?

Whatever happened to the shoulder charge?
The refined dynamics of blooter and barge,
To lace-wrapped boots and whalebone pads,
To cattanachio and macroon bars?
Whatever happened to the shoulder charge?

Whatever happened to the foul shy?
No Willie Woodburn banned sine die,
No 'feed the bear' or the Thirds gone bust,
No Chic Charnley's rapier thrust,
No flute and whistle with Alan Rough.
The Field of Dreams has turned to dust.
Whatever happened to the foul shy?[12]

PARADISE

I'm back in Dalmarnock in Springfield Road where, despite the lurking presence of the new velodrome, Stuart and I are heading for Paradise, that is, Celtic Park, or just Parkhead, home of Celtic Football Club. Maybe cycling is the pre-eminent Scottish sport of the future – joining snooker and elephant polo among sports at which Scotland has developed a pedigree – but Celtic are going strong, having reached the last sixteen of the European Champions League recently, beating Barcelona along the way. Strangely, Rangers, their greatest rivals, the other half of the 'Old Firm', have suffered a serious decline, being demoted to the third division because of financial irregularities. Celtic-Rangers matches were a big thing here once, attracting massive crowds. Stuart's granny used to live opposite the stadium. She claimed to tell whether Celtic or Rangers had scored a goal according to the way the china rattled on the sideboard! These tenements are nearly all gone now, even the slightly more prosperous terraces that boasted what the locals once called 'the lucky middens'.

Parkhead Cross, once a bustling centre of tenements, shops and pubs, is pretty dead today. Three pubs that once catered for locals and the thronging match day support are fairly run down. The Turnstiles is shut and looks almost derelict, The Springfield Vaults and the London Road Tavern only open normally at weekends, but today there is a little activity at the latter. From the dress of the men and women smoking outside, I guess that it is a funeral party.

The entrance to the stadium features statues of a famous triumvirate: Jock Stein, the legendary manager who died of a heart attack when Scotland scored the winning goal against Wales in a World Cup qualifer, Jimmy 'Jinky' Johnstone, the elusive genius on the wing (today, or maybe every day, someone has draped a Celtic scarf around his neck) and Brother Walfrid, a Marist Brother at the nearby Sacred Heart who founded Celtic Football Club in 1888 to raise funds for the poor and deprived in the east end. Apparently, he is to be played by Daniel Day-Lewis in a feature film about his life.

ENCOUNTERS WITH JOHNNY CASH, CHE GUEVARA, ETC

The overwhelming feeling here is not so much of a football park as a sort of religious shrine – and this heartfelt allegiance to the club continues nearby. The Calton, down towards the Barras and the Barrowland Ballroom, is the centre of Celtic mania and there are here various inflections of it to be found: the Braemar Bar advertises the world's only Johnny Cash Celtic Supporters Club – 'great music, great fitba' – Baird's Bar, once the epicentre of the Celtic universe (temporarily closed because of, I'm told, some discussions between the landlord and the police) sports, perhaps surprisingly, a selection of international flags which apparently represent the countries of various Celtic players. Others are less circumspect. The Hoops and the Emerald Isle are bedecked in green and white. Celtic memorabilia can be bought at Timland, which cleverly employs the logo of Timberland with the 'BER' replaced by a shamrock (also, of course, re-appropriating what was once a term of abuse for a Roman Catholic, 'tim'), a Barras stall called the Holy Ground, and a smaller shop, Cairdenach Eireann, which unashamedly hawks Irish republican propaganda.

I have a drink in Bar 67, the name of which refers to Celtic's greatest ever victory – their European Cup triumph of 1967. It is a cosy sort of place featuring murals of Celtic players and various pieces of memorabilia: a drum with an inscription to the John F. Kennedy Memorial Flute Band, a Palestine-Celtic flag (the politics of this allegiance are complex, but the connection is largely one of two marginalised, oppressed communities), an advertisement for the Volunteer Kevin Barry Flute Band, a scarf with the legend 'Georgie was the Best, Jimmy was the Greatest'.

That the lore and legend associated with Celtic is about more than just football is apparently in Calton Books, an independent book shop in London Road just beside Glickman's sweetie shop where I used to come for aniseed allsorts as a lad. Here Celtic Football Club, Irish republicanism, international socialism and local history merge seamlessly. There are not only books – mostly Scottish, but also encompassing quite a lot of international political and social theory – but also magazines, football programmes, hat pins and badges celebrating socialist heroes (John Maclean, Che Guevara, Robert Tressell, Ernst Thaelmann the German Communist, Staff Captain Joe McCann, an IRA volunteer killed by the Royal Ulster Constabulary) and t-shirts with various slogans: 'our demands most moderate are – we only want the earth', 'oberas a la victoria', 'resistance is not terrorism', 'unrepentant fenian bastard'! Brian, the custodian, is proud of his stock and chats away about it and his own upbringing in the area and his memories of Mile End when it had streets of tenements. I can ask anything I like, but for 'security reasons', I can't take his photograph.

It is in Calton Books that I suddenly get the connection between Che Guevara and Celtic. One of the books on sale is *When the Gorbals Fought Franco*, the story of J.J. Lynch, born in Ireland but raised in the Gorbals. Lynch was, of course, Che Guevara's father's name.

While I'm around here, I decide to take a very short excursion to The Braemar Bar. I'm fascinated by the names of Celtic supporters clubs. Some are named after old legends: Jimmy McGrory, Charlie Tully, Jimmy Delaney. Some after more recent stars: Henrik Larsson, Georgios Samaras, Didier Agathe, Tommy Gemmell, Yogi Bear. Some have stories to tell: The Lochgelly John Thomson Celtic Supporters Club is named after the Fife goalkeeper who tragically died on the pitch. The Eddie Duffy Celtic Supporters Club remembers a fan who passed away. The Casey Jones Celtic Supporters Club?

The Braemar Bar stands on a rather desolate corner in London Road but the exterior tries its best to be welcoming, two chalkboards have, alternatively, words for welcome in different languages and expressions in Glaswegian: 'D'ye fancy a wee swally?' 'Hawrawrerr', 'Shut yuir Geggie!'.

The building possibly dates back as far as 1845 although, as was often the case in the zealous sixties, the top stories of the tenement were condemned and demolished. There has been a bar here for a while but nobody knows quite how long. John Wallace has been the landlord for more than twenty years. He inherited the place from his uncle Cedric Fletcher and a painting by the gantry shows the bar as it was with his name inscribed on the corner façade and the man himself standing outside. He was a big man, 36 stone. John tells me that it took eight men to carry his coffin – or rather seven to carry and 'wee Matt to hang on to the end'.

There is a bodhran handing on the wall inscribed 'Johnny Cash/ Man in Black/ Celtic Supporters Club' and you can buy a badge with the same inscription. The story goes something like this. Some years ago there was a discussion among customers of the pub about whether Johnny Cash wrote *Fifty Shades of Green*, a song with obvious Celtic appeal. As it happened, Johnny Cash appeared in Glasgow in 1972 at the Apollo which had just been created out of the former Green's Playhouse. He decided to take a wander around some east end pubs and was able to answer the question in person. And the club is named after that occasion.

Nearby is Lynch's or the Old Burnt Barns, arguably the oldest pub in Glasgow. It has been owned by the Lynch family for years and still is. Delia Lynch shows me some of the paraphernalia collected by her father John: there is the figure of an Indian, a sculpted merman, the stuffed head of a buffalo, a painting featuring John Wayne and the cast of *The Quiet Man*, an image of the Statue of Liberty. There is a nice wood panelled back room as well as the function suite upstairs. However, it is here that the Celtic pantheon is exemplified, as there are various tributes – to Jinky Johnstone, John Thomson, Che Guevara, John Kennedy.

A little later that evening, I'm in the Tolbooth Bar at Glasgow Cross – a decent traditional pub with old advertisements on the wall and high windows with cut glass. It too, is a Celtic pub, and there is a singer. Republican favourites like *Back in Derry* (written by Bobby Sands) mingle with *The Fields of Athenry*, *Dirty Old Town* and *A Boy Named Sue*. Everyone seems happy – drinking, laughing, joking.

So, is this sectarianism? Well, sectarianism is not in fashion at the moment, singled out for zero tolerance by the Scottish Parliament. The *Scotsman* has conducted a poll which claims that the vast majority of Scots think sectarianism should be a crime (how can an '-ism' be a crime?). Football clubs are fined if their supporters sing certain banned songs. A recent trial for assault on the Celtic football manager seems to have hanged, farcically, on whether he was called a 'fenian bastard' or a 'fucking wanker'.

Yet, how can you codify such a thing? The fact of the matter is that an all-out attack on sectarianism risks attacking also genuine engagement with history, politics, culture and identity which are still at the heart of working-class communities, both Protestant and Catholic, such as Dennistoun and the Calton. And if that is stripped away, what is left?

BRIGTON

It is essential in Glasgow to be even-handed regarding the sectarian divide, so I head a little further south to Bridgeton, or Brigton, as it is commonly known in Glasgow. Bridgeton Cross, with its cast iron 'umbrella' in the centre, was once a busy and thriving local centre, but it is much quieter now.

There are a few pubs still in Bridgeton, although large areas around the Main Street have been demolished. Some bear the loyalist insignia to demonstrate their allegiance. The two most potent symbols of the Protestant cause are, of course, the union jack and the figure of King Billy. That is, William of Orange (William III of England and William II of Scotland) who fought wars in support of the Protestant cause. His victory over James II at the Battle of the Boyne was seen as quashing the Catholic cause and ensuring the Protestant succession to the throne. His other name, William of Orange, gave rise to the fraternal organisation known as the Orange Order or Orangemen.

My own religious background is unusual in that, as with many Glaswegians, my paternal grandfather came from Ireland. However, he was an Irish Protestant, and not a member of the Ascendancy – a working-class Dublin Protestant from Golden Bridge. I should, therefore, appreciate Protestant mythology more than its Catholic cousin, but I just don't find the lore and the iconography so alluring.

However, many do and Bridgeton Cross was the congregating spot for the Brigton Billy Boys, a Protestant gang led by Billy Fullerton, another 'King Billy'. More than a thousand folk attended his funeral in 1962. It is recorded in a poem by Edwin Morgan. There are still Orange Walks in Glasgow, notably on 12th July to celebrate the Battle of the Boyne (it is a public holiday in Northern Ireland). They are generally orderly affairs these days, although it is ill advised to try crossing their line even if you are in a hurry to get across the road.

Orange Walk

The march is punctuated
by commas (never a full stop).

These kings of causes won and lost
Brandish their sashes and banners,
Camp their coats outside a chapel.

Flutes and drums are battered and blown
Flags are fluttered and batons are slung,
All for the memory of a distant class and creed
In another land and another history.

Notes

1. See James Cowan, *From Glasgow's Treasure Chest* (R.E. Robertson: Glasgow, 1951).
2. Ian Begg is a noted architectural historian and I do appreciate his work, but I just don't think this building is right.
3. John Strang, *Necropolis Glasguensis with Observations on Ancient and Modern Tombs and Sepulture* (Glasgow, 1831). Buchan, Peter, *Glasgow Cathedral and Necropolis* (Glasgow, 1840).
4. Ian Spring, *Phantom Village: the Myth of the New Glasgow* (Edinburgh: Polygon, 1990).
5. The director was Russell England.
6. Tom F. Cunningham *The Diamond's Ace* (Edinburgh: Mainstream, 2001).
7. Alison Irvine, Mitch Miller & Chris Leslie, *Nothing is Lost* (Glasgow: Freight Books, 2015).
8. See Freddy Anderson, *At Glasgow Cross and Other Poems* (Glasgow: Clydeside Press, 1987).
9. From *At The Barras*, Harry McGee.
10. The original walk I undertook was just before the Commonwealth Games in Glasgow, which was regarded as a success. The athletes village and associated developments were to be a 'legacy' for Glasgow's future. Today, the area hasn't changed much.
11. See Neil Gray, 'The Clyde Gateway: a New Urban Frontier' *Variant*, 33 (Winter, 2008), 8-12. Note that the M74 is Britain's most expensive road. Regarding its extension, a report on its viability stated that it was expensive, unnecessary and would have an 'adverse effect on the community'.
12. Of course, to maintain the rhyme, 'sine die' has to be pronounced to rhyme with 'shy'. There is a precedence for this in a song by Adam McNaughton.

CENTRAL

THE HIGH STREET

Walking down the High Street from the cathedral, there is a great deal of Glasgow history but it is now found in abbreviated form – so much so, in fact, that you might pass it by without noticing. At the junction of the High Street with George Street and Duke Street on the left was once railway yards but now there is the beginning of a new housing development: Collegelands. The Molendinar Park Housing Association are promising to make this a leisure area with, apparently, the Molendinar itself bubbling through. Nothing much has happened yet, however. There is a wall with a poster advertising, I think, a pop band, that reads 'Danger! Poisonous Monkeys'. There was once a plaque on the wall near here indicating the one-time residence of the painter Sam Bough, but it is gone now. I remember I was impressed to learn that Bough was born in Carlisle. As a boy the only person I knew that came from Carlisle was my mother.

Before the railway, however, here stood the Old College, the first site of Glasgow University. That itself, however, was fairly new, built in the mid-seventeenth century (the university had been founded in 1451 as part of the cathedral complex). In 1870, nevertheless, it was unceremoniously demolished to make way for the expansion of the railway into the city. It is still remembered in the shape of the Old College Bar across the road from the site. This is one of a number of pubs that lay claim to being the oldest in Glasgow and it is likely that an inn stood on this site some time ago, although the building

is not that old despite a sign stating 'Glasgow's Oldest Public House, built circa 1515, Ancient Staging Post & Hostelry'. Apparently, perhaps the first ever inn in Glasgow once stood in the High Street just before the junction. It was called the Angel and the doorway consisted of an angel's wings.

A small, short street running down beside the Old College Bar may go unnoticed but was an important historical site. It was once known as Bun Lane, but is now Nicholas Street (after Saint Nicholas). It was also once known as Greyfriars Wynd and led down to the old Greyfriars Monastery (the Blackfriars were just down the road). There is a building on the south-east corner which is an ornate old bank in red sandstone with a sort of turret and a stern-looking worn stone figure atop. This represents Pallas, the goddess of wisdom, who featured on the seal of the British Linen Bank, which this building once was. Now it is a warehouse for a fruit and vegetable merchant. However, a plaque on the side wall shows some people gathered round an older house with the traditional crow-step gable that once occupied this site and it notes 'On this site stood the house in which the poet Campbell lived'. Thomas Campbell (1777-1844) was born in Glasgow and educated at the High School and the University of Edinburgh. Campbell is not generally well known as a Scottish poet and his work remains largely unsung. His best known poem was written in London and is titled 'Ye Mariners of England'. His most successful collection was *Gertrude of Wyoming* of which I have a little well-worn first edition. Apparently, despite the subject matter, it was largely written on the island of Mull and Campbell never visited America (although he did travel through Europe and met Wellington after the Battle of Waterloo). The Scottish influence on Campbell's work is largely underestimated and he did write about the Scotland (and Glasgow) of his childhood:

> Scenes of my childhood and dear to my heart,
> Ye green, waving woods on the banks of the Cart...

His poem, 'Lochiel's Warning', deals with the battle of Culloden and contains his most quoted words: 'coming events cast their shadows before'.[1]

Across the road, high up on a new block there is a gargoyle embedded in the wall and a plaque commemorating the site of the Blackfriars Monastery, but that is long gone. Before what might be called the first 'slum clearances' of the 1860s this whole area was crowded with tenements. The City Improvement Trust decided they must be demolished, not so much for the improvement of the area or the well-being of the inhabitants, but to make way for the railway. Thomas Annan, a Glasgow photographer was commissioned to photograph the area as a form of documentary before it was razed. Thus was created one of the most important Glasgow books of historical records – *The Old Closes and Streets of Glasgow.*[2] One hundred copies only were printed for Glasgow Corporation in 1900, some time after the photographs were taken (they had previously been displayed as a gallery show – a cabinet of curiosities for the well-heeled who saw the urban poor as 'aliens'). Nowadays a copy will set you back the best part of five figures, but thirty or so years ago, before Glasgow's history became an issue, you could pick them up for a lot less. It is impossible to exactly imagine what once was here, but a Glasgow librarian and antiquarian, Joe Fisher, tried to do so, mapping the individual closes and the directions of the photographs.[3]

Moving on, the bottom half of the High Street is unprepossessing these days, a motley collection of shops. Carruth's Grotto stood here until recently. For generations it supplied plaster saints, communion and confirmation gifts and other Catholic memorabilia. Further down, Benson's Beds is a fairly standard furniture shop, but I remember when it was one of those galleried department stores. One fairly new addition, however, stands out – The Blue Chair Café. This colourful place was founded a couple of years ago by a Scottish songwriter and his Australian partner – thus the Australian flag and the saltire feature equally outside. Below is written 'Home of the Bohemian chair: a space for performers and wordsmiths to share art you can't hang on a wall'. Outside are a few tables, one inscribed – 'Our heads are round so that our thoughts can go in either direction – Some French Guy'. The Blue Chair is open most hours and in the evening there are events – open mic, quiz nights, a flea market, philosophical discussions – to which you can bring your own bottle. The café takes its name from an Elvis Costello song:

> Well, it's my turn to talk, your turn to think
> Your turn to buy, my turn to drink
> Your turn to cry, my turn to sink
> Down in the blue chair, down in the blue chair[4]

There is an oil painting of the very man prominently displayed inside. The rest of the decor is best described as eclectic – squashed Irn Bru cans, an African mask, corners with toys and books piled up.

This is a popular and cheery place. Prompted by the hostess, Lorelle, a loquacious type with purple hair and nose piercings, the customers actually talk to each other! There is a blue chair situated in the corner for performers and guests are invited to write a poem when they are there and put it in a box for subsequent dissemination. So I think of the old closes that once were here and of this place now and I do.

Thomas Annan in the Blue Chair Café

Welcome sir, to the latest product of
The Glasgow City Improvement Trust.
Place your half-plate there, by the chiller.
Evian water (cholera free) but no vesta for
your cigar. Vegan approved paninis but first
visit our commodious restroom, wash
the collodion from your fingers and scrape
the grime from your boots. Don't hurry,
we have one hundred and fifty years.

GLASGOW CROSS AND THE SALTMARKET

The High Street comes to an end at Glasgow Cross. The Gallowgate turns to the left and the Trongate to the right. To continue straight on takes you into the Saltmarket and down to the Clyde – roughly following the path of the Molendinar from the cathedral down to the very earliest origins of Glasgow as a little fishing village on the river. Thus the name Saltmarket; salt was used to cure salmon (it was once a centre of textile production too and was called the Walkergait – from the practice of walking or 'waulking' the tweed).

In medieval times, markets were held here, although the original Mercat Cross was removed in 1659 (the current one is a reconstruction). During the sixteenth century, as Glasgow became more prosperous, merchants gathered here, and the Tolbooth was constructed. It served as the Town Clerk's office, a meeting place, a debtor's prison and the depot for coaches in and out of the town (the Gallowgate was the main thoroughfare in and out of Glasgow, London Road, which now also runs from the Cross being a much later amalgamation of country lanes). The main part of the Tolbooth building was demolished, rebuilt, then finally demolished in 1921. The only part that still stands is the imposing seven storey Tolbooth Steeple which has, for centuries, defied the 'improvers' who have continually tried to destroy historic Glasgow. As recently

as the late sixties its demolition was proposed as part of the extension of the Glasgow urban motorway. When this was opposed by
some, I believe it was suggested that the motorway could run
directly above the steeple, leaving a few feet between the two. The
steeple is closed and not used for very much now. There is a clock
face and, internally, a chime of sixteen bells provided by John C.
Wilson and Co of the Gorbals Brass and Bell Foundry in 1888.
Right by the steeple was once a low-level railway station. That is
gone now, but there is still a large vault in the centre of the road that
provides ventilation to the railway below – a sort of iron lung,

It is not generally well known that L.S. Lowry came up from
Salford to Glasgow in the forties and painted several scenes including the Finnieston crane and the Tolbooth. The little matchstick
men that inhabit his painting are reflected by the multitudes of men,
mostly in bunnets (flat caps) that occupy postcard scenes of the
Cross throughout the last century. This was always a popular place
to gather. There were sales and roups, recruiting fairs during the
depression and various watering holes to congregate in. At the
beginning of the Gallowgate, one of the best known pubs over the
years has been Chrystal Bell's, or, more precisely, Chrystal Bell &
Co. This opened in 1904 and was the result of a merger of two families – the Chrystal family, whisky merchants, and the Bell family.
Three brothers once owned a transatlantic ship named *The Three
Bells*. One of brothers, Finlay, became the proprietor here (for a
while, the pub was renamed The Royal Albert, for no apparent
reason, but it has thankfully now been restored to its original
name).

It is fair to say that there is nothing much I don't like about the
area around Glasgow Cross. There are many things to do here.
There are honest-to-goodness old Glasgow pubs – the Tolbooth,
the Empire Bar under the bridge, the Old Ship Bank – named after
the first of Glasgow's distinctive banks, founded by the tobacco
merchants, which once stood on this site – where the sing-alongs
are legendary, and the Lampost. This was once Graham's Bar and
I drank there years ago when the landlord was Barclay Lennie
(Len) who later became a well-known art dealer. Subsequently it
was taken over by the landlord of the Lampost (now demolished)
near the site of Duke Street Jail. The main feature of this pub was
an actual lampost in the bar. Presumably the pub had been built
around it. I also remember a small pub called the Moray Arms just
around from what once was the police station (customers were

sometimes invited to take part in line-ups – identity parades – for a couple of pounds). It still exists but is now called The Whistlin' Kirk, named after the episcopal church around the corner – St Andrew's-By-The-Green – which was the first to have an organ ('a kist o' whistles') installed.

A variety of shops are found in the Saltmarket. Actually just off the main thoroughfare but prominent with its curved frontage is Thomas Hay's Pet and Aquarium Corner, which has been there as long as I remember. Then there are tailors, a gallery and picture framers, newsagents and, notably, solicitors. These are largely criminal solicitors, as the High Court is further down the Saltmarket and the Sheriff Court just across the river. One, Scullion's, has a very distinctive sign consisting on a skull adorned by a barrister's wig and 'crossbones' which consist of a pair of handcuffs and what looks like a pair of lopping shears or a jemmy.[5] If, however, a felon cannot find solace there, then across the road is MOJO, or the Miscarriage of Justice Organisation. The motif of this organisation consists of the letters formed from a broken pair of handcuffs. This was set up in 2001 by Paddy Hill, one of the wrongly-convicted members of the Birmingham Six, and a Glasgow man, John McManus. Its aim is to assist innocent people in prison, where they are often traduced as troublemakers, and after their release, when they still suffer from trauma and isolation. In the words of Paddy Hill, 'you can take a man out of the prison, but you can't take the prison out of the man.'

Then there are the cafés, not boutique cafés that continually spring up these days, but traditional old working-class Glasgow cafés. There is the Criterion and the Coronation or, to be precise, Guido's Coronation Restaurant – 'family owned since 1939'. I used to come here as a boy after the Barras. My favourite was a bowl of peas soaked in vinegar. The doyen of them all, however, is the Val D'Oro, the oldest chip shop in Glasgow dating to 1875 (more recently a contender in the Gallowgate has claimed this distinction, but the claim is spurious, I am assured).

The Val D'Oro is much larger than it looks from the outside and is dominated by the imposing figure of Luigi Corvi, who runs the shop as his father did before him. The Corvis have had the place since 1938 and chose its current name with, presumably, the 'gold' referring to the colour of the fish and chips. Luigi Corvi, a bachelor, is dedicated to his chip shop and to opera music and, when the occasion demands it, he is known to serenade his customers with an

aria or two. Before that it was the Swiss Restaurant and was owned by another Italian family – the Beltramis, who are now noted in Glasgow through Joe Beltrami, the son of the shop owner, who died only recently. Beltrami was a defence solicitor and lawyer for, among others, the Thompson family. He reputedly saved twelve felons from the gallows and the watchwords among the criminal fraternity in Glasgow whenever they were charged was 'Get Beltrami'.

For some time before and after Pope Benedict's visit to Glasgow in 2010, a large drawing entitled *Glasgow Cross Crucifixion*, by David Adam, an artist from Brechin, was situated above the door of Val D'Oro. Luigi and Peter Corvi were in it, along with a junkie shooting up and a pickpocket. The Madonna was represented by Mary Paterson, one of the café's longest-serving customers and in the foreground a little girl forlornly reached up to Christ with a revitalizing bottle of Irn Bru.

The subject is prescient, as Glasgow Cross was once the place of execution, as indicated by the naming of the Gallowgate ('gate' or 'gait' in Glasgow street names indicates a walk). At a later date, executions moved a little down from the Cross, to the edge of Glasgow Green in the Saltmarket at Jail Square (there is no jail here now but the public mortuary remains). Perhaps the most notorious execution was the hanging and quartering of John Ogilvie at the Cross on 10 March 1615. Ogilvie was guilty of practicing and promoting Catholicism at the time when it was strictly proscribed. He was tortured, deprived of sleep and taken on a cart to the Cross where the sentence was enacted.

St John Ogilvie, who is Scotland's only post-reformation saint, was canonized in 1976. The submission was based on an incident that took place in Easterhouse in 1967 when John Fagan, a docker, was suffering from stomach cancer. His local parish prayed to the Blessed John Ogilvie for a miracle and the parish priest, Father Thomas Reilly, pinned a medal of Blessed John to Fagan's pyjamas. Fagan was inexplicably cured, the miracle was proclaimed in Rome and the canonization took place. Not everyone in Glasgow, known for its sectarian divide, was convinced by this and the matter was propounded when Fagan later suffered a relapse (in 1990 it was claimed that he recovered fully from cancer for the third time).

Today there is a strange marble monument to the saint on the wall of the Tolbooth, his face turned inwards away from the viewer, presumably to the heavens. Another little twist to the story occurred in 2010. The artist Peter Howson, one of Scotland's most prolific painters who once had a studio in the Gallowgate near the Cross, was commissioned to paint St John Ogilvie. Howson was known for his expressionistic portraits of Glasgow street characters and the tragic war in Kosovo (as well as an image of a muscular Madonna – the singer). It seemed like a excellent opportunity to construct something modern but within a realist representational tradition. The BBC made a documentary about the production of the paint- ing entitled *The Madness of Peter Howson*. It was well-known that Howson, an obsessional artist, suffered mental health problems. The commission proved problematic for him and he created and subsequently painted over many versions (claiming, fantastically, at one point, that the £30,000 he had spent on paint had driven him to bankruptcy). Eventually the finished painting was revealed to the public. Gone were the elaborations of earlier versions and what remained was a gaunt figure of a man with staring eyes looking sus- piciously like Howson himself, praying with a noose loosely round his neck. The painting can now be found in St Andrew's Roman Catholic Cathedral facing the Clyde. Believers can follow a simple liturgy and obtain a plenary indulgence from the church.

The Saltmarket was always a place of entertainment and convivi- ality and among the establishments found here in the nineteenth century were the Shakespeare Singing Saloon, the Oddfellow's Music Saloon and the Walter Scott Saloon. All were devoted to drinking and general high jinks and they all had pianos and pro- grammes of what was sometimes described as 'comic and sentimental' singing. The Shakespeare also featured a bowling alley.

On the corner of Greendyke Street, facing the Green, once stood Mumford's Theatre or 'penny geggie'. William Mumford, an

Englishman, set this up in 1834 and it featured 'mechanicals' or a mixture of actors and marionettes. It later became a general store and was demolished in 1902. You can still see a print of Mumford's Theatre on the wall of the Tolbooth Bar at the top of the Saltmarket, although the rest of the decor in this interesting pub with light streaming in from its high corner windows is a clanjamfry of all things Guinness! Interestingly, an inscription above the door reads 'City Improvement Trust 1906'. I presume that this refers to the tenements that were once above the pub.

The most notable building in the Saltmarket is the High Court, based partly in the Judiciary Court House. This was designed by William Stark in the early nineteenth century and it is stark in design, its Doric stone portico the exact proportions of the Theseion in Athens. It has been described as 'austere to the point of Calvinism',[6] so it is, I presume, sort of Graeco-Scottish. Around the corner in Jocelyn Square the 1994 extension to the High Court mirrors Stark's original with a circular Doric portico. Inside there is a classical, but Scottish, touch – words from David Hume's Enquiries *Concerning the Principal of Morals* sandblasted into the stone. Directly opposite is a more ornate affair – a sort of pastiche of the Corinthian order – which is the McLennan Arch. Removed from the top storey of the Athenium in Ingram Street to here in 1893, it now constitutes a dramatic 'front door' to Glasgow Green and through it you can see another structure that featured in the lore of local executions.

A large stone obelisk had been constructed on the Green in 1805 in commemoration of the Battle of Trafalgar (long before the Nelson Column in London). Bizarrely, it had been struck by lightning in 1810 and the top twenty feet or so severed and replaced. This event itself was commemorated by a painting by the Glasgow landscape artist John Knox, known for his panoramas and paintings of developing travel in Scotland featuring steamboats and tourists. The scaffold on the Green faced in its direction which led to a grisly expression – 'You'll die facing the monument' – meaning that one had the complexion of a rogue or scoundrel. Public executions were once a cause for celebration, refreshments were available and strong drink was taken. Broadsheets with blunt woodcuts and verses on the condemned man's last words and confession would be written and pedalled. In 1820, James 'Purly' Wilson, a weaver, friend of Baird and Hardie and member of the Friends of the People, a radical group who supported the work of Thomas Paine, was executed here. He had led a protest march from Strathaven to Glasgow. His unusual appellation is due to the fact that he was attributed, rightly or wrongly, with the invention of the purl stitch in knitting. The last public execution here took place in 1865, of one Edward Pritchard, convicted of murdering his wife and his mother-in-law.

Hanging a Man

Surely it is an occasion for a holiday,
Dr Pritchard to be hanged on the Green –
Facing the monument (they say).
The chapmen are full of verse,
Rhyming the felon into oblivion.
The noose perfects its twisted task,
Fresh from the Gourock Rope Works.

It is good to be alive this sunny day.
Bring your knitting, rotting tomatoes
will be hurled. Come along to see
The righteous vengeance of the Lord –
A man made into a ruckle of bones.
Mutton pies and butt beer will be served.
Rejoice and stay – until the death.

SCHIPKA PASS AND BARROWLAND PARK

Old ghosts may well haunt the Glasgow Cross area of Glasgow, but part of it is pretty new. Roughly opposite the Val D'Oro there is an iron railing and the ground to the north sinks about ten feet to where the little lane called Schipka Pass can be found. This was originally a passageway between the Gallowgate and London Road called St Andrew's Lane but sometime in the late nineteenth century it changed its name to that of a the location of a famous (at the time) battle of the Russo-Prussian war.

Until his death in 2004 this was the demesne of Dick Barton, father of Gary Barton and proprietor of Barton's Mini Barras. For years Dick peppered the walls with slogans and observations on the world and Partick Thistle Football Club. Favourites included 'Off the Peg: 2nd Hand Suits from the Middens', 'Lingerie Sale, Knickers Down'. and 'Opening Soon, Sheikh Ma Tadger's Massage Parlour'. But Dick would also be seen around the area of the Cross, often wearing a beret, a false moustache and a Partick Thistle scarf and accompanied by a golden labrador. He would carry a blackboard labelled 'Dick Barton, Private Dick' on which he would chalk his various observations on local events and the world in general:

PRESIDENT CLINTON, THERE'S A SUCKER
BORN EVERY MINUTE

RENT-A-GENT GIRLS, I'M FREE, I'LL WINE
AND DINE YOU AND VAT 69 YOU,

BIBLE JOHN? JOHN MCINNESS WAS GUILTY,
DNA FROM HIS BROTHER PROVED IT

Dick Barton's businesses were diverse. He sold fireplaces, owned a trophy shop and also ran a pool hall for while, which was also once the old Mecca Bar beside the Val D'Oro and which, I remember, had the reputation as the roughest pub in Glasgow. A television documentary in the eighties described it as 'the bar at the bottom of the slide' which amused the locals, although the Oxford Bar in the Gallowgate, now derelict, was also mooted. Dick died suddenly and tragically in 2004 and the buildings in Schipka Pass have been demolished. Today, however, they have been regenerated with the construction of Barrowland Park on the site.

Barrowland Park is an initiative to utilise an area of waste ground leading eastwards from the old Schipka Pass. It was part of a general city-wide project to improve the city's appearance ahead of the 2014 Commonwealth Games. Part of the wider Calton Barras Action Plan and costing over half a million pounds it was designed as a 'pop-up park' without any commitment to the use of the land in the longer term. This is made clear by a placard attached to railings beside another feature – an 'iconic Gilbert Mackenzie Trench Police Box (one of only six remaining) – which states 'Stalled Space: a community fit... for a wee bit.' Recently, the City Council has announced its intention to utilise the land for further development of shops and housing thus sparking a 'Save Barrowland Park' campaign. Going by the usual rate of change in the east end, however, it could be there for some time whatever transpires.

The most notable feature of the park is an artwork by Jim Lambie – The Album Pathway. This candy striped walkway winds its way east towards the Barrowland Ballroom and features the names and dates of nearly 2000 bands and individuals who have played here. Fancifully, it could represent the album spines in someone's vinyl collection. Some examples:

The Smiths
Lena Martell
Whitesnake
Super Furry Animals
The Proclaimers
Skunk Anansie
Shane McGowan and the Popes
Deadmau5
Billy Bragg
Lloyd Cole and the Commotions
The Chemical Brothers
Primal Scream

I recognise most, but not all of them, but to the music aficionado this could literally be a trip down memory lane and it is possible that someone has seen many, maybe hundreds, of these gigs. One Saturday afternoon I watch through the railings as a few drinkers from MacKinnons – one of the pubs in the area that keeps long hours, opening at eight in the morning every day – smoke outside

under a sign that reads 'Make Barrowland Park Permanent. Vote Tommy Ramsay for the Calton Ward', and various people wander

up the pathway. Everyone stops to read the names. It is a perpetual Glasgow conversation piece.

The Barrowland Ballroom still lights up its extravagant facade, with, supposedly, the largest neon sign in the country, periodically for concerts. The current building only dates to the sixties since a fire destroyed most of the previous incarnation, but the interior with its wood-panelled walls, saxophone inscribed linoleum and zigzag stairs is more reminiscent of the thirties. It features in a 2015 movie, *The Legend of Barney Thompson* directed by Robert Carlyle, as a bingo hall (the movie also features iconic Glasgow sites such as the Red Road flats and Bridgeton Cross). The Barrowland Ballroom is a survivor, adapting to the changing times. It was once a roller disco and is now a well-known concert venue. It is no longer, however, a ballroom. In that capacity it was infamous for a series of murders that has remained firmly lodged in the collective memory of Glasgow ever since. 'Bible John' was the name given by the media to a gentleman who used to frequent the Barrowland Ballroom in the sixties. He was youngish, polite with sandy hair and freckles. He smoked Embassy filter tips, drank Coca-Cola and did a mean two step. He often referred to the Bible and had an unerring ability for identifying ladies who were having their monthlies, strangling them in dark alleyways and stuffing used sanitary towels in their mouths. In 1968-69 three young Glasgow women met their end this way.

Bible John has never been identified and no-one ever charged with these crimes but, despite Dick Barton's attribution, it has recently been demonstrated that the convicted killer Peter Tobin is the most likely candidate for the these murders.

Barrowland holds fond memories for many Glaswegians who remember the many acts who have performed here. Stories about the ballroom abound. David Bowie, according to legend, stole one of the star lights from the ceiling when it fell at his feet.[7]

MERCHANT CITY

As you walk down the lower part of the High Street, you know that the Merchant City is to the right as there are large street signs telling you so and large wrought iron gateways, similar to those at the Barras and, it occurs to me, those that demarcate Chinatown in Soho, have been constructed. This small section of central Glasgow is so well established now that it is easy to forget that it is a comparatively recent invention, and the result of a particular branding exercise. Basically, the Merchant City is a smallish square of central Glasgow bounded by the High Street to the east, Queen Street to the west, Argyle Street to the south and Ingram Street to the north. The name Merchant's City was introduced sometime in the seventies, possibly thought of by the architectural historian Charles McKean. Previously it was just part of the city centre, known generically as the Tron by the locals. It was an undistinguished area of the city centred around the old Fruitmarket. The merchants referred to are often known as the tobacco merchants, who enabled the development of Glasgow in the seventeenth and eighteenth centuries through importing tobacco from the New World. As the Babbity Bowster banana warehouse demonstrates, Glasgow merchants did not deal solely in tobacco. Most inconveniently, however, and the reason why the moniker Merchant City is not universally approved of, is that they also dealt in slaves.

In the aftermath of the hype of the late eighties, a group of Glasgow writers, in opposition to the title 'Merchant['s] City' (probably, although some have suggested that the resemblance is coincidental) set up a loose co-operative called 'Workers City'. In a series of publications they railed against the excesses of Glasgow City Council and their associates. I had a small part to play in this debate as in my first book about Glasgow I suggested that the term 'worker' (and some of the industrial imagery that arose at that time) had problematic connotations in a post-industrial city with high levels of unemployment. One reviewer took this to suggest that I was opposed to the Workers City Group, which I was not. The writings of this period have stood the test of time and can now be found in their entirety on the internet.[8]

Anyway, I'm up for a dekko at the Merchant City and, one sunny weekday, I am in the Press Bar, which used to be beside the offices of the *Glasgow Herald*, to meet Johnny Rodger. No-one could be better qualified than Johnny to show me the Merchant City as he is Professor of Urban Literature at the University of Glasgow and he also lives there, in one of the converted warehouses in Bell Street. I like the Press Bar. I used to come here as a student at Strathclyde University, it being conveniently across the road from the English department. I remember it as being mostly the haunt of mature students. Leather jackets and beards were cool then (maybe they still are). It hasn't changed much despite the fact that the press themselves have taken a hike to more modern premises some time ago.

In the centre of the Merchant City is the Candleriggs. There was once a major department store – Goldbergs – here but it closed and then a building collapsed and that was the end of a traditional pub,

Granny Black's. Another, the Riggs Bar, soon followed. Now loosely designated Candleriggs Square in large wooden letters, this is basically a hole in the centre of the Merchant City. Selfridges bought the site intending to open a store but that has never materialised. As I pass by, there has been some fly posting on the boards. One is advertising a shop but I like the sentiment: 'People of Glasgow, You Deserve MORE!'

Around the corner, the old Fruitmarket is now a collection of eateries and bars, but none of them can hold a candle to the oldest of them all. Café Gandolfi has been here about as long as the Merchant City, since the seventies. It has kept its original simplicity but has expanded to include extra venues including the nearby fish restaurant. The owner and chief chef, Seumas MacInnes, hails from Barra and his motto is 'deagh bhiadh, deagh bheannachd' (well fed, well blessed). His philosophy is straightforward and his food blessedly simple. You can watch him preparing his recipes online and there is an excellent Café Gandolfi cookbook. Recipes from aspiring chefs nowadays read like *War and Peace* and say things like 'a good greengrocer will be able to obtain this exceptional ingredient, hand picked from young shoots in the first days of the new moon and preserved in jars crafted by the finest craftsmen in the far-flung Caucasus, bla, bla, bla... ' The Café Gandolfi recipes say something like 'Find the finest finnan haddie, poach in fresh milk, serve.' (OK, I have simplified a little.)[9]

If I have a quibble with the work of Seumas MacInnes, it is in his fascination with the Stornoway black pudding about which he has written a whole book, *The Stornoway Black Pudding Bible*.[10] This Scottish delicacy now has preserved status, like the Arbroath smokie or the Cornish pasty, yet I have no idea from whence it was derived. As far as I remember, black puddings were once just black puddings and they were made anywhere. It is, of course, a pungent blood sausage which I don't care for, yet it has somehow attained almost cult status. Seumas claims to be one of the first to employ it in the wider culinary universe (that is, apart from a component of a greasy fried breakfast) in the Café Gandofi in the eighties. In Gaelic it is called *marag dubh* which means, err... black pudding. Some canny Lewis men, however, decided they would like to corner the market in this dubious delicacy and in 2013 it was awarded Protected Geographical Indicator of Origin status which means in order to use the name it has to made near enough at Stornoway. And that is that.

There are memories of my university days around here: the City Halls, where I graduated and the Ramshorn Kirk, where I attended the University Theatre Group. Both have interesting arcana inscribed on the pavements outside that deserve attention at a later date, but for now, Johnny wants to show me some of the interesting

architectural features of the west Merchant City.

The oldest building here is Hutcheson's Hospital, glistening white in the sunshine, like an upside down ice cream cone which was endowed by the brothers George and Thomas Hutcheson in 1660 to provide for sick old men. The brothers are still there by dint of their statues, among the oldest in Glasgow presiding over a wider range of the citizenship who are provided for by the restaurant that occupies the premises.

There are other notable buildings, such as the Trades House, in Glassford Street, designed by Robert Adam, but Johnny wants to draw my attention to two buildings, both former banks, that you could call the little and large of Ingram Street.

The old Trustees Savings Bank with its Beaux Arts interior was designed by John Burnet in 1866 but was improved by his son who added a grand dome and an extravagant facade. St Mungo features here in the centre of the pediment and a couple of bending figures hold the whole magnificent weight on their shoulders as if they sculpted from the heart of a mountain and have been here since the beginning of time. It is a *piece de resistance* designed to demonstrate the splendour and solidity of the financial and fiscal stronghold of commercial Glasgow in the nineteenth century.

Next door, slightly plainer in an Italianate style but larger, is what is now the Corinthian, a bar, restaurant and club, but was originally the Union Bank, built in 1841. The facade features ten ladies, two with trident swords and the names of other branches of the bank in Scotland – Dundee Kilmarmock, Rutherglen, Perth, Ayr, Paisley,

Aberdeen – demonstrating its national provenance.

However, there is something that is peculiar about this building. Johnny takes me down a wide lane to the side and points that what seems the back of the building is also an elaborate facade. In fact, this was the front entrance when the centre of Glasgow industry was closer to the Clyde and the docks, but the main entrance was switched when Glasgow expanded to create the Glasgow grid around George Square to the north and west. You can find old Glasgow immediately to the south of this point, where there is the Merchant House, a renovated tobacco merchant's mansion, and the Virginia Galleries where tobacco and slaves were sold. Glasgow's association with the slave trade is deep rooted. Many Scots were owners of plantations and many Glaswegians had their personal slaves (the ownership of slaves here was only banned in 1778). A portrait of the tobacco merchant John Glassford (after whom Glassford Street was named) and his family now in the Burrell Collection had, at a later date, a figure of a black slave painted out. Immediately to the north, opposite a baronial style building that Johnny tells me was based on the architect's bible of the time, Billing's *Baronial Architecture*, is a more recent development – the Italian Centre, a complex of upmarket shops and offices and a few flats converted from warehouse buildings that has outgrown their use in 1991. This is sometimes seen as the epitome of Merchant City style demonstrating all that is good about Glasgow regeneration. There is a giant figure of Italia above the front elevation and there are three other sculptural peculiarities. John Street is protected by three figures of Mercury (nominated Mercury, Mercurial and Mercurius), two rather malevolently perched on the top corners ready to swoop down and one landed amongst the pedestrians, a rather louche youth displaying his classical lines to the shoppers.

These figures were sculpted by Sandy Stoddart, a controversial figure regarded as somewhat reactionary by the contemporary art scene. He was appointed Her Majesty's Sculptor in Ordinary in Scotland in 2008. He is perhaps best known for his rather ludicrous statue of David Hume dressed in the robes of a Greek philosopher in Edinburgh's Royal Mile. His model is John Mossman, the monumental sculptor, and he is devoutly opposed to modern sculptural practice. I have no particular feelings about his work, but I note that traditional monumental sculpture, under the patronage of the great and good, lacked any particular cultural or political motivation.

In the palazzo of the Centre is a contemporary sculpture that I like a lot more. Two simple figures of a man and a dog gazing towards the sky by Shona Kinloch. It is titled *Thinking of Bella*. Rather than distant mythological figures from the heroic age, they could, of course, just be ordinary Glaswegians.

THE TRONGATE

From Glasgow Cross, winding my way through the city, I am following in the putative footsteps of Saint Mungo, as his image is everywhere, from the more traditional version at the Cross through a metallic sculpture on the side of the Tron Theatre to the brightly painted version on the facade of the Gallery of Art. The city coat of arms, equally is omnipresent on buildings and railings. A few years ago, the artist Ashley Rawson designed an alternative coat of arms featuring chips, cigarettes and a ned giving the v-sign in place of St Mungo. It was accompanied by a little verse, 'Let Glasgow Perish': '... There's the bird that never flies, stuck by gum it vainly tries/ There's the fish that never swims, served with chips to Billies and Tims, etc'.[11] Unfortunately, Glasgow may be smiles better but it has a sense of humour bypass when it comes to the city's image, so it wasn't well received. Nevertheless, I have seen enough of these symbols and I'm struck by a similar fit of irreverence when I remember an Edwin Morgan poem that takes the city motto for a stroll ('Let gallows languish... Let gargoyles forage... Let Brasso furbish...) and decide to attempt my own version:

Let Glasgow Flourish
(scatological version)

By the poaching of the bird,
By the flushing of the turd.

By the filleting of the fish,
By the peeing of the pish.

By the chopping of the tree,
By the weeing of the wee.

By the throttling of the bell,
By the farting of the smell.

I'm in the Trongate now. The original Tron Church burnt down in the eighteenth century. The story goes that members of the Hell Fire Club, somewhat the worse for wear, broke into the Session House and added logs to the fire burning in the grate to see how much of the heat of hell they could actually bear. The current church was substantially redeveloped and extended in the 1980s and is now the Tron Theatre. Another redevelopment nearby is the Britannia Music Hall, or Panopticon. This was derelict for years before being renovated. It is advertised as 'the World's oldest music hall' and dates to the 1850s. Stan Laurel made his first appearance here in 1906. It closed in 1938 and lay derelict and largely forgotten for years until it was resurrected by enthusiasts. Funds for its preservation are raised in a shop around the corner in the High Street.

If the people of Glasgow once had a great affection for the music hall, it is rivalled by their love affair with the cinema. Across the road, down Tontine Lane, can be found an interesting artwork which reflects this. Douglas Gordon's *Empire* is a constructed neon sign featuring the single word 'Empire' as a mirror image.[12] It represents a scene from the Hitchcock film *Vertigo*. It was originally more conveniently sited in Brunswick Lane opposite the Mitre Bar and illuminated with a flickering letter to reflect the scene in the movie. Now it is unlit and isolated behind gates that are usually locked, but the bar sign from the Mitre Bar, now demolished, has followed it. Its current state adds it a certain poignancy that tallies with the decline of the traditional cinema which was once the staple fare of Glasgow weekends.

It was Douglas Gordon who first referred to contemporary Scottish artists as the 'Scotia Nostra'. Some of these set up Transmission Gallery in King Street, a little street of various shops that once seemed to be the start of a area of antique and collectibles shops but seemed to have somewhat died a death. This artist-run gallery was set up to challenge establishment control of the art scene in Glasgow.

So new Glasgow artists are ambitious, but are they also egotistical? One critic has described Glasgow as the 'leading producer of shoe-gazing neo-formalism'. And here is a guide as to how to be an artist in Glasgow: 'be unusual. sneer at stuff. sleep around. pour scorn. believe in yourself. become conversant with theory. join in. keep abreast of fashion. be slim. appear knowledgeable. fear proles. swallow your pride. be minimal. do the unexpected. never deviate. be outrageous but never impolite. be middle-class. appear out of nowhere. take drugs. reveal yourself. be cool. use people. never underestimate the opposition.'[13]

I've taken this quotation from a book edited by Malcolm Dickson and I have come to the Trongate to meet him. He has been around the Glasgow art scene for some time. He is director of Street Level, a photography gallery that features exhibitions and events, a small bookshop, an archive formed from the papers of Cordelia Oliver, the Glasgow art critic, and a workshop with darkrooms and digital

photography facilities. Malcolm has been the director of Street Level for about twenty years, since it originated in a small space up by the cathedral. The name itself indicates the ethos. Street Level is meant to engage with people on the street and with communities. Although there is an education programme running classes in everything from the collodion process to portrait photography to digital imaging, Malcolm sees the most valuable educational function as the work that is done in collaboration with outside initiatives.

Street Level is open to public membership and has a range of excellent facilities for all photographic purposes. Malcolm shows me round. One of the members, Lachlan, is digitising and printing some old negatives from the thirties as part of a commission. He shows us one. It is a picture of a shop sign advertising rupture trusses.

I have previously been to Street Level a couple of times, before the modernisation, and Malcolm and I recall an episode that is quixotic if not totally bizarre, concerning a mutual friend. Eddie Linden grew up in the Gorbals and had, according to his own testimony, a disadvantaged childhood being brought up as a 'poor, working class, Marxist, Catholic, Jewish homosexual.'[14] Despite this, after decamping to London he became, for many years, the editor of the poetry magazine *Aquarius* and champion of contemporary poets. A few years ago, to celebrate his achievements, a special edition of the magazine – *Eddie's Own Aquarius* – was produced and a launch in Glasgow, at the Street Level Gallery, was arranged. For some reason that I cannot remember, Eddie arranged for boxes of the magazine to be delivered to me in Edinburgh and assigned me the task of bringing them to the launch.

On the specified evening, I arrived in due time at the venue but Eddie was not there. At that time a friend of mine, Cy Laurie, a Glasgow folksinger and publican, owned a bar in the street, a cavernous place with a life-size figure of Robert Burns in the corner. That is where I found Eddie, accompanied by the eminent Glasgow writers who were to read at the event, all professors of creative writing at Glasgow University – James Kelman, Alasdair Gray and Tom Leonard. Strong drink had been partaken off (but not by Tom Leonard who is teetotal). It was fair to say that Eddie was a little the worse for wear and also Alasdair, who it could be said, was not only having some difficulty standing, but also avoiding falling off his chair.

As the start of the launch was more than imminent, I suggested that it was maybe time to turn up and, slowly, we weaved our way to the gallery where there was a full anticipating crowd and Malcolm, ready to video the readings. It was decided that it was politic that Alasdair go first which he managed, leaning against a wall. He proceeded to take a sheet of paper out of his pocket with a newly written short story and read it, repeating one section three times. No-one was sure whether this was for poetic effect or not (it wasn't). Having completed his performance, Alasdair was helped to his seat where he slept for the rest of the launch except for one waking moment to announce that James Kelman was quite right about something or the other.

Meanwhile Eddie was nervous, so I calmed him down by getting him a bottle of Stella Artois and, to his credit, he was quite lucid and gave a short speech and a reading of his poem 'City of Razors'. The other contributions were also, perhaps, controversial. Tom Leonard chose not to recite any of his better known Glasgow poems but instead delivered a more recent piece about politics in which the name Tony Blair appeared a lot interspersed among various swear words. James Kelman was clear and confident but chose to rail against Glasgow University and academics in general, of whom there were several in the audience. (All three were, I believe, in the process of resigning, or perhaps already had resigned from their professorships at the university.)

The denouement of this extraordinary event, which must have perplexed visitors eager to learn about the Glasgow literary scene, came as the speakers were almost finished. A loud crash was heard in the foyer. It turned out that some neds had run in, grabbed the box with the proceeds for the sales of the magazine and scarpered.

Street Level is part of a community that notably includes the

Glasgow Printmaker's Workshop called 103 Trongate. Also in 103 Trongate is a more exotic form of art. Sharmanka Kinetic Theatre features the works of Eduard Bersudsky who was born and worked in Leningrad but moved to Scotland in 1993. His work has been exhibited in the Trongate since 1996. Bersudsky is constantly creating new works from his base in the Scottish Borders but it still has a very Russian feel. One show is titled *Proletarian Greetings to Honourable Jean Tinguely from Master Eduard Bersudsky out of the cradle of Three Revolutions*. There are regular performances of the carved and constructed figures that make up the gallery and, if patrons wish to continue the Russian theme, they can go next door. Café Cossachuk is painted bright red and decorated with Russian folk art. The menu includes Golubtzi, Chakhokhbili, Tzimes, Plov, Gouvetch and that is quite a mouthful!

ARGYLE STREET

Argyle Street was once called the Westergait, but was named Argyle Street in the eighteenth century after Archibald Campbell, the third Duke of Argyll (the archaic spelling 'Argyle' was an alternative at that time). Campbell's only clear association with Glasgow was that he went to Glasgow University, but he was one of the most powerful men in Scotland at the time. Argyle Street today is almost as long as Duke Street, extending about two miles to the west where it joins up with Sauchiehall Street at Kelvingrove.

This part of Argyle Street is mostly known for shopping. Once the department store Lewis's (not to be confused with John Lewis) stood in the centre and you could get almost anything there. Before that the main store was called the Polytechnic.

There are a couple of things about here. Down Stockwell Street to the left there was (I can't find it now) a plaque on the wall identifying the site of a townhouse in which the Glasgow merchant James McGill was born. He is best known for founding, in 1821, McGill University, Canada's oldest university, which features among its alumni that noted actor William Shatner.

To the right, in Glassford Street, the Steps Bar is a small but interesting pub designed in the art deco nautical style. It features a stained glass panel of a Clyde-built liner.

Joining Argyle and Buchanan Streets, the Argyle Arcade is a remarkable space but the fascination is largely curtailed if you are not interested in its stock-in-trade, jewellery. The city best known for its arcades in the United Kingdom, Cardiff, has a much more diverse collection of shops. Pondering on this disappointment one night I have a vivid dream in which I imagine another arcade in the centre of Glasgow. I even dream the address – it is in Albion Lane, off Albion Street. I dream the shops, the stalls, the pub at the end, the upstairs gallery. I even dream the items for sale and the prices: a restored church font, old broadsheets, a glass collector's cabinet. When I wake up it seems so real that I believe that it must be there and must be visited. But then the clear light of day dawns and it once more recedes into dreams.

With an entrance in the Arcade and another in a little lane, Sloan's is a rather grand pub and actually a surviving coaching inn which also claims to be Glasgow's oldest pub, starting as a coffee house in 1797. The courtyard outside was once used for cock fights but now has a more subdued craft market. It has a downstairs bar and upstairs dining room and is well worth a visit.

Glasgow's street artists are in evidence throughout the city centre these days. Klingatron and Rogue One, to an extent, use stencils like Banksy, but, to my mind, the carefully crafted portraits in spray paint of Smug are the finest examples and Argyle Street is his territory. A corner site has been portrayed as a bar where the customers are various animals including an elephant and a shark. Round the corner in Gordon Street is a giant girl leaning down with a magnifying glass in order to pick something up. The area is used for storage by a nearby bar so it currently looks like she is grabbing

a barrel of beer. Further on, on the corner of York Street, is another gallus young woman, striding up the street with headphones on and smoking a cigarette. This is part of a larger installation called *Gallery*. Trompe d'oeil figures gaze at various representations of famous paintings. Hokusai, Dali, Munch, Pollock and Picasso are represented – and there is Leonardo's Mona Lisa, although a peculiarly Glasgow Mona Lisa with the SEEC and the Finnieston Crane in the background, and the ubiquitous Irn Bru can in her hand. Locals, apparently, call her the 'Mona Lassie'.

Argyle Street can be divided into three parts: the shopping centre, then the middle part, past Smug's gallery, in which there isn't much now except some new hotels, then the western part, which comprises the traditional working class district of Finnieston. However, I'm taking a sharp right, up towards Central Station.

CENTRAL STATION

Ask a Glaswegian where is the centre of the city and there is a good chance that he will opt for Central Station. The largest building in Glasgow, this is a landmark in more ways than one. Walking down Renfield Street towards the station entrance in Gordon Street, for years the night sky was lit by a large neon sign, some thirty feet high, advertising Barr's Irn Bru. To elaborate, this sweet orange-brown concoction is immensely popular in Glasgow and Scotland. Manufactured by A.G. Barr (founded in 1875) since 1901 in one form or the other, it was at one time going to be Iron Brew, but the shortened name was adopted in 1946. For many years it was advertised by Ba-Bru, a little black boy in a turban who featured on the sign and appeared in a comic strip in Scottish newspapers. However, for reasons of political correctness, poor Ba-Bru has effectively been airbrushed from the marketing history of the product and now the only exoticism associated with it is purely Clydeside with the adoption of the well-known advertising slogans: 'Scotland's Other National Drink' and 'Made in Scotland from Girders'. The rotunda below the sign variously also featured large signs for Bell's Whisky and Player's Cigarettes, but they are all gone now, replaced by one large neon screen advertising, when I pass by, smart phones, cosmetics and holidays in Dubai.

Central Station, massive portal to the centre of the city for hordes to people – commuters, tourists, businessmen teeming over its huge white marble tiled concourse through its wrought iron gates and canopies every day. The facade of the station and the hotel above dominates Gordon Street and this is a busy area mobbed with revellers at the weekend waiting quietly or otherwise in queues at the busiest taxi rank in Scotland. Newspaper vendors used to sell the latest issues here. In the early seventies, Glasgow had two evening newpapers – *The Evening Times* and *The Evening Citizen* – and the sellers would compete – raucously crying the papers, making 'Evening News' or 'Citizen' sound like strange wails from the underworld. A winter's evening at dusk, the streets lit with neon signs and

station lights, workers trooping out of offices, these cries and the continual chorus of roosting starlings is a memory that abides.

Central Station itself is massive and busy. It serves the south of Scotland, inter-city to London Euston and various stations in England as well as commuter services from both its upper and lower levels. Over 30 million passengers annually cross its grand marble-tiled concourse. The roof consists of over 48,000 separate panes of glass. The station is on several levels and actually was built (originally in 1879 by Caledonian Railway) on top of a village called Grahamston on the banks of the Clyde. Tunnels still exist, although blocked off, that led down the river and once transported goods but were also conduits for numerous rats which infested the station within living memory.

Paul Lyons is Customer Services Manager at the station, but has spent most of his time over the last year conducting tours of the station which have proved extraordinarily popular. The tours once promised to include the roof gangways but health and safety has scotched that so they largely now feature the lower levels of the station, mostly inaccessible to passengers. It says a lot for Paul Lyons's story-telling ability that he makes so much of what are in effect fousty-smelling and sometimes confined cellars, but he is nothing if not enthusiastic. He has grand plans for the station and points to features that do not yet exist – the wrought iron gates (painted black for the funeral of Queen Victoria apparently) are to be returned to their original livery. The mortuary that stored the bodies of soldiers returned from the First World War is to be inscribed with Mary Symon's poem 'The Soldier's Cairn'. A blocked-off now unused lower platform is to be opened up and to feature a restored train carriage. Theatrical master of the empty space, Lyons regales us in the vacant fusty basements with tales of things that are yet to come.

His narratives, however, are only partly to do with the fabric of the station; his real concern is with the people who have occupied it. The unsung highlanders and Irishmen who, for years, undertook the station's most menial tasks. The men who howked hundreds of tons of coal every week through the station's underbelly to lorries in Hope Street. The women who met their men returning from war with lit candles to burn the lice from their infested coats. His most horrific stories, however, are of the station mortuary where maggotty corpses transported from France where stacked. They had to be identified by their family, sometimes young women or girls, who were then responsible for the body and usually had to pay to have it carried from the station. Lyons suggests that some, too horrified by the situation to think straight, would sometimes name just about any body in order to get out. More welcome visitors to the station, perhaps, have been the celebrities who have passed through. Roy Rogers visited here with Trigger, and it is rumoured that they both had a room at the Central Hotel. The largest crowd, according to Lyons, turned out for Laurel and Hardy – 9,500 souls. Oliver Hardy, apparently, was shook by the hand so enthusiastically that afterwards he found he had lost an expensive wristwatch.

There are ghost stories about the station too, of which Lyons is rightly sceptical. Not so, however, the Glasgow branch of the Ghost Society. In 2013 they conducted a study in the underbelly of the station used mediums and a 'spirit box'. They concluded that a man possibly named McRae or Adams had shot his wife with a revolver in the boiler room of the station in the 1920s, supposedly for the insurance payment after he had lost his fortune in the Wall Street Crash. The whole thing is recorded on their website, but they admit that there is no corroborating evidence.[15]

The concourse of the station is a fascinating place to watch the world go by. On either side are various shops and the curved dark wood facades of offices and what was once the destination board before the electronic versions above the platforms were installed. A former office on the west side of the station is now the Central Bar. It overlooks the main concourse and the windows are dotted by neon signs consisting of a red star and the word 'Heineken'. So, it is the perfect place to sit at the window, imbibe what is probably a very good pint of lager (or Tennent's if you prefer) and tune in to the rhythm of station life.

Glasgow Central Rap

> station rap, station rap
> girders thick with pigeon crap
> footfall, marble hall
> see it all, see it all...

> Lyons sets out on his walk,
> walk the walk, talk the talk
> four thirty on the clock
> next train to Giffnock

passport-holder, skateboarder
suitcase filled for vacation
station rules violation

old men clocking students talking,
kitted out for hill-walking
Chir Mhor, Goat Fell beckon
evening ferry from Ardrossan

football fans, Billies and Dans
plastic cups of Costa coffee
bottle of Lannie from the offie

fine clothed, toffee nosed
designer bags (Princes Square)
Paisley lassies, shoulders bare
out in town for a tear

big square clock, couple talk
women pushing baby buggies,
men in bar, playing puggies

muslim woman in a veil
clutching bargains from the sale
fast food joints in a row
West Cornwall Pasty Co

station rap, station rap
girders thick with pigeon crap
footfall, marble hall
see it all, see it all…

The railway lines to the south of the station cross above Argyle
Street walled with an elaborate wrought iron and glass facade,
recently restored. The space underneath, lined with shops and the
entrance to the lower level station is famously known as the
Hielandman's Umbrella. Gaels from the Highlands of Scotland emigrated in large numbers to Glasgow in the nineteenth century due to
the Highland Clearances and, more generally, the urbanisation of
society. At first, along with the Irish for whom they were sometimes
mistaken, they were generally shunned and kept to their own

company. The Hielandman's Umbrella was, therefore, reputedly their meeting place. Ian Mitchell, a Glasgow historian has ingeniously devised a 'Teuchter Trail' which leads from here to places associated with the Highland Scot such as the St Vincent Street Church which still conducts services in Gaelic, the site of the old Highlander's Institute beside the Mitchell Library, to the top end of Sauchiehall which was notable as populated by Highlanders still in my youth.

Almost, but not quite, under the Umbrella on the south-west corner of the station building is the Twa-Heided Man. Paul McGinn is the landlord of this establishment opened about fifteen years ago since when, he says, it has been 'washing its face'. It is a pub dedicated to Paul's uncle Matt McGinn, a kenspeckle and well-remembered Glasgow character. McGinn was a socialist, performer and a serious songwriter, but his popular comic songs are best remembered on the facade of the pub – words from *The Wee Effen Bee* and the *Gallowgate Calypso* :

> Maggie, Nellie and Mary-Anne,
> Lizzie, Willie and Phil McCann,
> Get your jaiket and don't be late,
> Murder polis in the Gallowgate.

Matt deteriorated a lot in his later years and the last time I met him, at the Strathclyde University Union, he was in a bad way. Tragically, he died in a tenement fire in 1977.

A little further to the south, the railway crosses the river but two piers still stand untopped, remnants of an earlier crossing and they have been deployed for an interesting artwork by the Scottish poet and sculptor Ian Hamilton Finlay. Chiselled in the stone so that it can be read, with a little difficulty, by passers-by on the foot bridge are some words from the Sixth book of Plato's *Republic*:

ΤΑ ΓΑΡ ΔΗΜΕΓΛΑ ΠΑΝΤΑ
ΕΠΙΣΦΑΛΗ ΚΑΙΤΟ ΛΕΓΟ
ΜΕΝΟΝ ΤΑ ΚΑΛΑ ΤΩΙ
ΟΝΤΙ ΧΑΛΕΠΑ

They are accompanied by some words in English, perhaps by way of a translation:

ALL GREATNESS STANDS FIRM IN THE STORM

However, Johnny Rodger[16] points out that the true translation is more like 'all greatness is precarious and good things difficult'. Therefore, it runs almost contrary to the perceived meaning! So, inscribed on these obsolete stone obelisks is not just a celebration of civic pride in the bridging of the river Clyde by a latter day Ozymandias but a substantial question mark, in a period of deindustrialisation and change, over the nature of the city and the changes occasioned by time and tide.

THE HORSESHOE BAR

Central Station is handy for the up-market shops of Buchanan Street, including the 80s development Princes Square. However, just around the corner from Central Station, up a narrow street (almost a lane) called Drury Street stands an institution just as venerable, the Horseshoe Bar. This is the best preserved and most popular of the old Victorian and Edwardian drinking dens, or 'people's palaces',[17] as they have been coined. The structure of the bar is that of a factory for processing drinkers. There are two double doors at either end and a vast circular (or horseshoe-shaped) bar that is feted as the longest in the world. In the days when Glasgow was a city of a million people, hundreds of drinkers would be accommodated here, nearly all men on their way to or from work. The place is mostly still populated by men and you would be hard pushed to find it quiet with sometimes, for example on match days, several bodies deep at the bar.

Around the top rack of the gantry, constructed in 1984, are inscribed various quotations, from the *Holinshed Chronicles* to more recent times. For example:

> Total abstinence is an impossibility, and it will not do to insist on it as a general practice (Queen Victoria)

> Not drunk is he, who from the floor,
> can rise alone and still drink more.
> Drunk is he who prostrate lies,
> without the power to drink or rise
> (T.L. Peacock)

> He that would shine and petrify his tutor, should drink draught Tennent's in its native pewter (C.S. Calverley)

The bar is extravagantly decorated. A clock spells out the name of the bar, there is a large sculpture of a horse and a portrait of Queen Victoria that the locals call Les Dawson from a supposed resemblance to the comedian. There is also a mystery in the Horseshoe Bar. Around the high rack, there are several jars of a Chinese design. There is a wedge under one that ensures it is always at an angle. Don't ask why. Nobody knows. It just is.

John Whyte, an erstwhile proprietor of the bar, was a staunch unionist as the union jack motif on two panels in the window (they are not appreciated by all the customers), that originally came from another establishment, demonstrates. Across the road from the Horseshoe is another bar that is of the opposite persuasion. The Yesbar used to be the Vesbar taking its monicker from an Italian scooter, but the owners were so taken by the campaign for Scottish independence that they changed the name. Inscribed on the canopy outside is a quotation from Nelson Mandela: 'May your choices reflect your hopes, not your fears.' And the Italian theme is reflected inside where there are multicoloured tables, fifties-style posters in pastel shades and prosecco on tap. The faded posters feature reclining models and slogans such as 'Buy Coca-Cola', 'Twilight Lounge' and the rather risqué 'Come in for a stiff one. It's ladies night. Everynight.' It is a friendly place and, soon after logging into their wi-fi, I get a text offering me a free pizza.

GEORGE SQUARE

Further up the road in George Square the independence theme continues. Yes campaigners are parading saltires and banners. There is a connection with Nelson Mandela here too. Glasgow was the first city in the country to grant Mandela the freedom of the city and they also named the old St George's Place, near the old Glasgow stock exchange, Nelson Mandela Place. In 1993 Mandela came to Glasgow and addressed a large crowd with these words:

> ...It is a privilege to be a guest of this great city of Glasgow... The people of Glasgow were the first in the world to confer on me the Freedom of the City... Whilst we were physically denied our freedom in the country of our birth, a city 6000 miles away, and as renowned as Glasgow, refused to accept the legitimacy of the apartheid system and declared us to be free...

The latest slogan employed to market Glasgow is 'People Make Glasgow' and it is prominently displayed in giant letter on the side of what used to be the College of Building and Printing. Opposed to the blue of the saltires, pink is the chosen medium here and it is all around, on the public bicycles collected at stances around the city and taxis, which are painted pink. Taxi drivers have recently taken to giving customers postcards with a poem on them. Entitled 'Welcome to Glasgow', it is cornered with the Glasgow coat of arms and surrounded by the slogan 'People make Glasgow':

Our city's full of magic,
a European great,
with so much to be proud of,
we're going to celebrate...

Whenever you arrive here,
you'll see a smiling face,
you'll hear the Glasgow banter,
and feel a warm embrace.

Believe it or not, there is more than one of these poems, all attributed to 'A Glasgow Cabbie'. Well, at least he has the driving to fall back on.

Glasgow marketing slogans haven't always had the best reception. 'Glasgow's Miles Better' prompted the comedian Jerry Sadowitz to ask 'better than what? The snot in my nose?' 'Glasgow: Scotland with Style' was hijacked by the Glasgow Autonomy Project who produced posters which read:

Glasgow: Scotland With Style – PISH
poverty, inequality, low life expectancy
NAE MAIR PISH

The people of Glasgow have not always found the city so benevolent as it was to Nelson Mandela. Many older people have a folk memory ingrained into them of the time when armed soldiers and tanks confronted workers in George Square. What is sometimes called The Battle of George Square took place on 31 January 1919. In the aftermath of Red Clydeside and industrial unrest, the prime minister, Winston Churchill, fearing a Bolshevik revolution, sent tanks into the Square to confront workers

More recently, in 2011, an altogether different form of war was enacting in the Square. *World War Z*, a zombie movie starring Brad Pitt was filmed here with George Square and St Vincent Street the main locations. The city was chosen to fill in for Philadelphia where, apparently, taxes were too high to film although, with about 2000 local citizens employed as extras, one wag suggested, unkindly, that Glasgow was chosen for a zombie movie to save money on make-up.[18]

The most notable feature of George Square is the City Chambers at the east end and the white marble cenotaph with its two large lion figures at either side. As a young boy (around 1960, I guess) I came here to see the Queen. It was an unusually warm day and one of the Guards fainted in the street. The City Chambers is a huge, splendid building that also has been a film location, doubling as the Vatican in Charles Gormley's *Heavenly Pursuits*. It is commonly used for receptions for just about anyone visiting Glasgow and I've been there a couple of times. At one conference I was surprised at the magnificence of the buffet only to discover that, within minutes, it was whisked away to a reception in another part of the building. Pat Lally was head of Glasgow City Council when the city became European Capital of Culture in 1990. A controversial character who was nicknamed Lazarus because of his political comebacks, he was regarded by some as putting profit ahead of the interests of the people. He promoted the building of Glasgow Concert Hall, which became known as Lally's Palais and hosted international stars. At the height of the culture city hype I had a t-shirt featuring a character displaying his empty pockets and the slogan 'Nae Pavorotti for the Poveratti'.

Another issue the citizens of Glasgow have had with the City Council is their tinkering with George Square to make it more suitable for major events. The whitebeams that graced one side of the square were removed and there have been proposals to move some of the statues. These include Scott and Burns and the poet Thomas Campbell, James Watt, Sir Thomas Moore, the hero of the Battle of Corunna, Victoria and Albert and a couple of prime ministers. Not so well-known, however, is the statue of James Oswald, the Liberal MP. He stands in the north-east corner and holds out his hat in his left hand.[19]

It is not well known that Joseph Conrad spent some time in Glasgow when he was a seafarer (the *Narcissus*, as in *The Nigger of the Narcissus* was a Clyde-built ship). The story is that the Scottish novelist Neil Munro took him to George Square one night and told him he could become an honorary citizen of the city if he tossed a sixpence into Oswald's hat, which he duly did.

THE ANCHOR LINE AND THE ROGANO

Just around the corner from George Square in St Vincent Place once stood a notable feature – the St Vincent Street public lavatory. As part of the city's attempt to increase cleanliness and reduce disease, the first public lavatory was built in 1850. Many tenements had elementary shared toilet facilities, and lavatories – known colloquially in Glasgow as cludgies – were often basic. The first public facilities were merely stalls on corners, but soon they became more elaborate and were generally constructed underground. The St Vincent public lavatory, built in 1892 was the jewel in the crown of Glasgow's conveniences with five stalls, four water closets, two washhand basins and an attendants' room. It cost £472 to build and employed the finest porcelain from Walter Macfarlane and Co and, atop the entrance railings, lion's heads from the Caledonian Railway. At first there were entrance charges and the facility raised a record £157 27s 5d in 1912.[20]

And nearby was the Vesuvio restaurant, past of a chain owned by the Romano family. Thirty years ago this was a favourite haunt of football players and Glasgow councillors, leading into a famous controversy regarding graft and corruption. This is possibly where the expression 'the best councillors that money could buy' was coined. It is now a tapas bar, but immediately across the road, the Anchor Line is one of my favourite stops for breakfast. Yes, the whole hog, with the Stornoway black pudding and the Portobello (now, don't get me started) mushrooms.

The Anchor Line is actually the old offices of the shipping company, a beautiful building modelled in white. The interior features memorabilia from the heyday of the Line which shipped passengers all over the world but notably been Glasgow and the United States, promoting the close ties between America and Scotland. There is leather luggage with brass corners, posters not only featuring the massive projecting hulls of the ships themselves but Scotland portrayed in the best of tartanry with stags, mountains and kilted gentlemen. There are tariffs for the passages – a one way trip to New York costing between $250 for an inside cabin to $1,500 for a suite – and testimonies from various travellers and their relatives: 'my uncle, John Foley, was a quartermaster on the *Circassia* between Glasgow and Bombay', 'On 25 April 1873 my great, great grandfather's brother Francis Mavor, stood on Mavisbank Quay with his wife and ten children to board the *Castalia* to New Brunswick.' The ships remembered include the *Bombay*, the *Kirriemuir*, the *Elysia* and the *Transylvania*. A menu details a Farewell Dinner on board one of them: 'Consomme Beatrice; Dream Faubonne; Corned Ox Tongue; Pumpkin hartinee; Saratoga potatoes'. The whole place is a memorial to an age of more leisurely travel and to the thousands who emigrated to and from Glasgow to distant shores.

It is no longer possible to sail on the *Queen Mary*, built in Clydebank and launched in 1936, to New York but you can still vicariously experience some of the thrill. The Rogano restaurant is situated just off Buchanan Street opposite what it now a posh clothes shop with 890 (I counted them) vintage sewing machines in its windows. The Rogano, however, has been here a long time. It is a splendid survival of the thirties, its interior based on the dining rooms on the *Queen Mary*.

The Rogano is, I guess, pretty authentic, probably the only thing to have been removed is the cigar cutters attached to the tables. It is all walnut burr and bird's eye maple with friezes of mermaids and sea horses. Throughout the years, many famous celebrities from Glasgow and further afield have dined here – Jimmy Logan,

Rikki Fulton and also Rod Stewart, Kylie Minogue and Mick Jagger.

I am here with my old friend David Paterson and his wife Anne-Marie. We haven't seen each other for about 35 years so we have a lot to talk about and we are determined to push the boat out (sic) on a selection from the restaurant's traditional menu, continuously served, apparently, since it opened.

The famous Rogano fish soup is certainly a throwback to the thirties with none of the refinement or lightness of contemporary haute cuisine – a vast bowl of a brown fishy substance with six hard crispy croutons, a bowl of grated parmesan and a bowl of Marie Rose sauce. I presume that the sauce is for dipping the croutons and, eventually, in preparation for an encounter with a mid-Atlantic swell, I finish it all. My main course is the equally lauded Rogano grilled lemon sole. Apparently Alex Ferguson has it every time he is here. Neither is this for the faint-hearted. Not one of those tiny delicate little lemon sole fillets you dip in breadcrumbs and fry. It is massive whole fish on the bone succulent and tasty. The vegetables are a little disappointment, though, more an afterthought than an accompaniment.

A recent review has called the Rogano 'resolutely unfashionable' and the staff 'rude'. Maybe. My impression of the staff is a little stiff and formal but ever attentive – the wine bucket is situated by your table but at a little more than arms length, to emphasise, no doubt, that your glass will be topped up for you.

The Rogano is a time capsule well worth visiting. In here, you could well be in a Hercule Poirot movie so perfect is the assimilation of the thirties. The only thing that spoils it is, in fact, the diners, with their shopping bags, anoraks and rucksacks completely ruining the period feel. Today, we have certainly had our fill, but we manage to split a bottle of wine in the elaborate interior of the Corinthian in Ingram Street. Altogether a rewarding Glasgow dining experience.

QUEEN STREET AND GOMA

A few yards from the Rogano in Royal Exchange Square, the Gallery of Modern Art fronts on to Queen Street. It was originally a townhouse built for £10,000 by William Cunninghame, a tobacco merchant, in 1778. He renamed the street outside to match the tenor of his new residence – what was Cow Loan became Queen Street – after the wife of George III. Cunninghame then sold his townhouse to the Royal Bank of Scotland; when the bank moved in the building became a business centre and exchange, which was when the Corinthian pillars were added. Then it was a library established by the Glasgow Merchant Walter Stirling. And finally, in 1996, it became a gallery for the city's collections. The changing functions of the one building breathing different lives into it.

The most famous feature of Queen Street, immediately outside the gallery is the statue of the Duke of Wellington erected in 1844. This would go largely unnoticed if it weren't for the fact that it always exhibits a traffic cone on its head (today it is also adorned by a Hawaiian shirt). What was originally a drunken prank has now become an established tradition and a permanent feature (what, I wonder, would the city do if the notably contrary Glasgow public now decide to take it away). You can find the Duke and his cone all over Glasgow and the GOMA shop has various versions (along with the commonplace Irn Bru cans and Tunnock's Teacakes that seem to constitute most of Glasgow memorabilia these days). However, I decide to go in search of the real thing and I find him, at the top of Buchanan Street, all bronzed up and puffing on a electronic cigarette prior to his shift sitting on a rocking horse with a cone on his head. He does this for a living. Does it not get a little, well, boring, I ask. Och no, there are plenty of people coming and going.

When I visit GOMA, the front of the building features an instal-

lation. *We Love Real Life Scotland* by Ross Sinclair was originally exhibited in John Street by the City Chambers in 2005. It can perhaps be seen as a commentary on Robert Louis Stevenson's 'the happiest lot on earth is to be born a Scotsman'.

It is a set of illuminated neon signs. The central piece, which flashes on and off in segments contains the title of the piece. The main piece is accompanied by twelve others, all aspects of Scotland or Scottish history which can be grouped under people, events and traits: Robert Burns, Walter Scott, Bonnie Prince Charlie, Edwin Landseer, Queen Victoria , Harry Lauder/ Culloden, Bannockburn, The Highland Clearances/ Alcohol[ism], Failure, Parsimony.

Of course, you could look at some as pairs: Harry Lauder: Parsimony, Culloden: Failure, Edwin Landseer: The Highland Clearances. And, if Queen Victoria equals Balmoralism, for example, that could be linked with Harry Lauder too.

I like this piece. Obviously, the 'real life' is partly ironic, and what are contained therein are popular mythologies. The brash frontage of the neon signs emphasises too a sort of branding and popularisation of history. It raises question about what is real and, since this book is called 'Real Glasgow', I think about what would be the equivalent list for Glasgow: Saint Mungo, Jimmy Johnstone, Billy Connolly... the Battle of Langside, the Ibrox Disaster... Drinking, Hyperbole?

Prone to the endless curse of the academic, I am deciphering GOMA, but I am confused at what is currently inside. Apparently, the gallery had been criticised for not keeping up with some new developments in Scottish art and they have now tried to redress this with an exhibition called *Devils in the Making* that is to include, for the first time, both video and performance art. Well, they should have stuck to their guns! There are a couple of exhibits I find interesting, and several that are not, but it is the videos that leave me completely stymied. There is a video of an artist running after a tram loaded with suitcases. I am told this is a development of his earlier piece which featured him running after buses. There is an earlier piece (a classic, I'm told) which is a video of children holding their breath in a car whilst driving through the Clyde Tunnel. Then there is a narrative piece of an artist dressed, apparently, as Travis Bickle from *Taxi Driver*, walking through the streets of London in order to hand a petition (piece of paper) into 10 Downing Street. It reads 'We are the People. Suck on This'. Now, I know that 'we are the people' ('we arra peepul') is a catchphrase of supporters of Rangers Football Club, but does David Cameron? Anyway, any chance that this stunt could be taken seriously is spoilt by the fact that the artist is continually grinning on his way. Maybe he is smirking all the way to the bank.

Once there was another kind of art displayed around here. Before the days of video or even cinema the panorama, a giant circular painting displayed, usually in a circular building designed for the purpose, was a popular entertainment. One such panorama, of the Clyde at the Broomielaw, some four feet long and depicting over half a mile of the river, was painted in 1817 by the landscape painter John Knox. Many of the artists of the time dabbled in this, as well as painting wallpaper for grand houses, stage scenery and panels for the new steamships that sailed up the coast from the Clyde.[21] In the 1820s, popular subjects such as Waterloo and Trafalgar were exhibited in a rotunda in Buchanan Street and, on one occasion an 'entirely new panorama of... the Battle of Bannockburn... the whole painted on 16,000 square feet of canvas, the figures as large as life... being accompanied by a full military band... gives a complete sensation of reality. Queen Street was another location for the panorama *The Storming of Seringapatam in 1860*.

Towards the bottom of Queen Street there are mostly chain stores now, but there is one notable survival – Tam Shepherd's Joke Shop has been here as long as I remember and is cemented in Glasgow lore ('Where did you get a face like that? Tam Shepherd's?'). This part of the street also reminds me of a couple of places that are no longer here. The Bank Restaurant was the venue for the Tradition

Folk Club run by a gentleman called Miller Frondigoun. It was hard core traditional inspired by Ewan MacColl's Singer's Club in London. One of the main tenets was that everyone could sing which led to some intriguing performances. A couple of doors down, I remember (just), stood St Mungo Vintners, a fine old Glasgow pub in the art nouveau style with Doulton tiled panels by Margaret Macdonald, the wife of Charles Rennie Mackintosh. Of course, the city demolished it in the early seventies but the interior was bought and shipped to the States where, I presume, it has been reconstructed, although I can't trace it.

SAUCHIEHALL STREET

It is a typical day in Sauchiehall Street. A kilted piper is playing outside what looks like an inflatable police box accompanied by Darth Vader on the accordion, two drunken young men are performing a *pas de deux* down the street, moving out and in as if they are connect by an elastic band and, further on, two giggling young women are following a Dalek rolling down the hill.

Sauchiehall Street is always busy and was even more so in Victorian times as old photos, paintings and some early film always show it packed, with trams and trolley buses moving back and fore. The lower section is pedestrianised now and is all shops, while the upper section contains cinemas, clubs and eateries: The Dumpling Inn, Torres Tapas, Kama Sutra, Zig, Waffle Monsters, Budda. There is also a branch of Blue Lagoon, one of Glasgow's oldest fish and chip shops – chips, of course, being a much loved delicacy in Glasgow (as Joseph

Conrad famously said, 'a poke o' chips. Noo!').

There is a version of the famous art nouveau-inspired Mrs Cranston's Tea Room still in Sauchiehall Street and a little preserve of thirties Glasgow in the art deco Beresford Hotel, the King's Café (which seems to have been afflicted by a bit of marketing vandalism and now proclaims 'Steak cattle & roll @ Kings café') and the Variety Bar. The Variety has a fine thirties exterior and the interior is mostly original. The day I visit, they are projecting old movies on the walls (for effect, not for viewing. I recognise *Mildred Pierce*) and they are having an indoor barbecue. The pub rules are clearly explained on the wall: 'No tracksuits. No sunglasses (after dark). No winching at the bar'.

A little further up, the Royal Highland Fusiliers Museum is housed in a fine Edwardian building designed by the firm that nurtured Charles Rennie Mackintosh – Honeyman, Keppie and Mackintosh. It was, in fact, built for the photographers T&R Annan. Thomas Annan was long gone before its construction, but his son, James Craig Annan, also a noted photographer who developed the photogravure process whereby images are developed or printed from a copper plate that has been coated with a light sensitive chemical, thus allowing a deep range of tones and a very detailed finished print. Thomas Annan's camera features in the museum display.

The museum itself is cleverly organised and, more than a history of armed conflict, it focuses on the Glasgow people who enlisted in the regiment. There are records of deeds of bravery, awards, celebration and also brutal death. The various elaborate uniforms of the militias were, in their time, much more than a signification of service: they were both status symbols and a sort of performance in themselves, granting their bearers an identity in return for their service.

Interestingly, from the upper windows of the building, to the rear, can be seen Albany Terrace and a few of the Georgian townhouses that originally faced on to the street but became hidden behind the new facade as the street was straightened. The Centre for Contemporary Arts is nearby. It used to called The Third Eye Centre and was a focus of the contemporary arts scene, but it is a little more subdued these days. It has employed one of these hidden buildings to some effect by incorporating it into the bar. Round about here in the sixties and early seventies were two institutions that catered to youth. the Electric Garden was a famous disco (now it's called the Garage and features the projecting front end of a truck, painted various colours, (with a saltire during the independence referendum) and a pub called the State Bar, which had a druggy reputation in its heyday and was closed for some time. It is now restored to an impressive polished interior.

TWO THEATRES, TWO COLLEGES, AND A CONSERVATOIRE

Lauder's Bar on the corner of Sauchiehall Street and Renfield Street is a barn of a place and has been here since 1871. The name of course relates to Sir Harry Lauder who often performed a few hundred yards up the road at the last surviving of Glasgow's traditional music hall theatres, the Pavilion.[22] This is still a popular place and hosts some of the old stars; a poster advertises 'Sidney Devine Diamond Jubilee Concert'. Sidney Devine is an old Glasgow favourite who prompted the little verse: 'I wish I could sing like Sidney, I tried last night but I didnae. I thought it was fine but it wasn't Devine. I wish I could sing like Sidney.' Other oldies have had to be resurrected. There are tribute acts to Gerry and the Pacemakers and the Tremeloes and the Glasgow comic duo Francie and Josie are appearing, even though their original alter egos, Rikki Fulton and Jack Milroy are long gone. There is even theatre: Real Hoosewives in *My Wee Fat Glesga Wedding*.

Opera and more highbrow fare can be found up the road at the Theatre Royal. For years this was the headquarters of Scottish

Television and their first television broadcast, *This is Scotland,* in 1957, came from here. I was fortunate enough a while ago to come across a rare tape of this event. An interesting feature is that nearly all the famous Scots that are trotted out have anglified RP accents. Helensburgh is a theme, as John Logie Baird, the inventor of television came from there, so we are presented with two 'Scots' from there – Jack Buchanan, who went to school with Baird, and became known as a posh, sophisticated music hall artist with a top hat and cane, and Deborah Kerr, known as 'the English Rose' The only authentic (sic) Scot in it is an actor who plays an archetypal Glaswegian called Jimmy wearing a bunnet.

Music is well catered for here too. The old Royal Scottish Academy of Music and Dramatic Art has moved here and been renamed the Royal Conservatoire of Scotland. Recently, my friend Fred Freeman has been made Professor of Scottish Music here – a real coup in that his speciality is traditional music. Fred is a piper also, and he introduced me to the National Piping Centre next door which has an interesting display of piping memorabilia. There are two 'centres' for piping in Glasgow – this and the College of Piping nearby. The reasons for this are convoluted but say something about the intransigence of pipers![23]

COMMERCIAL GLASGOW

A knight's tour of the chessboard is as good a way as I can find to describe the best way to take in the next section of Glasgow on the other side of Sauchiehall Street.

South of Sauchiehall Street down towards Central Station lies the criss-cross pattern of streets that constitute Glasgow's commercial district. Echoing the prosperity of Victorian Glasgow ('second city' of Empire) the buildings here are grand edifices that reflect the standing of nineteenth-century businessmen. Designated the five richest streets in Glasgow, Gordon Street, St Vincent Street, West George Street, Buchanan Street and Hope Street contain the most elaborate architecture. Without going into too much detail, there are interesting examples of various styles and building techniques here – John Honeyman's mock Venetian Ca d'Oro in Gordon Street with its vast arched windows allowed by an early experiment with cast iron supports, Gardner's Warehouse, another cast-iron structure, prefabricated off site, James Salmon's Hatrack, so called because the Edwardians thought it looked like somewhere to hang your tifter, and countless others.

Each individually is worth a look but I'll single out two – both in Hope Street – that merit closer examination. These two buildings, however, are a contrast in styles and influences that could be typified as transatlantic and continental, which reflects Glasgow's trade and artistic concerns of the time. The Atlantic Chambers is a massive steel-framed office block formed in red sandstone designed by the noted Glasgow architect J.J. Burnet that dates from 1899. There are glimpses of the Glasgow Style in the decoration but also an obvious transatlantic influence which echoes Chicago in the fin-de-siecle. Muscular in all its attributes, the 'Atlantic Chambers' carved in large letters over laurels is flanked by two large bare-breasted amazons.

A little up the road on the opposite side is the more modest Lion Chambers – a really delightful and well-proportioned eight-storey office block built between 1904 and 1907 in the art nouveau style. Bright white in its heyday, this was one of the first buildings in the world constructed of reinforced concrete. Sadly, for the last ten years it has been left empty, covered in a webbing as reinforcement to stop falling masonry. Classified as dangerous, there have been various proposals to repair it but nothing has happened. It has been described as a rotten tooth in the otherwise prosperous Hope Street, and its neglect fails to give the lie to those who claim that Glasgow's preference has always been to finance new build rather than maintain its existing treasures.

A crane would be useful in the investigation of some of the buildings in Glasgow's commercial quarter, as many of the finest features, in the Victorian tradition, are high above the ground. In light of that it is perhaps not surprising that two recent books have focused on Glasgow's half-hidden public sculpture.[24] You can buy the books or, if you insist in craning your neck, at least take a deserved break in the Pot Still in Hope Street. A pint and a steak pie can be enjoyed in this pleasant little hostelry, but if you are in pursuit of stronger stuff, try a malt whisky. The massive gantry of the Pot Still features nearly four hundred different whiskies. The most expensive – a 24-year-old Glen Grant will set you back £74 for a dram – but there are lots of more reasonably priced alternatives. My preference is for the Islay malts, with their pungent, some say 'medicinal' tang of seaweed. Try the Laphroaig (pronounced la-froy-ig) the Caol Ila (clee-la) or the Bowmore (b'more). Enthusiasts can enrol here for whisky tastings or classes.

This whole area of Glasgow is still commercially orientated, but in recent years more bars and restaurants, many of them in the basements of the buildings, have sprung up. The Meat Bar has, cleverly, re-employed an old shop frontage and offers steaks of all kinds. Slightly further to the north of this area were once various clubs where businessmen could relax after work. The Glasgow Art Club in Bath Street has been going since 1867 but has occupied its swankier new(ish) premises since 1893. It is still a private members club and runs regular exhibitions, but has diversified into event and wedding hire.

The Blythswood, in Blythswood Square, is one of Glasgow's finest hotels in a grand Scottish style – its refurbishment employed 9000 square metres of Harris Tweed – but it was once, not so long ago, the Royal Scottish Automobile Club. Whether its swanky residents are aware of the Square's rather seamier history is unclear, but Blythswood Square was, for many years, noted as the night-time haunt of prostitutes. Also, in a house diagonally opposite the hotel, one of Glasgow's most famous murders took place.

In 1857, Pierre Emile L'Angelier, a nurseryman from the Channel Islands, was found dead of arsenic poisoning. Love letters discovered revealed an affair with a local socialite, Madeleine Smith, who had promised to marry him, but had her sights on a young man with better prospects. Smith was tried for his murder. The fact that she had been seen in a druggist buying industrial quantities of arsenic might have been seen as a settler, but the jury reached, surprisingly, that peculiar Scottish verdict of not proven, which was, apparently, cheered by the onlookers. Madeleine Smith subsequently became a socialite in England and the United States, married twice and died in New York City at the age of 93.

On a more pedestrian note, I found myself hungry here one morning. Around the corner from Blythswood Square, in a small basement, is Babu, the Bombay Street Kitchen, which has had, recently, rave reviews for its food. Not for Babu the velour wallpaper and piped sitar music of the usual Glasgow Indian restaurant. The decor consists of light bulbs in colanders suspended by plastic packing cases, basic tables and bright red plastic stools as if from a kindergarten. The walls are adorned with torn Bollywood posters. Although I'm assured the food is authentic, I'm surprised to note that the two ladies who serve me are about as oriental as Easterhouse. I'm here for breakfast and I really don't know what is eaten for breakfast in Bombay. It turns out to be something like a spiced omelette in a chapati wrap. I can honestly say it is unlike anything I have eaten before. It comes accompanied by their speciality organic Chai tea made in the Indian way (that is the milk and sugar are stewed in the original brew). It is sweet, spicy and hot. The first few sips are good but I soon realise that the entire cup is likely to turn me into a jelly baby, so I leave it. They do good lunch boxes and evening meals here too: pau vadu, ragda patties, bhel puri. I could check it out later, but maybe it is best left to the famous Diner Tec of the *Evening Times*, still going after many years, I think, who will roll up in his wheels with his moll.

BRIDGE TO NOWHERE, BANANA FLATS AND LEANING FOUNTAIN

In the ancient world, some thought that you could sail off the edge of the earth. At the top end of Sauchiehall Street you could be forgiven for getting that feeling, for here the urban motorway cuts a great chasm through the centre of the junction.

A notable piece of the original Charing Cross still survives in the form of Charing Cross mansions sculpted in red sandstone with a clock and various carved figures. This block curves round the corner like a banana and even the individual rooms of the flats therein have curved walls. Another original feature on the other side of the motorway is the Cameron Memorial Fountain named after the Liberal MP and teetotaller who promoted the Inebriates Act of 1898 under which anyone convicted of drunkenness three times would have their photograph circulated around hostelries. This was the precursor of current pub watch schemes. The terracotta drinking fountain, however, is itself a little unsteady, leaning at an angle due to subsidence.

Two features of the motorway itself, however, are distinctive. Firstly, there is the pedestrian walkway that leads from Renfrew Street to Woodside Crescent, seldom used as it goes where no-one particularly wants to go. Secondly, another warped concept of the planner's imagination – an elevated structure over and across the motorway following the line of Sauchiehall Street. Today there are offices constructed on it, but this was unused for years leading to it being called the Bridge to Nowhere. An inspection of the original documentation reveals that the Bridge to Nowhere was supposed to 'close in' the cross itself and feature a restaurant that offered a vista over the great motorway. It is a strange conceit of Modernism that a restaurant facing down into the chasm of a multi-lane motorway would be a local attraction. The vista would have featured the extension of the M8 towards the Kingston Bridge where, according to urban legend, bodies are buried.

Further to the south, there is an uninteresting complex of fairly new hotels, but just on the west side of the cross stands an impressive building. This is the Mitchell Library, owned by Glasgow City Council.

THE MITCHELL

The great poet Ted Hughes was so in love with literature, it was said, that he would get an erection just by entering a library. If so, he would have loved this place in the seventies. Its grand reading room with its massive ceilings, its giant sloped reading desks and its large folio catalogues with pasted-in slips. Add to that its journals section at the side entrance opposite the Highlander's Institute and, upstairs, the Glasgow Room dedicated to the literature of the city, and the Music Library, with shelves full of songs and treasures such as the scrapbook of the Glasgow folk song collector, John Ord.

The Mitchell Library was formed from a bequest of £66,998 10s 6d from Stephen Mitchell, a tobacco manufacturer, towards the creation of a public library with the provision that 'books on all subjects not immoral shall be freely admitted to [the library] and no book shall be regarded as immoral which simply controverts present opinions.' With the construction of the present building the intention was to create a library second only to that of the British Museum. For some time, with over a million volumes, the Mitchell Library was, in fact, the largest library in Europe apart from national libraries. James Cowan, the historian and columnist who wrote under the name Peter Prowler, noted in 1932 that the Mitchell had over 13,000 books on Glasgow, and, for example, 500 plus on shorthand and 300 plus on snooker.[25] Like many other Glasgow scholars, I loved this place in the 1970s and I wish I could revisit that time. However, the story of the Mitchell that I recount here is one of a sorry decline. The rot set in quite a while ago. One development was the decision to convert the old catalogue which, like the British Library, used paper slips pasted in large ledgers, to microfiche. The problem was that the individual slips were hastily arranged for photography and some of them folded over, obscuring titles. However much the library spent on their catalogue at the time, they still had enough left to order carpets with the city coat of arms for the reading rooms at a ridiculous cost. The apogee of their incompetence, however, came in October 1997 when, deciding to reduce their collection to save costs, the library put thousands of books into skips in the street. Antiquarian book dealers, students, and collectors were there in minutes.

Not all would agree with my criticisms of the Mitchell Library. It has been refurbished. It has a modern café where you can have a

cappuccino and a panini, a crèche for infants. The annual Aye Write
Festival is held here. Some of the expansive traditional rooms, such
as the Burns Room, are available for events, meetings and extra-
mural classes (although the jewel in the crown, the grand reading
room, is usually closed). It is, in fact, a good place to do many
things, take the kids, meet for lunch, brush up on your genealogy or
take a class in creative writing. Many things, in fact, as long as you
are not looking for a book!

The Earl of Rosebery, at the opening of the Mitchell Library in
North Street in 1911 (it was originally in Ingram Street) was lamp-
basted for referring to it as 'this cemetery of books'. His words have
proved prophetic.

It is a typical day upstairs in the Mitchell Library: assistants are
chatting, one is on her mobile lamenting the problems of 'her
cousin's weans'. A customer is sitting at a computer playing Candy
Crush. One member of staff is explaining to a customer why she
can't use her mobile to take a picture (well, not *explaining*, she
doesn't know why). I am there to look at a book that isn't very
special or very rare but, for some reason, I can't look at it because I
need both my passport and proof of address. I have previous here.
Once I wanted to look at bound volumes of local newspapers only
to be told that they were a bit delicate so I'd better go to look at the
copies in the British Library. On another occasion I simply wanted
to look at some of the books in their 'world-famous' Burns collection, but they had been 'lost' and I would have to wait until they
could afford someone to go down to the archive and find and catalogue them.

I cannot overemphasise the importance of the old Glasgow
Room. Charles Oakley, who wrote the definitive history of Glasgow,
Second City, recalls 'The really big moment in my career came when
I found my way into the Mitchell Library's Glasgow Room... there
were shelves and shelves of books about Glasgow, standing upright
and bristling with the challenge to read them.'[26] There is no
Glasgow Room these days, but a space dedicated largely to the
creeping affliction of family history with what is now termed the
'Glasgow collection'.

The Glasgow collection is an unholy mess. Books are shoved on
shelves, some lying on their sides, some crushed. Why it is still called
the Glasgow collection is unclear. There is one book about the perception of water in Britain which has little to do with Glasgow and
there is a whole section on Burns, which is tangential to Glasgow.

There are a great many novels and, in the non-fiction shelves, an undue emphasis on crime and football.

This, however, is just a loose impression. Undaunted, I decide to put my suspicions to the test. I choose twenty books that I would expect to find in a Glasgow collection (including one I have written myself) and search for them. I only find three on the shelves. Then I check the catalogue. In fact all these books are in the library but not on the shelves. There is, in fact, to be clear, plenty of space to display books, some are in the main area but others are in a partitioned space at the back. There are empty shelves and there are spaces where there could be more shelves. For some reason, a library that once boasted a whole Glasgow Room cannot now even adequately maintain a decent browsing collection of books on Glasgow. They are there, but they are hidden away. The sad fact is that it wouldn't even require an enthusiast like Joe Fisher to improve this situation: anyone with a basic knowledge of the history and culture of Glasgow could rectify it, but no-one has and, presumably, no-one cares. Somehow we have forgotten that a library isn't meant to be a prison (or a cemetery) for books. Great libraries were browsing libraries and the writers of great books were browsers. I cannot mince my words here. This feeble attempt at a Glasgow browsing collection is, quite simply, a disgrace.

TENEMENT

Not far from the Mitchell and overlooking the motorway is an extraordinary little museum maintained by the National Trust for Scotland – the Tenement House. Well, it is a museum, but it is also a house, a flat in an ordinary close in a very ordinary red sandstone tenement in Buccleuch Street at the top of Garnethill. It is also, as it notes, a home – you could live there, an many ordinary folk do in the other assorted flats in the same close. The fascinating thing about this tenement house is that the interior has been preserved much as it would have been in the early twentieth century, not all that long after it was built in 1892.

Miss Agnes Toward and her daughter, also Agnes, moved to the house in 1911. Mrs Toward was dressmaker, as a remaining brass plaque in the close testifies. The mother died in 1939, but Miss Toward, who never married, retained possession of the flat until 1975 (although she spent the later years of her life in hospital). Fortunately, the flat fell into the hands of Anna Davidson, the

daughter of an elder at Miss Towards's church, who was staggered to find that it had remained much the same for years – a sort of time capsule of tenement life. She sold it to the National Trust who opened it as a museum in 1983.

As you enter the close (the common entrance to tenement flats) it is clear that it a well-maintained stairway with a brass plaque on the first landing advertising 'Mrs Toward; Dressmaking; No Fitting Required.' The walls are partially tiled. The demeanour of the close itself was regarded as an indicator of the folk who lived there. The best were 'wally closes', with often elaborate wall (wally) tiles, some in the art nouveau style. Stairs and closes were cleaned in turn on a regular basis by the occupiers.

Tenements were the common form of housing in Glasgow from about the mid-nineteenth century, originally constructed of grey sandstone which was superseded by red sandstone in the 1880s. Nowadays most of the tenements which survived the mass demolitions of the 1960s and 1970s are of the red sandstone type. This tenement is a comparatively late model, but typical of many built in this period, mostly in the West End and the Southside.

The tenement house has been preserved as far as possible as Miss Toward left it, and some other features have been sympathetically restored. It consists of a hall, a bedroom, a parlour, a kitchen and a bathroom. The hall was the formal entrance to the property and has a large gilt-framed portrait of a Victorian gentleman, and a grandfather clock. The parlour is also elaborately bedecked. Wally dugs on the mantelpiece, portraits of family members and the ubiquitous Robert Burns, a piano and a table set for afternoon tea. The parlour was intended for visitors and sometimes it was hardly used otherwise. Some years ago, I visited Jack Short, the famous music hall performer and father of Jimmy Logan, at his tenement in Ibrox. The parlour was laid out with theatre memorabilia and awards from his career. Here he entertained showbiz visitors including, he told me, Bing Crosby. Jack, however, preferred to live in the kitchen which was completely ordinary and unfussy.

The rest of the rooms are more functional: the bedroom with its bed, washstand and fireplace (coal fires were the only means of heating the tenement and grates usually featured in every room); the bathroom, which is unusual in that few tenements actually had an indoor toilet (and doubly unusual in that it features a sort of primitive shower above the bath); and the kitchen. The kitchen is the most interesting feature of the house. It was the workhouse of any tenement especially in the days of large families. This kitchen is typical; a large black range and a coal bunker to fire it, a vast variety of cooking and washing implements and flat irons for the laundering. The proprietary products used in the maintenance of the household are still there: Brasso, for polishing brass, Zebo, a black lead polish for the range, Rinso, for laundry.

Although it appears quite small to the visitor, this was a superior sort of tenement, especially to be occupied only by one person (there is a bedroom and bed recesses in the parlour and kitchen). It does not, therefore, give an indication of the type of tenement living that most working-class Glaswegians experienced for over a century (although there is a another flat downstairs that has been adapted into a museum of tenement life in general).

Most tenement flats consisted of either a room and kitchen (that is two rooms, a bedroom and a kitchen cum living space entered from a small lobby) or a single end (effectively just one room with a bed recess). A lavatory was provided on the stair half landing – shared between several flats. Personal hygiene involved a tin bath in front of the coal fire – although public baths provided better washing facilities for working men.

It cannot be overstated that, not so long ago, these cramped spaces often catered for large families. Every inch of space would be utilised: pull out drawers beneath the beds in bed recesses would be used by babies or small children, even the lobbies were sometimes sleeping spaces. There was little privacy or, indeed, peace and quiet. In the second half of the nineteenth century many tenements were 'ticketed'. That is they were measured and licensed for only so many occupants. This was unpopular and unsuccessful in that the city's housing stock was just not adequate to provide for the ballooning population of a vast industrial city.

The daily routine of tenement life had to be well organised in such limited space. Women were largely confined to the daily grind of domestic life, although men had their fair share of toil – backbreaking shiftwork in the foundry or the shipyard.[27]

Ballad of the Tenement Close

Dress the weans, check their heads,
Strip the linen from the beds.

The lum reeks fiercely,
Till the day's work's done

Put the briquette in the fire
Fan the flames till they grow higher

The lum reeks fiercely,
Till the day's work's done

Make the pieces for the man,
Butter bread, plain and pan.

The lum reeks fiercely,
Till the day's work's done

Wash the stairs, clean the mop,
Bring the messages from the shop

The lum reeks fiercely,
Till the day's work's done

Boil the kettle, turn it higher,
Set the bath afore the fire.

The lum reeks fiercely,
Till the day's work's done

See the factor, pay the dues,
Meet the neighbours, share the news.

The lum reeks fiercely,
Till the day's work's done

Peel the tatties, make the tea,
Daundle the baby on your knee.

The lum reeks fiercely,
Till the day's work's done

Watch the lichtie light the light,
Settle in for the night

The lum reeks fiercely,
Till the day's work's done

The tenement is celebrated in painting, by artists such as Herbert Whone and James Morrison (more recently, by Avril Paton, whose *Windows in the West* takes a west end tenement block and displays little vignettes of family life through each set of windows) and in photography, mostly notably in, perhaps, the stark studies of Oscar Marzaroli. The old Ettrick Bar in Dumbarton Road is now called The Tenement and photographs of different styles and aspects of tenement buildings adorn its walls. Although the tenement, to some extent, still constitutes a common form of housing in Glasgow, the tenement as a way of life (as noted in the title of one of Frank Worsdall's fine books)[28] no longer exists but is instead instilled into the popular consciousness of the Glaswegian. Tenement life has equally been stigmatised as a life of unrelenting toil and celebrated by that form of romance sometimes called 'stairheid nostalgia', as in Duncan MacRae's pastiche of a music hall favourite *Ma Ain Close* with its chorus lament:

An it's oh, but ah'm longing for ma ain close,
It wis nane o' yuir wally, juist a plain close,
And ah'm nearly roon the bend,

For ma ain wee single-end.
Fareweel tae dear old Gorbals,
An ma ain close...

However, neither version is totally correct and the truth lies in the reconciliation of these two opposites. The fact is that many ordinary and extraordinary lives, in all their diversity, were lived out in tenement Glasgow. For those of us born there, there is a double whammy. Our childhood is not only lost in our past but the whole environment has been wiped out and only a shadow of it is preserved in archives and in literature and art. At the top of Garnethill, preserved in a quiet oasis by happenstance, is a small reminder of Glasgow's tenement legacy. The rest, the lost history of that great empire of stone, lives only in our memories.

Calendar

The wind has scorched the paper skin
From my calendar of Glasgow,
Exposing the days, letting in
The present with its selfish now.
The past, naked, has confirmed
It's dues, but all the dates demand
The honours they have singly earned.

Pages in their order turned,
Years gathered weeks, weeks gathered days,
We think we hold the future in our hands
But the future unseen waits
Then wisely speaks and says
In time, the stoniest empire burned
And quickly turned to sand.

Notes

1. See J. Logie Robertson, *The Complete Poetical Works of Thomas Campbell* (London: Oxford University Press, 1907).
2. Thomas Annan, *Old Closes and Streets of Glasgow* (Glasgow: James MacLehose and Sons, 1900).
3. See Kevin McCarra & Hamish Whyte (ed.), *A Glasgow Collection: Essays in Honour of Joe Fisher* (Glasgow: Glasgow City Libraries, 1990).
4. See http://www.elviscostello.com.
5. This has now been replaced by a rather more bland image of a floral style circle.
6. Charles McKean, David Walker & Frank Walker, *Central Glasgow: an Illustrated Architectural Guide* (Edinburgh: Mainstream, 1989).
7. Nuala McNaughton, *Barrowland* (Edinburgh: Mainstream Publishing, 2013).
8. http://www.workerscity.org.
9. Seumas MacInnes, *The Stornoway Black Pudding Bible* (Edinburgh: Birlinn, 2010). An interesting story about black pudding is that cattle drovers used to cut the cattle they were tending for blood to add protein to their breakfast.
10. Seumas MacInnes, *Café Gandolfi Cookbook* (Glasgow: Café Gandolfi, 2009).
11. Another product that attracted approbation was a poster for the Glasgow Games (the Commonwealth Games) that made fun of the events – for example, the 100 metres sprint featured a ned running away with a stolen television. This was sold by Glasgow Museums in its shops but was later speedily withdrawn.
12. See Craig Richardson, *Scottish Art Since 1960: Historical Reflections and Contemporary Overviews* (Farnham: Ashgate, 2011).
13. Malcolm Dickson (ed.), *Free Association* (Free Association: Glasgow, 2006).
14. See Sebastian Barker, *Who is Eddie Linden?* (London: Jay Landesman, 1979).
15. For a more detailed history of the station, see Michael Meaghan, *Glasgow Central* (Stroud: Amberley, 2013).
16. See Johnny Rodger, *The Hero Building: an Architecture of Scottish National Identity* (London: Routledge, 2015).
17. See Rudolph Kenna & Anthony Mooney, *People's Palaces* (Edinburgh: Paul Harris, 1983).
18. Another interesting movie shot in Glasgow was Bertrand Tavernier's *Deathwatch*. See Ian Spring, *Phantom Village: the Myth of the New Glasgow* (Edinburgh: Polygon, 1990).
19. Adrian Searle & David Barbour, *Look Up Glasgow* (Glasgow: Freight Books, 2013). Ray McKenzie, *Public Sculpture of Glasgow* (Liverpool: Liverpool University Press, 2002).
20. See Peter Kearney, *The Glasgow Cludgie* (Newcastle: People's Publications, 1985).
21. See Patricia Dennison et al, *Painting the Town: Scottish Urban History in Art* (Edinburgh: Society of Antiquaries of Scotland, 2013).
22. Kate Molleson et al, *Dear Green Sounds* (Glasgow: Waverley Books, 2015).
23. Glasgow Theatres were reportedly feared because of the ferocity of the audience. It was said that the top acts demanded danger money to play here.
24. Adrian Searle & David Barbour, *Look Up Glasgow* (Glasgow: Freight Books, 2013).
25. See James Cowan, *From Glasgow's Treasure Chest* (R.E. Robertson: Glasgow, 1951).
26. Charles Oakley, 'They Wrote About Glasgow: a Tribute', in McCarra & Whyte (ed.) *A Glasgow Collection: Essays in Honour of Joe Fisher* (Glasgow: Glasgow City Libraries, 1990).
27. See Helen Clark and Elizabeth Carnegie, *She Was Aye Workin': Memories of Tenement Women in Edinburgh and Glasgow* (Oxford: White Cockade, 2003).
28. Frank Worsdall, *The Glasgow Tenement: a Way of Life* (Glasgow: W.&R. Chambers, 1981).

SOUTH

GLASGOW GREEN

The ghost of Blind Alick is fiddling away as various dancers jig and reel. There's a scrimmage at a twenty-a-side football match played to the Glasgow rather than the Rugby rules. Punters are chancing their arm at quoits and pitch and toss, and rowers are racing on the river. This is an image of Glasgow Green in the mid-nineteenth century, at the Glasgow Fair, held every July since the twelfth century. The antics of the Fair are recorded in a broadsheet ballad, *The Humours of Glasgow Fair.*

> Had ye seen sic a din and guffawing,
> Sic hooching and dancing was there,
> Sic rugging and riving, and drawing,
> Was ne'er before seen in a fair.[1]

A favourite location for the Fair in Glasgow is Glasgow Green – a large area of grassland (originally quite swampy) granted to the people of Glasgow by James II in 1450. It still, arguably, belongs to the people and you can walk your dog, play football or join one of the rowing clubs on its banks. That it is a city property is marked out clearly by tinny versions of the Glasgow coat of arms attached to the railings.

The tradition of the Glasgow Fair still presided in my boyhood, and many businesses would shut down for the duration. A favourite trip was 'doon the watter' – taking the ferry (a steamboat originally) down the Clyde to Dunoon or Millport or Rothesay.

A remarkable painting by the landscape artist John Knox shows Glasgow Green in the early nineteenth century, thronging with people. It features soldiers, drunks, cock fights, tightrope walking, 'Wombwell's Grand Menagerie' and an anti-slavery booth. Amazingly, this painting was lost before turning up, unidentified, at an auction in 2013.[2]

The use of the Green as a democratic open space for public assemblies and protests is also an old tradition and, when the Council attempted to sell it off to 'leisure developers' in the early 1990s, groups such as Workers City and the Free University mobilised to prevent it.[3]

Today, however, the Green is all but empty – Glasgow deserted for the dubious pleasures of Benidorm or Alicante. Another image comes into my head. Old photos of Glasgow Green invariably show it festooned with washing. A clean open area for bleaching and washing was of great value in the old days of smoke and pollution, not to mention the prevailing Glasgow weather and it was an established right of the people of Glasgow to use it for such.

Glasgow Washing

Sunny
Put my washing in machine,
Soon it will be nice and clean.

Showery
Put my washing on the line,
Won't be back at least till nine.

Wet
Sodden through with acid rain,
Take it back to wash again.

Windy
Hang my washing out again,
Won't be back tonight till ten.

Stormy
Dig my socks out of the dirt,
Go to Primark, buy a shirt.

If the south of Glasgow is taken to mean south of the river, then it is an extensive area, not as intensively historical as the north of the river. To head south, you can cross the Clyde at several different points and, for the purpose of this investigation, I am taking three distinct routes to the south and, paradoxically, each has its origin north of the river. So my first route is via Glasgow Green.

The most conspicuous building on Glasgow Green is Templeton's Carpet Factory which, famously, in order to get planning permission, was modelled (well, the facade facing the Green was) on the Doge's Palace in Venice. In recent years, this has had various uses – as a business centre and partly as flats, but there is one use that could hardly have been expected. Part of it is the West Brewery, an enterprise set up by a German, Petra Wetzel, in 2006. It adheres to the strict purity regulations of German brewing and advertises itself with the slogan 'Glaswegian Heart, German Head'. Its flagship lager is called St Mungo. The brewery tour is a refreshing contrast to the tour of the vast industrialised Wellpark Brewery. The process is patiently explained to us by an enthusiastic young lady named Ellie Barbour who emphasises the purity and skill of the process: 'the brewer makes the wort, the yeast makes the beer'. The wort is made from mashed barley with hops added and the particular nature of it and the recipe used make the distinction between different beers before it ferments. Samples are readily partaken of before the tour party gather in the bar for burgers and more beer.

Glasgow Green has had its share of tragedy. Frank Worsdall, author of many books about Glasgow, was assaulted there – possibly in a homophobic attack – and later died. One of Edwin Morgan's best known poems, called 'Glasgow Green',[4] is basically about a homosexual rape. There has also been many a drowning in the Clyde – but there would have been many more if not for the work of the Glasgow Humane Society, housed in a gated building by the banks of the river, which was founded in 1790 by Glasgow businessmen. For the last 88 years, this has been run by a father and son, Ben and George Parsonage – George taking over from his father after his death in 1979. Between them it is reckoned that they have saved thousands of lives. In the old days there was more than drowning to fear in the Clyde. The waters would often be stained different hues depending on what poured forth from White's chemical works. It's products were so noxious that workers there were known as White's canaries, because breathing the stuff destroyed their aspiration so that they whistled. This level of pollution no longer attains and there are fish returning to the Clyde, and, quite recently, a whale was spotted in the city centre.

However, there is another tragic death recorded by the waters of the Clyde, one poor soul that Ben Parsonage failed to safe. That, however, is on the other side of the river where we find what is left of the Gorbals, perhaps the part of Glasgow that is best known outside the city itself. You can Auchenshuggle, Polmadie or Drumoyne all you like, but there is no district of Glasgow as evocative of the whole as the Gorbals. And its fame, or infamy, arose partly through one media representation.

THE GORBALS STORY

Alexander McArthur, a Gorbals baker, with the journalist Herbert Kingsley Long, wrote *No Mean City*,[5] a best-selling novel about gang warfare in the Glasgow slums published in 1935. The novel was lambasted for giving an inaccurate picture of Glasgow and the Glasgow libraries refused to stock it. In his later years McArthur was well known among the pubs in the Gorbals, but his mental health had deteriorated. He had written a play – *The Mystery of Gorbals Terrace* – which he believed had been plagiarised by another writer, Robert McLeish, who had written *The Gorbals Story*,[6] which had been performed by Unity Theatre. On the 3 September 1947,

McArthur was observed in a pub in the Gorbals inebriated saying that he was going to drink disinfectant and throw himself in the Clyde. The next day, his body was found, soaking, on the banks of the river. The contents of his stomach included Lysol, a strong disinfectant. Only two people attended his funeral.

The Gorbals has been well represented in literature and art ever since. There is even a ballet about it, *Miracle in the Gorbals*,[7] and it has been the subject of photographers – Bert Hardy, Joseph MacKenzie, Oscar Marzaroli – and artists such as Joan Eardsley. I'm meeting with the writer Colin MacFarlane. Colin hasn't lived in Glasgow for nigh on forty years, but he still writes about it – notably about his childhood years in the Gorbals. Colin and I seem to have a lot in common. We were both born in the Glasgow tenements, we are about the same age and we both write about Glasgow (indeed we have both written books about Glasgow with 'real' in the title). However, I think that the resemblance is superficial. Whereas I am intent upon debunking some of the myths of Glasgow, Colin is often intent upon perpetuating them. His tales of life in the Gorbals owe not a little to popular fiction. He calls one book *No Mean Glasgow*[8] with a nod to *No Mean City*. He appropriates the name of 'The Gorbals Diehards' from John Buchan for his boyhood gang (although there is a little wry comment in the book for the cognoscenti to make it clear he knows he is doing so). His work while entertaining is sometimes sensationalist. Somehow, I have managed to grow up in similar circumstances to him without witnessing a fraction (well actually none) of the chibbings, break-ins and murders he seems to have. I raise this issue with him and he agrees that there is a degree of 'journalistic licence' in his work. Despite this, he has a genuine nostalgia for the place. He also laments the erosion of the Glasgow dialect; 'mate', never known in my youth, now seems to be a term of endearment whereas the common 'jimmy' as a form of address is dying out.

Of course, there are many favourable representations of the Gorbals. Years ago I met, in the Clyde Supporters Club in Rutherglen, Eddie Perrett. An old man then, Eddie had written a book called *The Magic of the Gorbals*.[9] In order to recreate the streets he remembered, he had penned little drawings of each street with its shops and pubs. A similar sort of remembering was enacted a few years ago on the lower walls of some tower blocks (now demolished) at the top of Gorbals Street. Figures had been painted on the lower walls featuring the same shops and pubs and street signs.

So what was the Gorbals really like? I decide to call on the ulti-
mate authority – my aunt Mima. Along with my father, another
sister and two brothers, she was brought up in a tenement in
Lawmoor Street. She is unequivocal regarding her memories – she
was quite happy there. We are looking over a volume of old photos
of the Gorbals and she recalls many of the shops and factories. She
comes to one photo and points to a figure peering out of a window.
That, she reckons, was her grandmother, known to the family as
Granny Green. Granny Green had a superior sort of tenement, she
remembers, as it had its own toilet. Although it is one of myths perpetuated about the Gorbals that it was an area of inferior slum
housing, this was not the case. The Gorbals had a mixture of
housing, including the occasional Georgian terrace. The demographic was more mixed than is sometimes appreciated. It was a
coherent community, the size of a whole town, that served nearly all
the needs of its inhabitants within itself.

Well, what is the Gorbals like today? I take a stroll across the St
Andrew's suspension bridge, by the Parsonage house, resplendent
in blue and gold. There is a Gorbals heritage trail if you wish to
follow it, but part of what we are looking at are absences, sites where
something had once been. There is hardly a tenement left in the
Gorbals but there is some new housing, for example in McNeil
Street, where one building, designed by Elder and Cannon in 1999
has been described as 'a classic twentieth century combination of an
eclipse and a cloud'. If you wish, in the Gorbals, you can visit the
bones of St Valentine (well, some of them) preserved in a shrine at
the Blessed John Duns Scotus Roman Catholic Church.

There are a many more bones to be found, however, in the
Southern Necropolis. It is reckoned that, over the years, a quarter
of a million people have been buried here. These include Sir
Thomas Lipton, famous for his tea and his sailing exploits, Allan
Glen, who founded my old school, Hugh MacDonald, who wrote
Rambles Around Glasgow,[10] and Alexander Thomson, the architect.

One statue that everyone is familiar with is the White Lady. It is
a monument to the wife of a carpet manufacturer who was run over
by a tram. Her face is now pitted and decayed, but she will still turn
her head to follow you as you pass (I walk past several times,
snatching a look, but no joy).

I don't dwell too long in Gorbals today, but one last visit.
Lawmoor Street once ran the length of the Gorbals but there are no
tenements here now and the street itself has been grossly curtailed.

However, a little remains containing a couple of businesses and the most noticeable is a manufacturer of tiles who has, for some reason known only to himself, built a full-scale replica of Michaelangelo's David in his courtyard.

GOVANHILL, STRATHBUNGO AND CROSSHILL

My second route to the south of Glasgow starts just south of Central Station. There is a distinct separation, in many ways, between the Southside and the rest of Glasgow. If you head south from the Laurieston Bar, in fact, there isn't much at all for a way. A well-known pub called the Souwester sits on the corner of the railway near some bricked-up arches. Some of these spaces, underneath the tracks running south from Central Station have been opened up and used for small businesses, garages, furniture warehouses, etc, but most are unused. The most ambitious project for this 'hidden underground' of Glasgow followed Glasgow's 'year of culture' when a large space called the Arches became a venue for a spectacularly unsuccessful exhibition – *Glasgow's Glasgow*. The exhibition was originally to be called 'The Words and the Stones' and a book was published with this title.[11] But it was ditched when it became apparent that the acronym was 'TWATS'. The space later became a quite successful theatre and then a nightclub, but there were some allegations of drug dealing and the authorities removed its late licence forcing the venue to go into administration in 2015. There is still some indignation around about this, but the word on the street is that the police had more evidence than was actually revealed. Past Bridge Street subway station some musical entertainment still survives in this part of town as the former New Bedford cinema has been converted to the O2 Academy, part of a chain of music venues in the UK. It seats 2500 and forthcoming bands according to the frontage as I pass include The Libertines and The Vamps. Here it stands pretty well alone as the tenements and factories that once formed this area are gone. Bridge Street and West Street subway stations once served busy communities but now they are the least used on the Circle. A couple of streets to the right was the site of the old ICI paint factory on the corner of West Street and Tradeston Street. My father worked there in the sixties and took me to the snooker room in the cafeteria and to the annual staff Christmas parties.

The factory and much else that was here is gone, but an old school survives. This is Scotland Street School, designed by Charles Rennie Mackintosh, that is now preserved as a museum. With its antiseptic whites tiles and wide parallel staircases it is reminiscent of my own primary school. For a museum, it doesn't seem *distant* enough from my own experience for me to totally appreciate it, but the children who are here today, parading through the old cloak-rooms and sitting at the little desks, seem to be impressed. There are little features preserved – the scholar's box of cardboard coins, sentence cards, some transcriptions of children's songs – that bring back memories. Maybe there is something missing. A coiled tawse, perhaps, a reminder of the stern presbyterian discipline Glasgow schools were renowned for:

Ma wee school's the best wee school,
The best wee school in Glesca.
The only thing that's wrang wi' it,
Is the baldy-heided maister.

He gangs tae the pub on Setterday night,
He gangs tae the church on Sunday,
An' prays tae God tae gie him strength,
Tae belt the weans on Monday.[12]

A little further south you come to a knot of Asian shops and a pub projecting at the gushet forming part of what is known as Eglinton Toll. Eglinton Street was named after the Earl of Eglinton, noted for organising the Eglinton Tournament, a medieval revival festival which took place in Ayrshire in 1839 and was a sensation of its day. Whether there was ever a toll here is not clear, but an alternative name for the junction was St Andrew's Cross, which can still be seen faintly on the gushet tenement wall. Supposedly, the roads meeting here form a saltire, thus St Andrew's. Supposedly, also, they form a star and this may be why the pub is called the Star Bar. One reason that this was a busy pub and a well-known local spot for several decades, was the location of the Plaza Ballroom across the road.

Once Glasgow had over twenty dance halls. The Dennistoun Palais was the largest and the Locarno in Sauchiehall Street was

popular. They offered relatively cheap entertainment but, most notably, a mechanism to meet members of the opposite sex. There was a strict etiquette to the structure of the dances – two waltzes would be followed by two foxtrots with the opportunity to choose partners in between. Knots of boys and girls would gather to size up each other. If you were both good-looking and a good dancer you had it made. Of course, there was also a gang element and fights sometime broke out.

In time, with television and other new forms of entertainment, the dance halls declined and the Plaza was, to my knowledge, the last left standing – closing in the nineties and subsequently demolished (although the block of flats that replaced it still bears the name). The Star Bar is, apparently, now noted for its karaoke and musical entertainment, but to me and most of the citizens of Glasgow it is famous for its cheap lunches. A three course lunch here was 50p not so long ago but is now £3.00. Today, it is a pleasant enough though quite barren bar partially filled with pensioners at lunch time. I pay 50p extra for the breaded fish and, thus provided, head on my way

A little further down Victoria Road, there are more shops, and cafés and pedestrians. There is also the Victoria Bar, where Scottish football supporters still meet on their way to Hampden Park, an Oxfam Bookshop and a Bank of Scotland with a large sign above proclaiming 'Christ Died For Our Sins'. This area, Victoria Road crossed by Allison Street notably, is Govanhill and it is a sort of mixed economy area with a variety of grey and red sandstone tenements of differing values but also with a notable ethnic community.

In fact, since the nineteenth century, this area of Glasgow and the nearby Shawlands has seen an influx of other nationalities. Jews from Poland and Lithuania, Italians, Irish, many of whom came to work at the ironworks founded by William Dixon in the 1840s in Hutchesontown, famous locally as Dixon's Blazes. In the sixties, mainly, Pakistanis settled here to work in the steel and textile industries. Many second or third generation Pakistanis now have prominent roles in the wider community. Generally, the ethnic diversity in Govanhill has been a positive force in the community. However, the latest immigrants – Roma people mostly from Slovakia (there are an estimated 2000 in the area) – have starkly divided opinion among local residents. It has been alleged that they form gangs and are responsible for a range of things from midden raking through organised begging to child prostitution. Support groups have been set up to integrate the Roma into the community.

The ethnic diversity of Govanhill can be seen in the shops and cafés in around: Kelly's Bar, the Italian Caffe and the Sheerin Palace, in Allison Street, a popular no-nonsense authentic Asian curry house. One of the locals I know from the Horseshoe Bar has seen the change of demographic in the area. He jokingly calls Allison Street Alissonstrasse. Still, pubs in the area have Scottish or Irish monickers – the Life O'Reilly, the Hampden Bar – although one is now a halal restaurant. Strangely, to me, walking down Allison Street, it seems very much like an *old* Glasgow type of street: tenements and shops, women pushing weans in prams, men nattering on street corners, delivery men going about their business. An interesting sideline – James Mollison, the noted aviator and playboy was born in Allison Street. In the thirties he was married to Amy Johnson and they were popularly known as the 'flying sweethearts'.

Islamic radicalism hasn't been as much of a problem in Glasgow as in other large cities in the United Kingdom, but round about here, a few years ago, another type of radicalism flourished.

Pastor Jack Glass preached on the Southside for years until his death in 2004 at his own Zion Baptist Church. He was a staunch Protestant who believed that the Pope was the anti-Christ and campaigned against Catholicism and what he saw as blasphemy. He particularly detested Billy Connolly and his sketch called *The Crucifixion* in which the last supper is set not in Galilee but in the Gallowgate, in the Sarry Heid. Glass stood for parliament twice, once as a candidate against the papal visit to Scotland in 1982. In 2004 he was diagnosed with lung cancer and proclaimed that the devil himself had afflicted him. His last public statement was to declare that he had defeated the devil. He died shortly afterwards. The folksinger Dick Gaughan later penned a song, *The Devil and Pastor Glass* with the memorable last lines:

> ...Jack Glass fought the Devil,
> from the early hours of morning to the setting of the sun
> Jack Glass fought the Devil – looks like the Devil won.[13]

Around the corner from Allison Street, Victoria Road comes to a dead end at the leafy gates of Queen's Park and the architecture is considerably grander as we are between two conservation areas: Crosshill to the left and Strathbungo to the right.

Strathbungo is now a highly desirable residential area of Glasgow, although at one time it was simply regarded as a slightly less salubrious and cheaper alternative to the West End. Strathbungo was once called Marchtown, the name surviving in March Street. No-one really knows why it developed the name Strathbungo. It is too far away from any river to be a 'strath' and 'bungo' is puzzling unless, as some suggest, it is a corruption of 'mungo'. There are a variety of nineteenth-century villas and terraces here, but the most notable is Moray Place (named after the Earl of Moray, a protagonist in the nearby Battle of Langside). This was designed by the Glasgow architect Alexander 'Greek' Thomson who lived here until his death in 1875. Thomson is a perplexing figure. A marble bust of him in the Kelvingrove Museum, his faced framed by curly hair and a grand beard, could perhaps be Grecian, but the stylistic elements in his architecture are often Egyptian and he even took an interest in Mesopotamian, Ottoman and other architectures. To see an interesting display of the elements of his architectural embellishments all carved in wood, you have to go not to Glasgow, but to Edinburgh where a public house – Thomson's Bar – has an interior decorated in the distinctive Thomson style. The Alexander Thomson Hotel can be found in Argyle Street, but there is no apparent connection apart from the name.

Thomson was not typical of the eminent architects of the nineteenth century. A devout man, he seldom left Glasgow and never set foot abroad. His company took on a variety of projects throughout the city and ranged from grand villas to tenement terraces. Moray Place gives a good indication of his style of housing which is based on classical proportions, repetition and symmetry (a style which is said to have influenced Frank Lloyd Wright). If you check the internet's most prolific encyclopedic site regarding Thomson, it notes that his work was little appreciated during his lifetime and also after his death until his reputation was revived in the fifties and sixties. This is certainly no exaggeration. Once Thomson's tenement buildings peppered this area, down Eglinton Street into Allison Street (where one survives). Between 1959 and 1981, Glasgow Corporation systematically demolished most of them. Even today, his work is not well preserved. Since a fire in 1965, his landmark church building, the Caledonia Road Church in the Gorbals, has been left derelict. His Egyptian Halls in Union Street and been empty for some time and, although it is apparently being renovated, it is now completely hidden behind one of those gigantic sheets that consists of a photographic image of the building behind. Other buildings have fared better: Holmwood House in Cathcart, one of his finest villas, has been restored by the National Trust for Scotland. His St Vincent Street Church, an imposing edifice on a steep slope running down from Sauchiehall Street, has been restored although there was a recent slight hiccup when part of the spire fell down through itself. Today, Alexander Thomson is fêted by some but has, largely, not been well served by his own city.[14]

QUEEN'S PARK

To the east of Strathbungo, not so well known but containing a few villas and terraces of note is the conservation area of Crosshill which borders on Queen's Park.

Designed by Sir Joseph Paxton and opened in 1857, Queen's Park was one of many parks created by the expanding city to provide leisure space for the citizens. The name is, perhaps, a nod to Queen Victoria but really derives from Mary Queen of Scots whose troops fought at the Battle of Langside nearby. At the time, prospective tenants of the yet to be built tenements and villas facing the park paid pretty prices for the assurance that their outlook was protected. Queen's Drive cuts round the north end of the park and Balmoral Crescent is typical of the more lavishly ornamented tenements here. It has curved glass in the windows, elaborate carvings including the figures of classical muses, wrought iron railings and lampposts topped with large globes. In the centre of the terrace, two doors have been painted a deep purple which should be out of kilter with the rest of the terrace but instead gives a striking and pleasing emphasis to the feature, especially as they are framed with pots of colourful plants and flowers. An unusual feature of the block, often unobserved, is the figure of the Statue of Liberty high up on the eastern corner, minus its characteristic torch which may have fallen into the hands of a particularly intrepid thief. A feature of one

nearby house is a lamppost featuring the Glasgow coat of arms. This signified that the Lord Provost lived here. They were supposed to be removed after the incumbent left, but there are several scattered around the city.

These pleasant and well-preserved flats with their leafy outlook hide a brutal secret. In 2008 a professional Glasgow woman, Moira Jones, had returned from a night out with her boyfriend, parked her car in front of her flat and was assaulted and abducted by a 33-year-old Slovakian with a history of violence. He dragged her into the park, raped her, beat her to death and left her body under a bush.

I am headed to the other side of Queen's Park to the gate diametrically opposite. This facade of the park, down Pollockshaws Road, is probably what I remember best from childhood. On one corner is the Langside Hall which now belongs to the City Council but was originally built in 1847 as a bank and stood in Queen Street until it was rebuilt here, stone by stone in 1901 at a cost of £18,000. Opposite that, however, is a sight that most Glaswegians will recognise. It is the colonnade and domed clock face of the Corona Bar, which looks older but, in fact, dates to 1912. This was a good old-fashioned Glasgow pub, but has now had a make-over and been renamed, for no apparent reason, The Butterfly and the Pig. Even more contemporary entertainment is also indicated on the gable-end of the tenement above advertised an adjacent venue – the Shed, 'entertainment hub of the Southside'. An interesting feature above

both doors of the Corona is an open hand, palm outwards, with a cross superimposed. This relates to the nearby area of Crossmyloof, now probably best known for its skating rink. The unusual name simply comes from the old gypsy expression 'cross my loof' – that is 'cross my palm (with silver)' to request money for services or for luck. The actual figure here, however, relates to a slightly more complex legend regarding Mary Queen of Scots – that she called on the power of a rosary or cross in her hand for victory in the Battle of Langside.

However, I am heading across the road to a more modest location. I'm at the Glad Café again which I enter through a corridor. It is a darkish venue in late morning, although there are bands, poetry readings and other arty events in the evening which, I suppose, would be cosy enough. Today, there are only two mothers with babies and me. I fancy a glass of wine but I'm told that they are not licensed at that time of day so I order a speciality tea. It takes the two assistants so long to deliver it that I wonder if they have gone to Assam to pick the leaves.

Anyway, I am here to meet May Miles Thomas, the filmmaker, and she is the sort of person to enliven proceedings. Endlessly informative, switching from topic to topic, May is not slow to express her opinions in a rich Glaswegian on the abilities of contemporary art students ('they couldn't draw their airse along the floor') or the difficulties in obtaining funding for creative projects in Scotland ('I didnae have a dug in that fight', 'all they were offering was heehaw to Garngad').

May has come some way from her upbringing in the tenements of the Southside. She now lives in a townhouse in Strathbungo having previously worked making short films and advertisements in London and Berlin. For a time she lived on the classical terraces of Calton Hill in Edinburgh but felt the necessity to return to Glasgow. She toyed with the idea of buying half a Greek Thomson villa, but now here she is, not far from where she was brought up.

May currently has two projects on the go. She is making a short film about the unearthing (or hopefully the unearthing) of the Cochno stone,[15] just outside Glasgow in West Dunbartonshire. This Bronze Age flat stone is one of the best examples of cup and ring carvings in the world. No-one knows what the symbols signify but it a fascinating and beautiful thing. Amazingly, after it was discovered in the sixties, archeologists from Glasgow University decided to bury it under three feet of soil as they believed they couldn't

guarantee its safety. Now there are plans to dig it out, perhaps create a permanent monument (although the fact that it straddles private and public land doesn't help) and record it more fully. A Spanish company have shown an interest in making a complete full-scale reproduction.

The second project is a feature film based on the life of her mother-in-law who was a geneticist involved with experimental labs and some clandestine activities during and after the last war. May has collected some of her possessions after her death which is using to construct some sort of factual/ fictional narrative about her life: a torn Christmas card, a photo of Bengalese finches in the head of a spoon, a skein of auburn hair, a transgender gingerbread cutter.[16]

However, I am more interested in May's work on Glasgow and I have asked her to take me to somewhere she filmed for *The Devil's Plantation* that means something special to her, and today she is taking me a walk around Queen's Park.

May came back to Glasgow shortly after the Moira Jones murder and she remembers the park being closed. The police did a finger-tip search of the whole park, she tells me, making it, for a while, the most examined and perhaps the safest place in Glasgow. Clearly that episode has given May a slightly different slant from her child-hood memories. Entering the park, one of the first things we come across is the poetry rose garden. This was constructed after Glasgow hosted the World Rose Convention in 2003 and the theme is Scottish poets. On this day, the roses themselves look sadly bedraggled and I wonder how well they have been tended. May points out a large carved stone around which the words of one of Hugh MacDiarmid's most quoted poems have been inscribed:

> The rose of all the world is not for me.
> I want for my part
> Only the little white rose of Scotland
> That smells sharp and sweet
> — and breaks the heart.[17]

It is a little verse I know well but I realise that I often misquote it, especially getting the second last line mixed up to try to force a rhyme.

As for the rest of the poets, there has been a fairly eclectic choice which is detailed on a plinth: they range over five centuries from Robert Henryson to George Mackay Brown. There are Gaelic poets – Duncan Ban MacIntyre and Sorley MacLean; female poets – Violet Jacob and Marion Angus; and Robert Fergusson and Robert Burns are there, but no Walter Scott. Two poets, James Hogg and Robert Burns, have been chosen for a special compliment – they have their own dedicated rubbish bin. As often in Glasgow one is left wondering what numpty in the City Council came up with such an idea.

CONGRATULATIONS!!!
YOU HAVE BEEN SPECIALLY SELECTED FOR A PRIZE

IF YOUR NAME IS
J A M E S   H O G G
R O B E R T   B U R N S

THEN PLEASE TELEPHONE THE NUMBER BELOW*
TO RECEIVE YOUR PERSONAL MEMORIAL LITTER BIN

*calls will be charged as detailed below; other providers'
charges may vary and are likely to cost more

The more interesting part of the park, however, rises uphill. There are foundations of an old bandstand, but the focus of events, concerts and fairs has been relocated to a sort of natural bowl. At the top of the hill is a mast and a viewpoint with a plaque indicating some of the city's historic sites. Here is one of the points where

Harry Bell conjured up his prehistoric site alignments. Aware of the critics of ley line theory who have, sardonically, lined up contemporary features such as telephone boxes, it suddenly occurs to me that the most obvious and natural alignments on this skyline are between high-rise blocks: Red Road to Sighthill to Moss Heights, etc. I wonder what some future archeologist, ruminating over the ruins of this great city, would make of it all.

At the top of the hill here is the oldest part of the park where a large mound is said to have been a Norman castle. May points out a rather inconspicuous stone circle among some trees – six stones around a large puddle. These could be prehistoric or they could be part of an encampment related to the Battle of Langside. Harry Bell apparently brought his pieces up here and felt an energy emanating from the stones which he described as 'smooth, polished-looking, sympathetic to the touch'. I sit on one but only feel a little damp.

We descend via a glasshouse. Outside there is the figure of a panda carved out of a tree stump. Inside, however, there is more exotic fauna. This is the reptile house. A sequence of glass tanks are arranged around the walls and in the centre space. The first tank contains a pair of copulating tortoises, the others variously a blue-tongued skink, a red-headed agama, a death stalker scorpion and other creatures of dubious attractiveness. Many of the tanks, however, are empty and a few contain insects that have been encased in plastic. May says it is a sort of subsidised crèche like the

Tramway – but I'm not sure I would bring the kids here.

Further on we skirt some allotments and I'm quite surprised to see that one contains chickens. May, however, can trump that. Apparently someone was fined for keeping pigs here and slaughtering them on the spot. We pass through some trees into what May says is called Area 60, supposedly for the preservation of wildlife, but now used, on and off, as a gay cruising ground. She points out the bushes where the Moira Jones murder took place. Down around there, she tells me, she often finds (among the usual hypodermic needles, etc) the little figures made from twigs etc that could be charms or hexes. It's like the Blair Witch Project, she says. She attributes some of it to the druids of Rouken Glen – cousins, no doubt, of the druids of Sighthenge.

Walking down to exit via the Queen's Drive gates after visiting Queen's Park with May I get to thinking. The tour seems to complement the somewhat eerie films that first made up *The Devil's Plantation* or the black and white photographs that are accessed via May's Glasgow website. Queen's Park, in essence, gives me that peculiarly Glasgow feeling that contains a mixture of tranquillity and anxiety.

Queen's Park

Fingertip-felt swathe of Glasgow green,
Guarded by the death stalker scorpion,
Lair of the Rouken Glen druids, home
To the James Hogg memorial litter bin.
Your municipality is abundant but,
What secret terrors tumble therein?

THE TRAMWAY

I'm visiting the Tramway for a specific purpose although I thought I was already done with it a while back when I was there with Gerry Hassan to talk about his book on mythologies of modern Scotland.[18] The Tramway is an old tram shed on the Southside that once housed the Museum of Transport. I remember coming here in 1971 to see the Apollo 10 moon module and a piece of rock from the moon. In the nineties, however, it was converted to an arts centre, with a cinema, performance spaces and a café bar. Peter Brook called it 'an industrial cathedral that connects art with humanity'. That may be, but it is not a very prepossessing space. It still looks industrial and the café is like a works cafeteria. There is an interesting enough landscaped garden entered via an alcove with a model of Clyde, the Glasgow Commonwealth Games mascot. The most interesting feature, however, is the view from the garden of the giant gleaming Sikh Gurdwara or temple, opened in 2013.

I'm here to see the Turner Prize exhibition, for that most prestigious of artistic prizes, perhaps piggybacking on the previous success of Glasgow artists, has decamped here this year from the Tate in London. To start with the omens are not good. The whole thing seems designed for children. The guide to the exhibition features questions that seem to be addressed to an eight-year-old. When you exit the exhibition, you can write comments on a little slip that, when inserted into a machine, rings a bell.

However, on to the exhibition itself. Well, I would say it was a waste of space, but the space is hardly wasted at all. This enormous erstwhile home of trams and buses, with its stone floor still traversed with tram tracks and now redolent in whitewashed walls and partitions, has practically nothing in it.[19]

One corner is taken up by the most interesting exhibition, that of the winners – but this is more like a warehouse or shop than a piece of art. In the opposite corner is a room with computer screens featuring interviews and tables covered in books which are meant to comment on the content of the piece but seem largely unrelated to me. There is a large empty space in the centre in which nothing is happening but is set aside for a performance which seems to consist of the incantation of a fairly random selection of words.

One other central exhibit is a room of identical chairs onto which fur coats have been placed – well, not just placed, their linings have been sewn into the backs of the chairs. They are intended to be, I suppose, a sort of empty people (although not a very interesting collection of empty people since they all wear the same coats). My observation is at odds with one reviewer who describes it as like 'the post-scarper cleared crime scene/function room of a raided mafia baptism breakfast.' Really?

There is another room where you can listen to videos of the artists talk about their work. The artist video, I note, has developed its own peculiar genre. It consists of shots of them in slow motion or time lapse in dreary post-industrial settings interspersed with them in their studios waffling in a pretentious and meaningless way. Yes, I'm afraid cynicism has entered the building, and grumpiness isn't far behind.

The Glasgow Miracle might indeed be worth talking about, but the fact of the matter is that has mostly won its colours from the Turner Prize connection; that annual celebration of anti-art – sculptures made from elephant dung, empty rooms with lights going on and off. God alone knows what the general Glasgow public think of this sorry show.

Once there was great art in Glasgow. I remember Glasgow School of Art degree shows in past years with, for example, the surreal narrative paintings of Stephen Campbell, the carved wood constructions of Tim Stead, or the delicate frosty portraits of Alison Watt. I'm fed up with the current breed of Glasgow artists – the whole shebang of them – running after trams, sitting in their bedsits in Strathclyde, holding their breath in tunnels.

Don't get me wrong here; conceptual art is fine if it has an interesting concept. The stuff here doesn't. I ask Mungo, my pet monkey, to generate some new exciting concepts and he does so *ad nausea*:

> Louis Vuitton handbags stapled to restaurant tables.
> Silk pyjamas stitched onto bedclothes.
> Agent Provocateur panties dangling from bedsteads.
> Bowler hats cemented to hatracks.
> Blackberrys bolted to desks.

The genesis of the Glasgow Miracle is often ascribed to a lecturer who instructed his students to focus not on the product but on the process of being an artist (would you like to go to a restaurant in which the chef is focusing on being a chef?)

The dereliction of ideas and creativity in contemporary art practice is distressing, and it has percolated down to students. I've seen a degree show in the past year (not in Glasgow, however) in which I couldn't find a single praiseworthy display. The situation is reid rotten, as we say in Scots. My opinion is that, since the practice of art is at best ignored by those who do not think it is important it must be promoted by those who know that it is. Maybe the maligned Glasgow Effect project is the final nail in the coffin for the whole school of what might be called 'non-art.' And perhaps it is time for Glasgow, once again, to be at the forefront of an artistic revival.[20]

FIELD OF DREAMS

Long ago small boys with litanies on their lips of the great Scottish teams of long ago would have wet dreams about the sacred turf I'm heading to now. Once Scotland were a football team to be feared. My father always said that the Scottish team of 1966 would have won the World Cup, but they were thwarted by the inconvenient fact that they failed to qualify. True enough, they trounced the holders, England, in their first game as champions. In 1967 Scottish club football was at its zenith. Celtic famously won the European Cup, Rangers were in the final of the European Cup-Winners Cup and Kilmarnock in the semi-finals of the Inter Cities Fairs Cup. That was as good as it got.

Disappointments followed. There were false dawns. We went on the road with Ally's Army to Argentina in 1978 on a wave of unwarranted optimism expecting to win the World Cup. It was the worse foreign investment since the Darien Scheme. Nowadays, we don't even qualify to take part in the World Cup.

The nadir for Scottish football was under the management of the German Bertie Vogts who, as they say in Glasgow, couldn't manage a menage. We couldn't beat the Faroe Isles and it was unkindly suggested that maybe we should take on the Scilly Isles, or even the Summer Isles, which were uninhabited. Subsequently we fell to a world ranking below that of the Cape Verde Islands and Burkino Faso. In the eighties, B.A. Robertson sang the words:

> I have a dream, if dreams come true,
> Then Bonnie Scotland, I'll play for you.

A couple of decades later, it was rumoured at least, some players were scunnered at the thought of playing for their country.

Nevertheless, the Tartan Army, some say the best supporters in the world, haven't given up. I'm heading to their spiritual home, and the home of the Scottish Football Museum, Hampden Park, the Scottish national football stadium, across the Southside, skirting the new £842m Queen Elizabeth Emergency Hospital which, because, perhaps, of its futuristic shape, the locals have optimistically nicknamed the Death Star.

I have fond memories of Hampden, although the first game I attended there ended in an ignominious 3-0 defeat to a then unheralded Dutch team. Two highlights of my visits were to games which, for reasons I can't remember, were untelevised – thus, unusually, remaining in folk memory, which is not a bad thing.

Just after the 1978 World Cup, the champions, Argentina, came to Hampden. The team was full of big names and an untried 17-year-old whose name was Maradona. We couldn't get the ball off him and we were handed a consummate lesson in the art of the game. The Scottish fans stayed to applaud a lap of honour by the winners.

Another occasion was the Celtic-Rangers Dryborough Cup Final (strangely, enough, the only Celtic-Rangers match I've ever been to). Davie Cooper, a Rangers legend, who died suddenly and prematurely at the age of 39, scored one of the most amazing goals ever seen. If I remember correctly, he caught the ball in the air near the bye-line, flicked it over the head of one player, then another, then volleyed in into the top corner with his left foot.

As I approach Hampden a tune comes into my head. Some wag once wrote a parody of the song *The Day We Went to Bangor* called *The Day We Went to Hampden*. I can only remember one interesting expression:

> On the way back, I fell out with Jack,
> And I gave him the dandruff decider.

Hampden Park is the Scottish national stadium but actually belongs to Queen's Park FC who also play there. Queen's Park are the oldest football club in Scotland, founded in 1867, and have the rare distinction of being the only amateur club in the Scottish league. They dominated the game in Scotland for years after their formation, winning the Scottish Cup on ten occasions and featuring in the FA Cup final twice. For the first international played between Scotland and England in 1872, the entire Scottish team were from Queen's Park. The glory days are over, but the club is still around, playing in their black and white pinstripes, which earned them the nickname the Spiders.

Today, however, I'm not here to see a match, but to visit another attraction. The Scottish Football Museum opened in 2001 and is a prime tourist attraction in the city. In its galleries you can see the Scottish Cup and vintage memorabilia from the beginnings of the game, watch videos of great goals and marvel at the Hall of Fame, which currently features 99 footballing legends: Archie Gemmill, Kenny Dalglish, Denis Law, Derek Johnstone, Maurice Malpas, etc.

The best part of your visit, however, is the stadium tour, starting in the home dressing room. Your heart palpitates and the hairs rise on the back of your neck as you listen to a recorded team talk from the ex-Scotland manager, Craig Brown. But the finest moment is a chance to jog down the tunnel and emerge onto the sacred turf in front of 60,000 cheering fans (well, you have to imagine them). The final pleasure is a chance to have the speed of your shot recorded and receive a Hampden Hotshot certificate. I do OK, but nowhere near the legendary Peter Lorimer who could propel a football at over 90 miles per hour.

Football, or 'fitba', is close to the heart of Glasgow, at least to male Glasgow, and you won't hold many conversations in the city without it coming up. It too, has a dark side, once tainted by sectarian violence, the game is now discredited as leading to incidents of domestic violence commonly, after big matches. These two problems remind me of a couple of jokes: Kenny Dalglish, a Protestant, had signed for Celtic but was alarmed when the crowd started calling him a 'pape'. 'Don't worry, son,' said Tommy Gemmell. 'I got used to it, it disnae bother me now.' 'But,' said Kenny, 'you *are* a pape!' Wife says to husband, 'Sometimes I think that you love Rangers more than me.' 'I love *Celtic* more than you!'

Glasgow humour is a tool to disarm serious issues, but perhaps we can become a little too obsessed with our allegiances at time?

Evermore

1965 wis just magic. Big Jock Stein took over at Parkheid. The start o twenty years o quality fitba: Jinky Johnstone, Yogi Hughes, Danny McGrain, oor Kenny, wee Cherlie Nicholas.

PARKHEAD HERALDS NEW ERA

It wis great. We wir unbeatable. The huns couldnae touch us. Then 1967 wis even mair magic. Estadio Nacional, Lisboa: Celtic 2 Inter 1. A blooter frae Gemmell an a nifty sidefoot frae Chaumers.

LISBON LIONS HEROES OF EUROPE

Shankly sed tae Jock, 'Yere immortal, Big Man.' Ah merried Agnes and then we hid a wean. Ah caed him Simpson Craig Gemmell Murdoch McNeill Clark Johnstone Wallace Chalmers Auld Lennox. Then we went tae Argentina fur the World Club Championship, an ye wouldnae believe it. Thae animals tried tae tear us apairt. They spat oan Boabie Lennox an they tried tae cripple wee Jinky. Then they kicked Simpson oan the heid. Ye wouldnae credit it, the fucking Argie referee ordered a replay an he sent fowr o oor boys packing fir nothing. An then he gave them the gemme even though it should hae been abandoned. Sick. Whit we should hae been:

CHAMPIONS OF THE WORLD

Onyway, 1970 wis magic agin. We gubbed Leeds United, the pride o fucking England. Then we goat to the final agin. Feyennord, some wee Dutch team that yed nevir heard o. I couldnae believe it but. The tie goes tae extra time an then; big Billy McNeill pits his haun up in the penalty box, next thing we're oot the gemme, 2-1. Ah kicked in the telly, goat rid o Agnes... Fuck...

But then things goat better. Soon we hid Dalglish. Then in 1977 he ups an he's aff.

KENNY KING OF THE KOP

Well, I didnae blame him in a way. But ah'd goat Simpson Craig Gemmell Murdoch McNeill Clark Johnstone Wallace Chalmers Auld Lennox a budgie an ah'd cawed it Kenny. All just couldnae staun the sight o it efter that. The wean widnae stap greetin aw night.

The next few years werenae bad. Sort o up an doon. But then in 1985 ye wouldnae believe it agin. The Big Man goes an cops it. Scotland goat a penalty against the taffies an Cooper, a fucking teddy bear, pits it away. So the Big Man has a fit an draps deid.

ALL SCOTLAND MOURNS ITS HERO

Scotland goat tae the World Cup, but they were soon papped oot. But something wisnae right Ah just couldnae get it oot o ma heid. So, as a sort o homage, ah dies ma hair green. Then ah goes doon tae the hock shop and ah gets a wee gun aff o Shuggie – a luger he ses. Ah goes tae the post office an ah hauds them up, just like that Butch Cassidy, an ah goes an gets a flight oot tae Buenos Aires. An then ah finds that wee bastard o a referee an ah shoots him deid. A bit over the top, mebbe, bit he wis way

OUT OF ORDER

The ither day, Simpson Craig Gemmell Murdoch McNeill Clark Johnstone Wallace Chalmers Auld Lennox came to visit me. He asked me to caw him Ronnie. He brought me a Wee Red Book. Ah see that the bhoys hiv goat the double agin

SILVERWARE RETURNS TO PARADISE

'Da,' he ses, 'dinna talk pish. Yir no in an Argy concentration camp, yir in fuckin Leverndale.'

Ah looks at him.

'Gonna keep takin them wee sweeties,' he ses. 'Mebbe they'll let you oot fir next season.'

CARRICK QUAY

I have crossed the river Clyde twice to head to the Southside of Glasgow. For the third and final time, I intend to take to a more circuitous route from the city centre, heading west along the Clyde walkway and then across the river by boat to Govan.

It is a dullish day of small drizzle when I make my way to Carrick Quay in Clyde Street just around the corner from the Scotia. There are some better quality newish flats here – their facade like the prows of ships facing out to the Clyde. Carrick Quay is named after the *Carrick*, an old sailing boat that was moored here for donkey's years. It was one of the first developments of the nineties (begun in

1989 actually) and heralded a new wave of executive flats, but never totally took off and there are still properties here commonly available for sale.

As for the boat, a clipper ship built in 1864, the *HMS Carrick* was employed for years by the Royal Navy Volunteer Reserve Club and sometimes hosted events and parties. However, it partially sank twice and was eventually towed to the Clyde coast where it sat for some time until the hulk was put on a boat and sailed down to Adelaide from whence, originally named *The City of Adelaide*, it had once sailed under its own steam (or, rather, sails).

My intention is to follow the Clydeside walkway for some way and then cross over to Govan, but first to gather my two attendant demons. First of all, on the wall of a nondescript building, a giant

underwater Dalek. Well, he has been described as a giant, and he certainly dwarfs the Finnieston crane that appears on the shore behind him. But that could just be the effect of perspective. To me, he is kin to the Dalek sliding down Sauchiehall Street, a thoroughly Glasgow Dalek.

Secondly, nearer the banks of the river, is a long tiger painted out of fire, it seems, by the artist Klingatron. Armed with these familiars, I am heading off along the walkway, but the elemental battle between fire and water is suddenly settled. The skies open, it is chucking it down.

SQUINTY BRIDGE, ARMADILLO
AND HYDRO

After drying off with lunch, then, I'm back on the trail but heading
another way via Finnieston to the riverside and Docklands.

Ok. I'm almost lost. Well, not lost. I know where I am but just
don't know how to get where I'm going. It's the damned motorway
again. Getting where I'm going is a bit of a task as there are numer
ous dead-ends and it is necessary to negotiate both the railway and
the motorway. But, after a while, via a few office blocks, warehouses
and the odd new hotel a strange site appears, a large metallic wall
with continual perforations, like a polished and embellished tin can.
This is the wall of a car park and beyond it is the Hydro, and we are
wandering into a landscape that could well feature on some futuristic film set or an Iain M. Banks novel.

However, before we get to the future, there are some reminders
of the past. The Finnieston Crane is probably just about the most
famous landmark in Glasgow. 174 feet in height, it is the only one
of several giant cranes left on Clydeside. Its main function was to
lift locomotives constructed in Glasgow onto ships to be sent all
over the world (apparently there are some Glasgow-built locomotives still running in India). Until quite recently, I believe, it was kept
in working order, but now stands purely as a symbol of Glasgow's
industrial past. The steel plaque on its side gives its origin: 'Clyde
Navigation Trustees Crane no. 7... Covans Sheldon & Co Ltd,

Carlisle 1931'. This is the structure from which George Wylie suspended a straw locomotive to symbolize the demise of heavy industry in Glasgow. After the artist's death in 2013, a giant question mark was suspended as a tribute to him.

A little further on, a large round stone building now houses restaurants and bars. This is the Rotunda, which was once the entrance to a pedestrian tunnel under the Clyde (it is mirrored by another on the other side.). It was shut down for years, but in my youth, I believe, urban adventurers found a way in and walked, with the aid of torches, under the river.

The three most recent features here, however, are all of one ilk. The Clyde Arc, opened in 2006 is a road bridge with a distinctive curved design which, with its cross supports, now forms another commonly employed image as a silhouette on the skyline. Because it crosses the river, unusually, at an angle, it is known locally as the Squinty Bridge. A similar propensity for nicknames has led to the main hall of the Scottish Exhibition and Conference Centre (the Clyde Auditorium) being called the Armadillo because of its segmented roof. Next to it and more recent, opened only in 2013, is the SSE Hydro (no-one has thought up a suitable nickname yet, although it looks a bit like a giant flying saucer), its gleaming

segments, arranged, in opposition to the Armadillo, horizontally. In the best Glasgow tradition, it is designed to be bigger and better, seating over 13,000 as opposed to over 10,000 in the Armadillo. Acts accommodated her recently have included Adele, Rod Stewart, and Lady Gaga.

The day I visit, this is an unpopulated landscape, part of but not part of Glasgow. No-one very much inhabits here but every so often the enormous car parks will fill up, hordes of concert-goers will come and go, followed by legions of cleaners and stage setters and part of Glasgow will be enthralled, for a short time, by some media-hyped performance from another continent. Although it is impressive sight, and a credit to Glasgow, I'm sure, I have never been here and probably never will (unless Elvis can make a come-back), so I don't really have much to say about it.

Further on, following the Clydeside Walkway and dodging countless bicyclists with mobile phones, some of the old docks has reverted to nature: rosebay willowherb, thistles, umbrella tress, dandelions and dock leaves have taken over. I'm heading a little further west – to the Riverside Museum, effectively Glasgow's museum of transport, which has taken over from an earlier incarnation in the Kelvin Hall.

RIVERSIDE

A firm supporter of Dr Johnson's old adage that being on a boat is like being in gaol with the additional risk of drowning, I am some-what intimidated by my first encounter at the Riverside. Hesitantly stepping on board, I take pictures but I don't get too close to the edge; an erstwhile rock climber, I could ascend the loftiest pinnacle, but I'm a total wimp confronted by a skin of dark calm damp.

The *Glenlee* was launched in Port Glasgow in 1896, but shortly afterwards her name was changed to the *Islamount*. After years circumnavigating the globe as cargo ship, she was deployed by the Spanish Navy as a training vessel. In 1992 she was purchased by the Clyde Maritime Trust, refurbished and brought home to the Clyde,

one of only five Clyde-built sailing ships still afloat in the world. And here she is now, parked outside the Riverside Museum. She is a spectacular sight and in good trig, painted red, white and grey with black squares along the side. This is supposedly a tradition from the old days whereas merchant vessels tried to appear as if they had cannon on board.

The whole thing is a fascinating experience and almost as nerve-wracking as going down Big Pit, the Welsh mining museum. The hold of the ship is much larger than you expect (you could almost have a game of five-a-side in it) but that was for the cargo. The crew lived in tiny constructions on the deck – the poop deckhouse for the officers and the main deckhouse for the rest. There is a 'hospital' – a space just about big enough for a bed, a 'head', which is a toilet, and a galley, a little more commodious than the others. The whole place could be awash in a storm. There is a reproduction of a painting of the ship listing seriously and giant waves bashing her while the seamen trim the sails. The thought alone is terrifying. Men were sometimes lost overboard and injuries and disease were common, making the hospital a very crowded place.

The maritime theme is continued in the main museum. The Riverside Museum, designed by the influential contemporary architect Zaha Hadid, cost £74m and opened in 2011. It stands at the confluence of the Clyde and the Kelvin and its jagged profile juts out towards the river, like the prow of a ship or the form of a wave (fitting for Glasgow's new 'flagship' museum).

Internally there is much to admire: there is the history of Clydeside construction of engines from the Finnieston ferry to the *Lusitania*, Henry Bell's *Comet* to the *QEII*. There are Glasgow trams and buses and carriages and bikes. Cars are displayed on the Arnold Clark Car Wall. This is a peculiar conception; surely walls weren't designed for cars and vice versa. However, it isn't too bad. What I baulk at is the display of the collection of ship models. Once these inhabited a whole hall in Kelvingrove museum, set apart in their individual cases, lit from above, sailing on their own imagined sea of glass. It was my favourite exhibit as a boy. Now they are displayed on top of each other, poorly lit and lacking the grandeur they deserve. Couldn't Glasgow have afforded just a little more of Hadid's carefully designed space?

However, there is no doubt about my favourite part of the museum, the reconstructed Glasgow street which is a slightly expanded version of the original in the Kelvin Hall. It is replete with offices and shops and vehicles. There is Ovinius Dam's photography studio and Devine's Gowns and Mantles. There is a bootmakers, a cabinetmakers, a saddlers, a pawnbrokers, a café. Then there is a reconstructed subway station and a pub. In the cobbled street stand a hearse and two horses and a baker's wagon.

It is a testament to old Glasgow, a Glasgow that is long gone, or is it? The Rendezvous Café, with its booths of stained glass and its marble-topped tables is from Duke Street. It was founded by Giovanni Togheri from Tuscany and was open from 1929 to 1985. There is every possibility that I visited it as a child. The saddler's shop features a video of a saddler at work and I realise that it is the father of a girl I once went out with. The pub, however, offers the greatest shock. It is the reconstructed interior of The Mitre, which once stood in Brunswick Street (the original site of Douglas Gordon's Hitchcock set) and in which I would occasionally have a drink. Interestingly, The Mitre wasn't very old before it was moved. It was only opened in 1927. However, it fits in very well here in this pastiche of various periods in Glasgow's past.

For me, this street is a reminder of both a communal and a personal past, it is a sort of perfect simulacrum of a Glasgow that maybe once was and it is, in fact, comforting. I could stay here all day, and it could only be improved if you could actually get a pint of beer in the pub.

CLYDE WATERS

Another way to cross the Clyde is to take the free ferry that crosses to Govan in the summer months. As the little boat chugs across the flat water on a grey day, I reflect on the futuristic landscape on either side of the river. It is now a view familiar to just about everyone in the region – and on a daily basis. Just as the headquarters of the main newspaper, like the *Daily Record*, decamped to the banks of the river some time ago, the television companies have now joined them and both the BBC and Scottish Television headquarters are there. The morning news every day features the landscape of the Clyde – old and new – the Finnieston crane and the Clyde Arc.

This little ferry is the only one still running across the Clyde today, but there were once eleven ferries in all.[21] My father would take me, as a small boy, back and forward across the river on them. I always remember him here. But the Clyde of my father's day was the old Clyde of the great shipyards: Harland & Wolff, A. & J. Inglis, Barclay Curle, Yarrows. They are gone now and I wonder what my father would make of the new Clyde vista, like something from a sci-fi epic. I guess that the Finnieston crane would be the only thing he would latch on to. There is a way in which the terrain of the city sometimes becomes a mirror of an emotional landscape. There are a couple of lines in the poem 'Glasgow' by Alexander Smith:

> ...From terrace proud to alley base,
> I know thee as my mother's face.[22]

I once took this as the key for a poem about my father, the Clyde, change and death.

September Song

> From tumbled block to weedy waste,
> I know you as my father's face.
>
> My father's face was hard and mild,
> Lined with dreams of man and child.
>
> Do not disdain my father's name,
> If other faces seem the same.

Do not distort with praise or pity,
The rheumy heart of this mean city.

Oily water puddling meets,
Settling stones of rain-struck streets.

September embers final blow,
September's song lays summer low.

. . .

Clyde's waters flow too crousely now,
Furrows fleece the schlammy brow.

The body feels through steel-wrought plates,
The spirit's source in silence waits.

Do not lie soft in greenless dust,
Do not lie hard in river's rust.

Necrotic dust its measure takes,
Memory's seed the future makes.

My father's gaze is fixed and still,
The city burns beneath its will.

GOVAN

Disembarking the ferry, I'm in Govan and my first port of call is the
Glasgow Science Centre. Built in 2001, this has always been something of a white elephant. I find it generally uninspiring, mostly full
of interactive exhibits for children, some of which work. It is best
known for its observation tower, however. Built at a cost of £10m,
and 137 metres high, this is claimed to be the tallest fully rotating
freestanding structure in the world. Magnificent views of Glasgow
and its surrounds can be had from here. Well, that would be if it
worked! Dogged with problems for years, it has hardly ever func-
tioned, earning it the nickname 'Faulty Tower'. After refurbishment,
it opened again in July 2014 but there are still problems with lift
doors, etc. So, come the summer season in March, it may or may

not take you to a dizzy height.

My guide through Govan is my old friend John Cowan, who has lived here just about all his life. Best known now, probably, as the birthplace of Sir Alex Ferguson or as the sit-com home of Rab C. Nesbitt, it is fair to say that not so many years ago Govan was in a sorry state – a thriving working class area of tenements, ship-builders and dockers had been reduced to a shadow of its former self, a clutch of houses, off-licenses, tanning parlours and court solicitors. However, there have been improvements. As well as the new ferry, Govan has a radio station – Sunny *Go-van* (originally an ironic nickname for the place), a heritage centre in the home of Fairfield Shipyards, which has also been converted into office space, and an innovative community website, *GetIntoGovan*. From it, among other things, you can download the Govan Trumps playing cards featuring famous Govanites – Alex Ferguson, Owain the Bald, Mary Barbour, John Elder, King Dyfnwal, Margo MacDonald, etc. Another interesting aspect of Govan is that it has two surviving junior football teams that mirror Rangers and Celtic – St Anthony's and Benburb.

However, before visiting the more recent heritage of Govan, a visit to the far past. Surprisingly, Govan was once a settlement on the Clyde that rivalled Glasgow itself, with its own saint, Constantine, to rival Kentigern. Govan Old Parish, occupying a site which traces Christian worship back to the sixth century, and now a full-time museum, hosts the sarcophagus of St Constantine and some remarkable Celtic carvings found in the area. There is also a

rare collection of five hogback tombstones. These large strangely-shaped stones get their name from their supposed resemblance to the bristled back of a pig, but they were possibly meant to represent houses – earthly or heavenly. They are probably the product of Vikings who inhabited this area around the tenth century.

Govan was once much more widespread. Early maps show what we now know as Govan as 'Mekle' (large) Govan, while Little Govan was on the south side of the river Clyde directly opposite Glasgow Green. Govan Burgh once covered a great deal of the Southside of Glasgow and had a population of over 80,000. It was, however, to the dismay of some Govanites, annexed by Glasgow in 1912.

The grand municipal past of Govan can still be encountered through Govan Burgh Hall and, opposite the Black Man and Brechin's, the Pearce Institute which still holds a range of classes and activities for Govanites. An interesting event took place here on 10-11 January 1990. At the behest of the novelist James Kelman, Noam Chomsky was invited as the keynote speaker at a conference titled 'Self Determination and Power'. Contributors included George Davie, the philosopher, Derek Rodger, the editor of *Scottish Child*, and well-known local musicians, artists and writers such as Alasdair Gray and Tom Leonard. The event was captured on film by Malcolm Dickson and has recently been the subject of a book with schematic drawings by Mitch Miller. It seems quite extraordinary today, sitting in Brechin's Bar, that not so long ago it was the centre for discussion groups on cutting edge issues in politics and representation.[23]

A little further west, the Fairfield Shipyard gates, once thronged with working men at lousing time, are now represented by a strange sculpture that looks like some sort of insect. The exhibition at Fairfield Govan gives a good account of the history of ship-building and of Govan in general: there are Govan Burgh pennies, tokens and medals, a depiction of the Govan Fair in which the Govan Queen was traditionally preceded by a ram's head, and drawings by the well-known war artist, Muirhead Bone, who drew the shipyard in 1917.

It is actually a sunny day when we see all this. John and I sit for a while at the Aitken memorial fountain by the Cross, now gleaming gold, black and red after a recent restoration where some teenagers are toying with a football and a man is apparently exhibiting his home-made version of Munch's *The Scream*. Then we take a pleasant walk down the landscaped riverside walkway. There may be problems of social deprivation in Govan, but it is still a community and its history can still be treasured.

GALGAEL

Well, it is a another dark, dreich damp winter's afternoon and I am walking down the uninspiring top end of Paisley Road West back towards Govan for no reason other than the geometry of the Glasgow buses. Circumventing a dreary industrial estate I head down past the grand thirties facade of Ibrox stadium, the home of Glasgow Rangers football club, impressive by its sheer length rather than any architectural excellence. Towards the east end a light pierces the gloom illuminating a statue of John Greig, an iconic Scottish footballer and erstwhile captain of Rangers. Unlike the exuberant figure of Jinky Johnstone at Celtic Park, this is an altogether more sombre tribute, as it is a memorial to the Ibrox disaster. On 2nd January 1971, a new year had just dawned and Rangers were playing Celtic at Ibrox. At the end of the game, a capacity crowd streamed down the stairways and, at one point, some fell and a crush developed. 66 fans, some children, died, mostly of asphyxia. I remember my mother frantically trying to phone my uncle, who was at the match but unharmed. The names of the victims are inscribed at the memorial and there are tributes. Today, some flowers and scarves are scattered around and, a little further, at the gates to the stadium, there are some more scarves, flowers and written tributes for an ex-Rangers footballer, Arnold Peralta, who has been shot dead in his native Honduras.

Around the corner is Ibrox subway station and across the road Fairley Street – named after the area of West Dunbartonshire adjacent to the Cochno Stone – a rather dreary collection of warehouses and used tyre merchants. This, however, is my destination and one doorway is well-lit and welcoming.

This is the home of the GalGael Trust where the old Govan tradition of boatbuilding is alive and well – albeit on a smaller scale than that perpetrated by the shipbuilders of the great yards. GalGael is a combination of two Gaelic words: 'Gal' meaning foreigner or stranger, and 'Gael', a native Scot and in this dichotomy it epitomises a mix of rural and urban Scottish tradition – a highland spirituality and a working-class Govan solidarity.

It was founded in the nineties by Colin Macleod, aka the

Birdman of Pollock or, for his letters to the press, Quiet MacLOUD, a craftsman and environmentalist; himself a sort of hybrid – born in Australia to parents with a Highland background, but brought up in the working-class housing estate of Pollock. Colin died tragically of a heart attack at the age of 39 but his widow, Gehan, still runs the Trust. The traffic came to a standstill in Govan for the procession of his coffin, itself carved in the workshop here. However, his spirit is still evident, not least in his life size carving of a sea eagle that is suspended above the entrance desk. Other carvings are prominently displayed – some utilitarian, some decorative: there is a model of a birlinn, an elaborate music stand, beautiful carvings of Celtic symbols and the Scottish coastline in profile, eagles and fish and, above the desk, the suspended figure of a sea eagle, as wide as the height of a man, carved by the founder.

GalGael is an open organisation for the benefit of the people of Govan. Many have suffered the ravages of unemployment, drink and drugs or mental health problems. They come here to learn the patient skills of working with wood and the workshop is largely dedicated to this purpose, although some parts are rented out to raise funds: a bespoke furniture maker, an enterprise constructing individual boxes for limited editions of malt whisky. Outside is a sawyer's yard and wood drying kilns. GalGael will collect felled trees and make them into timber for their own use. They also sell firewood and kindling and have a craft shop – all geared towards the funding of their community project.

Beginners start with the manufacture of small items, but the major part of the enterprise is boatbuilding, and this is what has largely caught the popular imagination. Colin MacLeod's first project was to construct a miniature version of a birlinn, a traditional Hebridean craft. Its iconic outline is best known as a repeated motif in Celtic jewellery such as the highly collectable brooches created by Alexander and Euphemia Ritchie.

Today's constructions, however, are even more ambitious. In the centre of the workshop – near completion after twenty months of work – is a fishing boat, a Loch Fyne skiff, to be launched on the Clyde soon. There are other boats including small rowing boats. Some are sold, but often the members of the workshop get to sail them – appreciating the practical uses of the vessels created by their craftsmanship.

Lead boatbuilder is Ben Duffin. Ben studied linguistics at the University of Edinburgh but, preferring a hands-on occupation,

headed to the west coast of America to learn boatbuilding. On retuning to Scotland he found GalGael and it is now his daily occupation and his passion. GalGael is a busy place – I am not the only writer or academic who has to be shown around. The workshop, adorned with carvings, old ropes, smelling of newly sawn timber, is inspirational and I almost feel like chucking my pen (well, my laptop) and taking up a chisel or two myself.

Voyager

The words of the gallant sons of the Gaeltachd,
The heart of a stump of a tree uprooted from a garden
    in Drumoyne,
The hands of an unemployed plumber who has seen better days.

All to make a moment when, on a day fresh with wind,
a perfect keel precisely slices the surface of the Clyde.

GRAND OLE OPRY

Hey ho, it is pay packet Friday and I'm set to round off the Southside of the city with a night on the skite. Down Paisley Road West I pass the rather nondescript pub that is now the Merchant's Quay but was once the New Regano (the spelling, apparently, to differentiate it from the Rogano) and also the Sportsman's Bar. But for a while in the seventies it was Jim Baxter's, owned by Slim Jim Baxter, the Rangers and Scotland football legend, best known, perhaps, for playing 'keepie-uppie' with the ball in the 1967 international against England. Baxter, to the end of his career, was not so slim and had well documented problems with drink and gambling. Pub landlord was not, arguably, the best profession to enter. He died in 2001.

But the finest of the pubs around here is the Old Toll Bar, and that's where I'm heading for a quick stiffener before donning my metaphorical stetsons and six guns, for a night at the Grand Ole Opry. The Old Toll Bar is another of Glasgow's prominent Edwardian watering holes with an elaborate mahogany bar and antique pub mirrors. One advertises 'finest pressure filtered whisky', a throwback to the days when there wasn't time to wait for the malt to mature.[23]

Traditionally, tolls were where a fee was collected to transport goods. Bars at tolls had special privileges for travellers. A more recent tradition in Glasgow (up to about fifty years ago) was the bona fide traveller law. In order to get a drink on a Sunday, you had to demonstrate that you were actually travelling somewhere. This could result in serious drinkers often 'swapping' villages to meet the three mile restriction.

Founded in 1974 and located in an old cinema in Govan Road, the Grand Ole Opry is the largest club of its kind in the United Kingdom. A couple of decades ago, it was busy every night of the week. Today, at weekends at least, it still makes a fair fist of things. It has a liquor-fuelled bar, with quick-draw service and a chuck wagon to feast on burgers and beans.

Some of the customers are geared up – those jacket fringes like a bad haircut, spurred boots, creations from sequins and rhinestones. There is music, both types, country and western, some line dancing, and a shoot-out. Well-worn faces with names like Tucson Tam, The Justifier, and Four Coffins Cathy. Tonight, a party of lassies are out on a hen night, dressed to the nines and scoffing Jack Daniels and Diaquiris. There are some grizzled old sods too, with their haufs and haufs. The common theme seems to be enjoyment. Everyone looks happy, even beneath some extravagant facial hair. There is music, with old favourites like *Johnny B Goode* and the more adventurous get up for what we call in Glasgow the jigging.

The band play in front of a large projection of a Western scene

and you can feel yourself receding into the distance of the desert.
The evening concludes with the playing of the club's anthem, *The
American Trilogy*, and the ceremonial folding of the flag by well-
trained regulars. Why, I ask myself, is Glasgow so fascinated by
the cowboy tradition? It could be the Western patter, the sentimental nature of some of the songs, but I think that it is mostly
the battle against adversity – those simple little narratives about
overcoming obstacles, fighting for your rights, blazing new trails.

The Ballad of Tombstone Tam and the Camlachie Kid

He was out on the spree, in the Grand Ole Opry,
    Where they ca'ed him the Camlachie Kid.
He said Eskimo Nell, It's me on the bell,
    For I've won at the dugs fifty squid.

Aw lipstick and curls, the Castlemilk cowgirls,
    Little Lou, Big Lizzie and Bessie.
They were oot on the batter, and full o' the patter,
    And the floo'er of them aw was called Jessie.

He was quick on the draw, thought that Jessie was braw,
    And he knew that he just had to bag her.
To her he did toddle, says you're jist like a model,
    From the back o' a can o' lager.

Coming out for a cig? Getting up for a jig?
    His patter was pure dead gallus.
But she said naw, you're getting hee-haw,
    That's from me, and from Senga and Dallas.

Short, ugly and fat, with a ten gallon hat,
    And stinking of stale beer and tobaccy.
He was Tombstone Tam, a bit of a bam,
    And he fingered the Kid from Camlachie.

He said, hey pal, you're eyeing my gal,
    I'd sure like to give you the boot.
I'll show you the door, or it's oot on the floor,
    You and me for a bit o' a shoot.

Caw for your mammy, if you're up for a rammy,
You must think I'm saft and glaikit.
You're a lickspittle runt, so I'll tak a punt,
Come on lads, haud my jaiket.

Well the Kid sure was quick, and he gave it a lick,
Expecting his opponent concedin'.
But it wisnae enough, the gun just gave a puff,
While the bullet from Tam put his heid in.

Ah weel, said Tam, I don't give a damn,
You'll never see me tak a dive.
If you shoot from the hip, I'll give you a tip,
Make sure that your ammo is live.

Well the sod's taen its fill, up there on Boot Hill,
Fast Fred and Saskatchewan Sid,
Trigger Tom Clancy, Nantucket Nancy,
And the one ca'ed the Camlachie Kid.

Notes

1. The chapbook is preserved in the National Library of Scotland. See http://digital.nls.uk/chapbooks-printed-in-scotland.
2. The painting was subsequently bought for Kelvingrove Art Gallery and Museum.
3. See Mitchell Miller & Johnny Rodger, *The Red Cockatoo: James Kelman and the Art of Commitment* (Dingwall: Sandstone, 2011).
4. Edwin Morgan, *Collected Poems* (Manchester: Carcanet Press, 1996).
5. Alexander McArthur & H. Kingsley Long, *No Mean City* (London: Corgi, 1994). For details of McArthur's death, see Seán Damer, 'No Mean Writer? The Curious Case of Alexander McArthur', in Kevin McCarra & Hamish Whyte (ed.) *A Glasgow Collection: Essays in Honour of Joe Fisher* (Glasgow: Glasgow City Libraries, 1990).
6. Robert McLeish, *The Gorbals Story* (Edinburgh: 7:84 Publications, 1985), with an introduction by Linda McKenney. Other well-known writers who wrote on the Gorbals include Ralph Glasser: various volumes combined in *The Ralph Glasser Omnibus* (Edinburgh: Black & White, 2005) and George Gladstone Robertson, *Gorbals Doctor* (London: Jarrolds Publishers, 1970).
7. *Miracle in the Gorbals* (1944). Story by Michael Benthall, music by Arthur Bliss.
8. Colin McFarlane, *The Real Gorbals Story* (Edinburgh: Mainstream, 2007), *No Mean Glasgow* (Edinburgh: Mainstream, 2008).
9. Eddie Perrett, *The Magic of the Gorbals* (privately published, 1990).
10. Hugh McDonald, *Rambles around Glasgow* (Glasgow: John Smith, 1910).
11. *Glasgow's Glasgow: The Words and the Stones* (Glasgow: Glasgow District Council, 1990).

12. See Ewan McVicar, *One Singer One Song: Songs of Glasgow Folk* (Glasgow: Glasgow City Libraries, 1990).

13. See http://www.dickgaughan.co.uk.

14. Gavin Stamp, *Alexander 'Greek' Thomson* (Glasgow: Lawrence King Publishing, 1999).

15. See http://www.devilsplantation.co.uk/blog/tag/cochno-stone.

16. See http://www.elementalfilms.co.uk/

17. Hugh MacDiarmid, *Collected Poems* (Edinburgh: Olwen & Boyd, 1962).

18. Gerry Hassan, *Caledonian Dreaming* (Edinburgh: Luath, 2014).

19. The shortlisted artists were Assemble, Bonnie Camplin, Janice Kerbel and Nicole Wermers. The prize was awarded to Assemble.

20. For a detailed survey of 'The Glasgow Miracle' and recent art in Glasgow see Sarah Lowndes, *Social Sculpture: the Rise of the Glasgow Arts Scene* (Glasgow: Stopstop, 2010). Lowndes chronicles the social and communal rise of the Glasgow arts scene which had cultural and political ramifications. I admire her scholarly account, not least for its chutzpah, but I lament the lack of lasting artworks that derive from that period. For a critique of contemporary arts practive, see Peter Goodfellow (ed.) *The Treason of the Scholars* (London: Panter and Hall, 2015).

21. A full list of Clyde passenger ferries is: York Street Ferry (York Street to West Street); Clyde Street Ferry (Clyde Street, Anderston to Springfield Quay); Hyde Park Ferry (Hydepark Street to Springfield Quay); Stobcross Ferry (Finnieston Quay to Mavisbank Quay); Finnieston Ferry (Finnieston Quay to Mavisbank Quay); Kelvinhaugh Ferry (Yorkhill Quay to Prince's Dock); Govan Ferry (Ferry Road, Partick to Water Row, Govan); Meadowside Ferry (Meadowside Street, Partick to Holm Street, Govan); Whiteinch Ferry (James Street, Whiteinch to Holmfauld Road, Linthouse); Renfrew Ferry (Yoker to Renfrew); Erskine Ferry (Dunbartonshire to Renfrewshire).

22. See Hamish Whyte (ed.) *Noise and Smoky Breath: an Illustrated Anthology of Glasgow Poems 1900-1983* (Glasgow: Third Eye Centre, 1983).

23. Mitchell Miller & Johnny Rodger, *The Red Cockatoo: James Kelman and the Art of Commitment* (Sandstone, 2011).

WEST

A VERY QUIET STREET

Within the purview of Miss Toward's tenement flat, if not in actual sight, stands another, more spacious flat, across the gash cut by the M8 in West Princes Street. And just around the corner from it, you can find the Carnarvon Bar, a nice Edwardian pub which still has an island bar with jacket hooks, a segmented ceiling and pendant globes. It is dark-panelled and well-lit, cheap beer, country music and cheerful banter. It is a good refuge on a wet day – like a pub rather than a living room decorated by Ikea and Cath Kidson.[1]

Further up from the Carnarvon takes you to the west end of West Princes Street, which is a lengthy street heading all the way to Kelvingrove, but the lower part has only a suggestion of a faded grandeur. Queens Crescent has a walled garden that sports the remains of an old fountain, now overgrown with plants but maintained to a respectable standard. Most of these Georgian townhouses are offices and there is an ethnic feel to the district. Round the corner is an Islamic Centre with knots of bearded men congregating and a Chinese medical centre. The tenement flats at the bottom end of West Princes Street are no great shakes, some straggly plants grow out of walls and window buttresses. Some of these flats are now occupied by students, including one that has a special place in the history of Glasgow..

In fact, not so long ago, for a while, the Carnarvon was the Oscar Slater and the tenement flat round the corner (now occupied by students from nearby Glasgow University) was the scene of a famous murder of a spinster, Miss Gilchrist, for which a German Jew, Oscar Slater, was unjustly convicted and later pardoned.

In 1908, Marion Gilchrist, a relatively well-off spinster of 83, was found murdered in her tenement flat. A brooch was all that was missing from the premises. A while later, Oscar Slater was discovered to have pawned a similar brooch. It turned out that the brooch was not the one purloined in the murder but the police, prompted by public indignation at the murder of an old woman, proceeded anyway, and Slater was prosecuted and jailed for the crime. The police hardly come out of the case well and it pains me to say that the Superintendant at the time, John Ord, was implicated. Ord was a folk song collector, a historian of Glasgow and a generally interesting character.[2]

After Slater's conviction, a detective involved in the case, John

Trench, took a special interest. He was the subject of general approbation, but others involved included the criminologist William
Roughead and Sir Arthur Conan Doyle. Various theories were
posited some of which incriminated members of the Gilchrist
family. Several books have been written about the Slater case over
the years including one titled *A Very Quiet Street* (a description of
West Princes Street by a witness in the case) – a strange rambling
meditation on the murder by Frank Kuppner.[3]

In 1928, Slater's conviction was quashed. He married and settled
in Ayrshire, dying in 1948. The case still remains popular in
Glasgow lore and is the subject of a rare bit of Glaswegian rhyming
slang that you still hear now and then – 'see you Oscar [Slater =
later].'

Back past the Carnarvon, skirting the motorway and turning
right, beneath the heights of the Park district, leads you into
Woodlands Road and towards Glasgow University. At one time
three pubs here were popular weekend haunts of students – the
Arlington, the Halt and the Three in One. Only the Arlington still
stands, proudly proclaiming 'established 1860', but the Halt, probably the most popular in its time, has been taken over by West
Brewery and replaced by West on the Corner, a very different beast.
The Three in One had a rather chequered past with a reputation for
drug-dealing. It was resurrected as the Uisge Beatha, but that is no
longer there. Thankfully unchanged, however, at the end of the road
is the Doublet, erstwhile haunt of students and Partick Thistle
supporters. With its stuccoed walls, timber beams, Tudor struts,
horse brasses, copper jelly pans and bed warmers it is much the
same as it was in the seventies and a good enough place for a pint
of Special and a mince pie.

One surprising remainder of old Glasgow in Woodlands Road is
the Annan Gallery. This is still run by the Annan family and has
been around since the days of Thomas Annan in one form or the
other. You can purchase here reproductions of Annan's old closes
printed from the original plates.

The red sandstone tenements around here are often let to students although some are starter homes for young couples and there
is a small ethnic community too. Across the road from the old Halt,
however, there is another type of tenement dweller! A small podgy,
extravagantly bearded man in a giant stetson sitting astride a two-
legged horse standing with its legs crossed.

The statue, erected in 1992, is a tribute to the cartoonist Bud

Neill and his most famous creation Lobey Dosser (in Glasgow parlance someone who couldn't even afford a room in a tenement room and kitchen and had to doss in the lobby). Lobey Dosser, his horse Elfie (El Fideldo) and the villain Rank Bajin inhabited a peculiarly Glaswegian corner of the wild west called Calton Creek where Lobey was the resident sheriff. I remember the various cartoon strips that appeared in the *Daily Record* in my youth. Some were alien, like The Perishers or Modesty Blaise, but others were more familiar. Angus Og was a lovable islander from the 'Utter Hebrides' drawn by Ewan Bain who lived in Milngavie. Lobey Dosser no doubt struck a chord as the parlance of the wild west has always been popular in Glasgow.

VOLTAIRE AND ROUSSEAU

In the words of Virginia Woolf, 'secondhand books are wild books... vast flocks of variegated feather.' There is an aviary and a half at my next stop just round the corner from the Doublet and across the river Kelvin in little Otago Lane, winding down to the river. Run by Joe and Eddie, the famously taciturn McGonigle brothers, Voltaire & Rousseau has been purveying secondhand books for over forty years. This is not an elegant antiquarian bookshop. It is part of an old stables with books stacked every which way to the extent that inching your way between them is an adventure in itself.

You could bottle the smell in this place and sell it to book lovers. I go just to look but come away with a couple of ballad books. I think I may already have them but, what the hell, they're a bargain.

Otago Lane itself is a strange, almost rural byway in the busy West End and it is under threat from developers to the extent that a Save Otago Lane campaign has been launched. Yet its bohemian charm remains. A recent addition is the Tchai Ovna House of Tea. Not only can you sample exotic teas here with names like Moon Palace, Dragon's Eye and Honeybush, but you can order vegan food and smoke a hookah! A rather odd story about the Lane is that, a few years ago, a man died in a small flat above the bookshop. Amazingly, there was no record of him anywhere. He had no employment, no income and subsisted just on hand-outs.

Not far away, in Great Western Road, is Caledonian Books. This is a fair enough secondhand book shop but a bit dull. All the books are nicely shelved, properly ordered and at just the right price. However, a few years ago something quite astonishing happened here.

Every collector of books has a dream, that may occasionally be partly realised, that they will come across something special one day, hidden and unrecognised in a bookshop. The all singing, all dancing find of the century took place in Caledonian Books. It was a volume of original lost watercolours by William Blake.

The whole episode is well documented as there was a bit of a barney about who the volume actually belonged to. In 1743, William Blake had produced twenty watercolours for a book called *The Grave*, by the Scottish poet Robert Blair. One had turned up in a gallery in the United States and, of the other nineteen, only twelve were known from the plates in the book. In 2005, Paul Williams, a book dealer from Yorkshire, found the nineteen watercolours in a portfolio in Caledonian Books where they had been part of a house clearance and bought them for about £1000. They were subsequently to fetch around £8m. A complex battle regarding ownership entailed which resulted in the book shop, Williams and another dealer sharing the profits.

Brian Moore, in his novel *The Great Victorian Collection*,[4] relates a marvellous dream sequence in which his protagonist, a collector, imagines himself amongst a fantastic collection of once lost antiques. To me the story I have just related is a glimpse of such a dream. What any collector hopes for one day is a great discovery such as this. It is almost magical and Walter Benjamin recognised such an epiphany when he called a collection a 'magic encyclopedia'.

CURRY ALLEY

The lands around the Kelvin were once owned by the Gibson family, and Gibson Street, leading from the top of Woodlands Road to University Avenue, is a fairly average sort of street with some shops and restaurants. When I was a student, however, it was known as Curry Alley. Glasgow has a long and spicy history of the provision of Indian cuisine and the Glaswegian obsession with the curry has never waned. This, however, is where most people believe it all began round about the late sixties. The three I remember are the

Shish Mahal, the Shalimar and the Koh-i-noor. None of them are here now, although the Shish Mahal moved to nearby Park Road. The Koh-i-noor, or the building housing it, famously collapsed into the Kelvin; it still exists as a buffet restaurant near the Mitchell.

The daddy of them all, however, was the Shish Mahal, founded in the sixties by Ali Ahmed Aslam, known as Mr Ali. When I was a student we would queue up outside here on Friday nights to be squeezed around a small table for a biryani or a khorma or a bhuna. The Shish Mahal still exists and it still has a loyal following. However, it also has a more substantial claim to fame. Legend has it that Britain's favourite curry, the brutally orange chicken tikka masala, originated here. Asif Ali claimed that his father invented it one night in 1971:

> On a typical dark, wet Glasgow night a bus driver coming off shift came in and ordered a chicken curry. He sent it back to the waiter saying 'it's dry'. At the time Dad had an ulcer and was enjoying a plate of tomato soup. So he said why not put some tomato soup into the curry with some spices. They sent it back to the table and the bus driver absolutely loved it. He and his friends came back again and again and we put it on the menu.[5]

More recently, in 2009, a Glasgow Labour MP, Mohammed Sarwar, requested that the city be given EU Protected Designation of Origin status for tikka masala. So, did Glasgow invent the world's most popular curry? As sure as Stornoway invented black pudding.

Today, Glasgow has many more curry houses. Mother India and The Little Curry House are highly regarded, and Mister Singh's, in Sandyford Place at the top of Sauchiehall Street, is run by the flamboyant eponymous television chef and is a quirky hybrid with staff dressing in kilts and turbans. It featured as a location for the movie *The Big Tease* (1999).

Glasgow's love affair with Indian cuisine continues. But throughout the city a curry is not a curry. It is a 'Chic Murray'. Chic Murray was a notoriously droll Glasgow comedian with a penchant for one-liners: 'I got up this morning. I like to get up in the morning; it gives me the rest of the day to myself', 'I crossed the landing and went down the stairs. Mind you, if there had been no stairs, I wouldn't even have attempted it', 'If it weren't for marriage, husbands and wives would have to fight with strangers'. There have been many famous Glasgow comedians: Tommy Lorne, whose catch phrase was 'in the name of the wee man', Lex McLean, a famous bluenose, Hector Nicol, who wrote songs for various Scottish football clubs, Billy Connolly ('the Big Yin') and, more recently, Kevin Bridges, an affable young man from Clydebank. It is a moot point whether there is a particularly Glaswegian sense of humour. If there is it a rather wry version. The following joke is, apparently, only understood by Glaswegians: Man goes into pub with poodle. Landlord says 'Only guide dogs allowed.' Man says, 'It is a guide dog, I got it from the Council.' Landlord says 'Don't be daft, poodles aren't guide dogs.' 'Ah tellt them, Ah tellt them... ' he says.

THE UNIVERSITY

Turn left at the top of Gibson Street and you're at the University –
or rather Glasgow University, as there three universities in the city
now. Glasgow, however, is indisputably the oldest, the fourth oldest
university in the English-speaking world, founded in 1451. The
first thing you see when turning into University Avenue is the bulky
eminence of the Student's Union or what was known as the Men's
Union as it originally only admitted men (women had a separate
union). The diehards held out until 1980, when, threatened by dire
repercussions from the Sex Discrimination Act, they gave in. In its
roisterous heyday, the male-only cellar beer bar was as close to a
wild west saloon or a medieval banqueting hall as you could get.
Packed with young men consuming the cheap beer at alarming
rates, nightly there would be the quaffing of ale from yards. The
secret of successful speed drinking, apparently, is to suck the beer
in. The record for sooking a pint, I believe, was about three
seconds.

Females were allowed in upstairs for occasional discos for which
there was an entrance fee, but some of the lads thought it was better
fun to climb in through the library window and open the back door
for free. I remember, unfortunately, after confessing to being a rock
climber, being roped into this one night. At a later date, my friends
became officers of the Union and they had keys, so we would let
ourselves in and play snooker all night.

The students of Glasgow University have a right to elect a Rector. In the past, rectors have included eleven prime ministers, but that all changed and I remember my student colleagues campaigning to elect Arthur Montford, the Scottish football commentator. More recently, rectors seem to have been a mixture of TV personalities and political dissidents

Round the corner in University Avenue the main building of the University itself, prominently situated on Gilmorehill, is a neo-gothic extravaganza with symmetrical quadrangles and a soaring central tower. It is also home to Scotland's oldest museum, the Hunterian, founded in 1807 by the physician William Hunter. It is possibly best known for Hunter's anatomy collection, but there is a great deal more including a substantial Mackintosh collection which includes a reassembling of the interiors from Mackintosh's house in Southpark Avenue (demolished some time ago). Surprisingly, this has been encased in a concrete exterior as part of a building adjacent to the University Library. The shapes of the windows still remain but it is nothing like a Victorian terrace – and the front house opens (if it did open) out into space about ten feet above the ground.

KELVINGROVE

Rising above Woodlands Road is the hilly area of Glasgow known as the Park. Centred around Park Circus, these gracious early Victorian terraces are the epitome of townhouses for the wealthy in the second city of Empire. Many were converted to offices, but there is a return to their earlier residential use, mostly through flat conversions. The Park School for Girls used to be a notable feature here. My school, being boys only, invited them to our annual school dance, although we always thought they were a little too posh for us.

The Park district overlooks Kelvingrove Park, probably the finest of the Glasgow parks by dint of its hilly aspect and the fact that a river runs through it. It was originally called the West End Park and contains notable monuments: the Stewart Memorial Fountain, topped by Scott's Lady of the Lake – a sop to early eighteenth century romanticism, a bandstand, statues of Lord Kelvin, Thomas Carlyle, Joseph Lister and others, and, tucked away in a corner, the Suffrage Oak, planted to commemorate the granting of votes to women in 1918. There is also a bowling green, and when we were students, we would have a game on occasional sunny days.

The park was the site of a notable suicide (or was it?) on 15 January 1918. The previous night Fred Shaw, who performed under the stage name of Mark Sheridan, had performed as Napoleon in the revue *Gay Paree* at the Coliseum Theatre. Mark had had a successful career; best known for the music-hall song *I Do Like to Be Beside the Seaside*, there were suggestions that his latest performance had not been universally appreciated and that he had been barracked by the notoriously difficult Glasgow crowd that night. He had arranged a noon rehearsal for the 15th but did not turn up and later that day his body was found near the river in Kelvingrove Park with a bullet wound in his forehead and a Browning automatic pistol lying nearby. He was buried in Cathcart cemetery and the death did not seem to unduly inconvenience his widow and the mother of his five children who took over the direction of the show, found another Napoleon and continued with the tour. The official verdict was suicide caused by depression, yet there are still nagging doubts. He had made arrangements for the few days ahead, the bullet wound seemed inconveniently situated for a suicide, and Kelvingrove Park, even at that time, was known as a meeting place for gay men and some of the theatrical community were known to frequent it.[6]

That mystery remains but there is another personal and theatrical connection that springs to my mind. When I was taking Theatre Studies (I liked the theory; I didn't act) at Strathclyde University, my tutor and Director of Drama, and head of the Strathclyde Theatre Group, was Hugo Gifford. In 1981, for no known reason, he was found dead, apparently of hypothermia, in Kelvingrove Park.[7]

Kelvingrove Park was the site of three of Glasgow's four great exhibitions, in 1888, 1901 and 1911 (the other, in 1938, was at Bellahouston Park). When I was a boy, my grandmother gave me a little medal for the 1901 exhibition which I still have, along with a collection of memorabilia for all the exhibitions which I have now amassed.

My next visit is to what was built for the 1901 exhibition with the proceeds of the 1888 exhibition and is now known as Kelvingrove Art Gallery and Museum. I remember Kelvingrove well, as it was a favourite boyhood haunt, with my parents, on a school trip, or later on my own.

It has changed since then, reopening in 2006 following a three year renovation. Part of the concept of the revamp was to banish the old rigid taxonomies of the Victorian universal survey museum and introduce a structure that was more thematically and narrative-based. Also the place was made more child-friendly; some paintings were hung at a lower height, captions were enhanced to contextualise the objects and make them more understandable (there have been some suggestions that they are also addressed to children). This is seen as more accessible and egalitarian. There were many mixed feelings about this among the visitors and, shortly after the re-opening, the influential *Burlington Magazine* compared Kelvingrove to a 'kindergarten'.[8] Whatever the cause, however, the evidence shows that attendance actually *fell* by more than twenty per cent in the year after the refurbishment. Only, I suggest, in Glasgow could a large sum of money have been spend with so little return.

I, too, have mixed feelings. Perhaps I was an unusual child, but I rather liked the austerity of the old approach. The museum and art gallery seemed to me a place to be regarded with awe, rather like a cathedral. I couldn't have imagined running around playing with toy-like interactive exhibits. But my preferences are rooted in a different era with perhaps a different regard for the treasures of history.

The thematic approach to the artworks can work as well. The Scottish section that mixes paintings and historic artefacts and tells a compelling story through the centuries of improvement (and the Highland Clearances) to romanticism, culminating in a fine view of Horatio MacCulloch's masterpiece *Glencoe*, with the shining eyes of the startled deer in the centre staring directly at the visitor, is a success, as are some of the other small sections.

One thing is missing, however. I wander round the upper galleries twice, clockwise and anti-clockwise, simultaneously folding and unfolding the floor plan and scratching my head. I am searching for my favourite paintings to show my partner – the Renaissance paintings, the most valuable in the collection, including Botticelli's *Annunciation* and Bellini's *Madonna and Child*. My quest, however, is in vain. They are just not there.

Possible explanations race through my head. My memory is faulty. They have been moved downstairs. Surely, surely not even the city of Glasgow could have lost millions of pounds of art treasures. So, I decide to ask an attendant. 'Where are the Renaissance paintings?' 'On loan.' 'What, all of them?' A nod of the head. Next stop is the central information desk. 'Where are all the Renaissance paintings?' 'On loan.' 'On loan where?' 'In America, I think.' 'And are they coming back?' A pause. 'Yes...' A pause. '...but not for a long time.'

Well, the older I get, the more pedantic I get. Therefore, I set myself the task of finding these paintings. Traditional art web sites don't help. They tell me that they are still in the collection at Kelvingrove. So I email the gallery and I eventually get a reply from the Curator of European Paintings. Yes, they have been in America, but they are now back home – that is, back home in the storage facility at Nitshill. They are thinking, however, of new ways of making them accessible to the public. And I thought they could just hang them up on the wall somewhere! Sadly, the emphasis, to my mind, has moved from the display of precious objects to corporate culture, functions, events and most other things rather than the traditional function of an art gallery.

Botticelli?

Botticelli? Not on your nelly.
Bellini? Have a panini
Raphael, well, well, well…

Museums and art galleries have recently been accused of crass and patronising dumbing down and institutional vandalism. This is not peculiar to Glasgow and it is perhaps a reflection of a developing tendency in contemporary museum practice. Tate Britain has also been accused. Some critics see this as part of a wider neo-liberal agenda and one entitled a review of the revamped art gallery 'Blairism on the Walls at Kelvingrove'. As for the 'improvements' to Kelvingrove, the people of Glasgow have had a say. *The Evening Times* conducted a poll and discovered that a large majority of its readers preferred it as it used to be before the renovations.

Glasgow Museums in general has a history of controversy that also encompasses, for example, the Riverside Museum, which was accused of institutional bullying. The most scandalous of all is still entrenched in the minds of Glaswegian critics of the establishment and is known as the Elspeth King Affair. Elspeth King, aided by her partner, Michael Donnelly, had effectively transformed the People's Palace into an leading community museum – despite scant funding from an establishment that didn't value the city's own culture – when she was effectively sacked from her job as curator by Julian Spalding, director of Glasgow Art Galleries and Museums. It was suggested that he didn't care for the fact that she was Scottish, working-class, female and a critic of, among other things, the dreadful waste of money that was the *Glasgow's Glasgow* exhibition. King continued with her successful career in gallery management outside Glasgow and Spalding also lost his job, but the controversy is still a sore memory for many Glasgow folk.[9]

BYRES ROAD

When the Merchant City wasn't even a gleam in anyone's eye, Byres Road, with its eclectic mix of shops and bars, was where we came for some weekend frivolity. And you still can, to visit Tennent's or the other bars, browse in the charity shops, including the Oxfam Bookshop and record shop, or find a delicatessen or a trendy clothes shop. It connects Dumbarton Road with Great Western Road and trams used to come up here – you can still see the brackets for the lines on some of the red sandstone tenements. I'm here with some friends on a sunny summer's day and it is the West End Fair. Just about everyone is paraded down Byres Road with costumes, banners, musical instruments. There is an enormously long Chinese dragon sashaying its way down the road and the West Enders are having a party. Another banner advertises The Ubiquitous Glasgow E Steampunk Society, whatever that is.

The Hillhead Book Club, where I'm having a drink, has a bit of an identity crisis. There are no books to be seen. Today it is a bar café with a sort of flea market going on up on the balcony. The balconies give a clue to its original use, which was as a cinema. The Hillhead Picture Salon or Electric Theatre, dating back to 1912 with its art nouveau style facade, was one of the earliest picture halls in the city.

On a hot day like today we fancy an ice cream and there is no shortage here. All with an Italian flavour – Nardinis, Sputinis, with a vintage scooter in the window – but the oldest of them all is the University Café, run for generations by the Verrechia family. William McIllvanney set his influential crime novel, *Laidlaw*,[10] here and noted 'the university café smacked of the 1930s'. It is still much as it was and not a bad place to stop off. A peculiarity is that, to go to the loo, you have to collect a large key, enter the adjacent close where you find an old-style Glasgow cludgie. Years ago, I remember being in here when an old lady in a dressing gown came in. The staff gently escorted her back across the road to the Western Infirmary from where she occasionally escaped.

Just by Hillhead subway, you can deviate to the left or the right. Left is Ashton Lane, which is a social hub for the West End. There is a cinema and fashionable bars and restaurants: Brel, Jinty McGinty's and the Ubiquitous Chip – known simply as 'The Chip', it is a collection of bars on different levels which has been popular with West-enders since it was opened in. You will find writers and artists around here, and also professional football and rugby players.

Turn right and you will be in Dowanside and Ruthven Lanes, a network of vintage and antique shops. You can search for retro clothes in Starry Starry Night or just about anything else in small shops piled high with either antiques or junk depending on your

point of view. It is an ecumenical sort of place – one shop owner has an orangeman's sash and an album of orange songs displayed next to a signed Celtic strip. The bottom end is a little more upmarket. Liz McKelvie's shop, The Studio, taking up two units is a splendid selection of late-Victorian and Edwardian Glasgow style furniture and artefacts. A more recent addition is (Un)fine Art, a fascinating and quirky shop selling contemporary art pieces including Damien Hirst.

These lanes are not residential, but some feature fashionable mews houses. At the beginning of 2016 a strange story hit the press. A couple had paid over £600,000 for an A-listed mews apartment and then promptly demolished it – which was not only an act of vandalism but completely against the law. Who knows what the outcome will be.

LIVER AND ONIONS AND LIOS MOR

My final stop in Byres Road is a nod to nostalgia. Once students from the University, weary of the raucous chaos of the Students' Union beer bar, would come here on a Saturday night and two pubs, across the road from each other, to my mind, stand out – the Rubaiyat and the Aragon. In the seventies these were extremely popular pubs and, although more expensive than the nearby University beer bar, they offered a (possibly) more civilised alternative. Also, remember, in those days, cheap supermarket alcohol was not available. A can of beer from an off license could cost more than a pint in a pub.

The Rubaiyat was developed from a tearoom in the fifties and was noted for its 'Bowl of Night' bar, named after a line in Omar Khayyam's poem. It is no more, but the Aragon is still there and much the same. Surprisingly, it was only opened about 1970, converted from a butcher's shop. Today I am the only customer. The pub sign, a sickly-looking head of the Duke of Aragon pondering over a book, looms ominously above the door. I have no idea how it got its name. It is a fairly ordinary, undistinguished pub, not doing so well these with the lease up for sale. Yet, in the early seventies there would be queues outside here every Saturday night, waiting for a chance to squeeze in uncomfortably for a pint. Times have changed – Tennent's Bar just up the road, monopolises the local custom, and the Curlers – now part of a student chain designated

by a sign featuring Edvard Munch's *The Scream* – is popular with students.

I could continue down Byres Road from here and take in another popular pub at the junction with Dumbarton Road – The Three Judges, noted for its real ale, – but instead I intend to cut diagonally across to meet Dumbarton Road at its junction with Hyndland Street.

Hyndland Street is short but interesting. Towards the top is Cafezique, a bistro converted from an old high-ceilinged shop. The sign outside proclaiming 'Hargan's Dairy' is well worn and makes a notable contrast with the sleck chrome bar. This is a pleasant place to share a bottle of nicely chilled sauvignon blanc, or indeed, to dine. You can get an all-day breakfast here of puddledub bacon, Stornoway black pudding and Aberfoyle pork and herb sausages, or lunch with various concoctions of granola, yoghurt and haloumi cheese (which I have heard of) or boquerones, sobrassada and Jo Hilditch British cassis (which I haven't).

Alternatively, across the road there are a couple of galleries and a nice thirties café – the Rio Café – converted into a bar. There is a giant ice-cream cone outside and the promise of quality burgers inside. My destination, a few yards down the street, offers more basic fare. The Quarter Gill is a totally unreconstructed typical Glasgow man's bar, not especially notable for anything, but the rear part of the bar is now designated Kirsty's Kitchen, and here the landlady cooks up traditional home fare (just like your mother made) for about a fiver a plate. Liver and onions, peas, carrots, creamy mash and gravy washed down with a pint of Tennent's lager. 'Fan dabbie dozy', as they say in Glasgow.

Opposite the Quarter Gill, across a paved area, is another bar
and I am going there to meet Ranald MacColl, is an extremely tal-
ented artist, for years cartoonist for the *Daily Mirror*. He
campaigned for the statue of Lobey Dosser in Woodlands Road and
produced the books of Bud Neill's cartoons after they were largely
forgotten, he tells me, by getting blown-up photocopies from the
Mitchell Library and then tippexing out the fuzz and interference.
Now Ranald spends most of his time as a designer of bar and
restaurant interiors. His first job in Glasgow was the revamping of
the bar just across the road that was to become the Ettrick for the
Colin Beattie, property developer and owner of a chain of bars in
Glasgow.

Colin Beattie who, in his media appearances, comes over as a
large, quiet-spoken, genial man, could be regarded as the saviour of
Glasgow's pub trade if it weren't for the inconvenient fact that there
are some in Glasgow who see him as the heir of a gangster dynasty.
His father, Colin Beattie senior, known as 'Big Coalie', who died in
2015, was reputedly Glasgow's most formidable hardman.
Nowadays, his son rules roost over a tranche of Glasgow's finest
eateries and watering holes but controversy still dogs him. He is
quite famous, or infamous, in Glasgow. One, probably fanciful,
story I am told is that he bought a whole building that once
belonged to City Bakeries for the 'CB' monogrammed stained glass.

The Lismore was once a fairly run down pub called Mullan's
with an Irish bias and, Ranald tells me, Colin's original concept was
to make it an Irish theme bar. Ranald persuaded him that it should
have a Scottish theme and boast a malt whisky selection, even
though malt whisky drinking was in its infancy at the time. The
name Lismore – or Lios Mor in Gaelic – was actually taken from
Lismore House, an Italianate villa in Kelvinside built originally for
the German consul in 1860 (now owned by a housing association)
but the choice was serendipitous as it turned out. Ranald's family
had originated in the island of Lismore, near Oban off the coast of
north-west Scotland – famous as the seat of the bishops of Argyll
and noted for its medieval monastery, castle and ancient broch.
Ranald took the theme of highland history, especially the Highland
Clearances which decimated the population of the island – in the
mid-nineteenth century the population was around 1400, by the
end of the century most were gone (today there are about 200 folk
still there) – and created a testament to this part of Scottish history
in the construction of a space that can only be regarded as a

complete work of art, a *gesamtkunstwerk* in German, in which all the various aspects and details make up a whole.

The exterior of the pub is eye-catching, the walls bulge out, constructed, Ranald tells me, from bent plywood, and the pub name – inscribed in English and Gaelic – tilts towards you. The overall effect is reminiscent of the prow of a boat.

Inside is a mixture of preservation and innovation. The original stone wall has largely been preserved but the bar has been rebuilt with slots for malt whiskies as a special feature. Craftsmen have painstakingly carved and constructed every feature of the woodwork and traditional materials including knotted rope and wrought iron have been employed for features. The flooring is a timber called purple heart sourced by Ranald in an east end salvage yard where it had been wormed. It was laid, sanded down, and over time has attained a glowing patina. Most notably, the doors and windows were constructed with a nod to *fin de siècle* Glasgow style and a series of six stained glasses windows were commissioned from the artist Yvonne Smith. These tell the story of Lismore and its eventual depopulation and employ historic motifs such as little white flowers – St Moluag's flower, named after the patron saint of Argyll and founder of the monastery on Lismore. Variously, lime from lime kilns and grain is loaded on a cart indicating the island's previous prosperity, families are portrayed packed and ready to leave, a blacksmith plys his trade. The final and most striking panel shows

an exile, pen in hand, leaning over a ledger. Behind him is a map of the United States and below him an eviction notice; both indicate the journey he has undertaken along with thousands of other Highland Scots at the time. Unfortunately, because of the character's resemblance to an American movie star, this is known to the locals as the Al Pacino window. There are other subtle nods to the island and Highland tradition. At various points on the exposed stone walls are carved three words in Gaelic:

TREUBHANTAS = BRAVERY
ONAIR = HONOUR
DILSEACHD = LOYALTY

The tenor of the place changes, however, in the smaller bar at the back, raised a little from the front bar. This was once a storeroom but Ranald decided to convert it to a 'dark room' or *rumdubh*. This, while sharing some of the decorative features of the front, is a more recondite space. There is a little stained glass above the back entrance but the design is abstract rather than narrative. Ranald points out a couple of additions not in his original plan – a goat's skull, a ship's binnacle – but fit in well enough. One of his own choices, however, was the design of the walls, which are a sort of pastiche of tartan, rendered (by Ranald himself) as slashes of dark green, blue and purple (sub species Timorous Beasties – the popular but radical local design company – he tells me).

Most visitors to the pub note and comment on the interesting design of the gents lavatory. The three urinals are variously dedicated to the instigators of the Highland Clearances – George Granville, the Duke of Sutherland, Patrick Sellar and Colonel Fell. Users are invited to 'show them the respect they deserve'. However, the chief focus of the *rumdubh* to my mind, is that it serves as a gallery for the extraordinary montages of Colin Wilson. The artist has taken elements relating to island life – old photos, mussel shells, fish hooks, torn letters, the shells of oystercatcher eggs, bits of fish crates, razor clams, seaweed, a fish net float, a fiddle shape whittled from a bit of wood – and evoked the lifestyle of Lísmore. The images are both beautiful and poignant. Some have captions – one is labelled 'island of bent grass, land of barley; everything is plentiful', another is accompanied by poem from Iain Crichton Smith, 'The Final Sadness', beginning 'Why do I weep…'[11]

I never met Colin Wilson, but he was, by all accounts, a weel-kent character around the pubs and restaurants of Byres Road. He was an eclectic artist and his influences were various: *Alice in Wonderland*, film noir, The Brotherhood of Ruralists. Colin's chaotic lifestyle had settled a little when he produced the work for the Lismore as he had been gifted a studio in Ruthven Lane with a small bedroom above. Tragically, in February 2002, the studio caught fire and Colin, trapped in the bedroom above, died. His premature death only serves to give the sometimes ghostly images in the pub an extra poignancy.

Rumdubh

All the parts of the island have drifted here,
Through time, tide and the memory of man:
Hamish Munroe (drowned); his image,
An orange faded fish net float,
The icy sting of rope-burned hands,
The notes of a reel blown from a fiddler's bow,
The salty tang of sea lips licked,
The sea-wracked smell of a barnacled boat,
The death white skull of a petrel,
The St Kilda mouse (extinct),
A prayer lost in the wind's hard blow,
Bent grass and barley, land of plenty,
The final churching of a cracked bell.
And they have been formed upon these walls.

All the parts of Glasgow have also drifted here,
Through thoughts, dreams and the memory of man:
The sudden gloom of a close on a sunny day,
Crackling of a trolley bus spur,
The uniform geometry of a Sally Ann band,
Demolition dust's dry choke,
The unpredicted contents of a lucky bag,
A streetlamp halo's soak into the foggy night,
A pub queue's daft banter,
The scliffing of worn school shoes,
Pat Roller and Lobey Dosser
The terse cacophony of an Orange Walk,
Buttonholing patter of a Barras trader.
And they have been formed upon these pages.

PARTICK AND FINNIESTON

Just a skip and a jump from the Lismore, a large red sandstone church serves monthly for the meetings of the Partick Folk Club. Nowadays most folk clubs are just a succession of concerts by big name artists with occasional floor spots but the Partick Folk Club is different. It harks back to the days when folk song wasn't just an entertainment but a political statement, a way of life almost – those innocent days when a matter of great import was whether Bob Dylan was really a folk singer, and were electric guitars an abomination.

Here everyone sits in a rough circle around some tables with their drinks (there is no bar but if you bring a carry-out you will be provided with glasses – and a cup of soup at the mid-way break). The founder of the club and occasional host is Mick West whom I have known for donkey's years. Mick is a big man with a powerful voice who is the singing tutor for Sgoil Chiùil na Gàidhealtachd or the National Centre of Excellence in Traditional Music up in Plockton in the far north west. Despite impaired mobility these days he makes his way to the club by public transport most weeks during term-time. Today he is belting out a song about one of Scotland's socialist heroes:

> There was nane like John Maclean,
> The fighting dominie...

There are other contributions – traditional classics, newly penned pieces, jokes: 'My doctor prescribed viagra. I said "will it help my sex life?" He said "No, but it'll stop you rolling out of bed at night".' It is a great night but the audience are not in the full bloom of youth. I am slightly shocked when my old friend Barbara, on the door, tells me I get a concession.

Heading out of here and further west, Dumbarton Road has a mixture of small shops, traditional butchers, hardware, etc and more recent innovations: Tinlink Unisex, Sweeney's Paninis, organicplus. The Glaswegian penchant for silly humour is exemplified by the dry cleaners Partick-Ular (contender for the worst pun with the Duke Sweet in Duke Street, the restaurant Turnip and Enjoy and Glasgow's Miles Batter (a fish and chip shop). A notable establishment has a long-serving display of false teeth and the title 'Glamorous Geggies' with a brass plaque inscribed 'J.P.B. Wood

B.R.I.L.L. Finest cosmetic dentist technician in the world'. Old Glasgow is well represented here. Pubs have their allegiances – the Dolphin (Celtic), the Rosevale (Rangers). There are also signs of gentrification – further west there is a choice of more up-market eateries: the Roastit Bubbly Jock Café (Scots for a roast chicken) and, of course, Velvet Elvis. That is, however, just about the western boundary of fashionable Partick. Further west you have to pass under the urban motorway and, although there are still shops, they begin to peter out. My mission, however, is in search of a different type of retail experience.

Anita Manning's Great Western Auctions has achieved a sort of cult status thanks, largely, to the venerable Anita herself. She took over the auction house over twenty-five years ago and was, reputedly, Scotland's first female auctioneer. Her celebrity, however, and the popularity of auctions in general, is largely due to television exposure on the various antiques programmes. Today, I have come to buy something (a portfolio of antique maps) but there are about 250 people here most of whom buy nothing at all. They are seated in rows of chair (serious buyers seldom sit) and are here, presumably, to catch a sight of Anita, who obligingly wanders around the hall. Auctions are great places for finding almost anything. Today we have a Victorian poster advertising 'the Hide of Chummy, the extraordinary Elephant and other Waxworx', a Wheatstone concertina, a theatre bill signed by Sir Harry Lauder and sundry other items of interest.

I have ventured beyond the trendy part of the West End. If I head to the other end of Dumbarton Road, however, I come to Kelvingrove museum and the meeting of Argyle Street and Sauchiehall Street, these two mighty streets joined by Radnor Street, the shortest street in Glasgow. This area, around the top third of Argyle Street, is the northern part of Finnieston. Old grey sandstone tenements line the street and there are shops and bars as there always have been, but this traditional working class stretch of road has seen a radical revival in recent years and is now undoubtedly fashionable Glasgow. So fashionable, in fact, that *The Times* recently selected it as one of the 'hippest' places to live in the country. Nearly all the traditional pubs of the top part of Argyle Street have been converted to fashionable bars or restaurants: the Crabshakk, Porter & Rye, Pickled Ginger and the Gannet, which opened in 2013 and has won numerous awards for its quality Scottish food influenced by the west coast of Scotland and the Hebrides.

At the top end of Argyle Street, however, I am in a cosy bar bistro called The 78 (the theme is musical, after old gramophone records) to meet Sylvia Allen. Sylvia has eked a living from her art for years and her work is in demand. Her painting style is colourful and impressionistic. She paints still life with flowers and some country landscapes, but her best work features Glasgow and, although it might seem hard to believe, she puts oodles of colour into the greyness of city street scenes. She also has a remarkable technique that injects movement into her cityscapes. Her best work seems to draw you into to the scene. I imagine it as I imagine, say, Buchanan Street

at dusk; the lights of the shops and the shoppers and pubgoers min-
gling. She exhibits at the Billcliffe Gallery, founded by Roger
Billcliffe, who is a noted curator, art historian, authority on Charles
Rennie Mackintosh and promoter of Scottish art in general.

After a couple of beers, Sylvia takes me to her flat around the
corner in St Vincent Crescent. This serpentine, late classical terrace
is one of the finest of its type in the country but, for many years,
was neglected and run down perhaps because of its location, away
from the fashionable west end. It is now the centre of a conservation area. Sylvia's flat is beautifully decorated and designed. It
mostly serves as a gallery for her work and it is a little haven of fine
Glasgow art.

GREAT WESTERN ROAD

Great Western Road is exceedingly long, leading from Queen's
Cross all the way to the outskirts of the city. The bottom end is a
motley collection of shops selling fruit and veg, beds, motorcycles,
etc, but one small premise stands out. This is the outlet for
Timorous Beasties, an interior design outfit founded in 1990 by Ali
McAuley and Paul Simmons, graduates of Glasgow School of Art.
In 2004 they scandalously released their Glasgow Toile, a fabric
wallpaper that inverted the traditional pastoral idylls to feature an
altogether set of city scenes: The Necropolis, a junkie shooting up,
the Armadillo, a ned peeing from a park bench, tower blocks,
teenage mums with prams, etc. They still sell that and a range of
other off-the-wall designs. You can buy a roll of wallpaper here for
over £1000. Honest.[12]

Continuing on, you cross the bridge over the Kelvin. Kelvin
Bridge itself was constructed in 1891, but old photos show that
there were once two bridges here, one winding through the arches
of the other. Further on, two main features of Great Western Road
are churches on either side of the road. Both have been adapted to
different uses. On the right, Lansdowne Church is a successful
theatre; on the left what was the old Kelvinside Parish Church has
become Oran Mor, Colin Beattie's flagship enterprise. It is noted
for two fantastic initiatives. Firstly, it is festooned with epic murals
painted by Alasdair Gray. Alasdair took on the commission for, as
he put, the average wage of a skilled artisan. Secondly, it also features theatre with its lunchtime series called 'a play, a pie and a

pint', founded in 2004 by Dave MacLennan, an old-time associate of the Citizen's Theatre.

Across the road from the Oran Mor is the Botanic Garden. Not as grand or as well funded as its counterpart in Edinburgh, it grew from a similar inclination – that of wealthy merchants to import exotic plants, either out of scientific curiosity, or to display their wealth. This is still a favourite spot for Glaswegians to relax. Its main feature is the Kibble Palace – a vast glasshouse actually built for someone's garden. John Kibble was a Victorian photographer and scientist and an eccentric who cycled across Loch Lomond on a floating bicycle. He sold the 'palace' to the Botanic Garden in 1871 and it was re-assembled there in 1873. Various events have taken place there over the years including the inauguration of Rectors of Glasgow University. The evangelists Moody and Sankey appeared there and it was reckoned that there was an attendance of 25,000.

You can still find a trace within the Garden of the ruined platforms of old Botanic Garden Railway Station. Built of red brick with two golden domes shaped like onions in the Russian style, the station building itself was a notable landmark until it was destroyed by fire in 1970 having been variously a café, a nightclub and a plumber's shop.

Further on we come to Cooper's Corner. Cooper's were a major grocery chain last century and their store, with its large clock tower and a cupola stands on this corner. The name is also inscribed in brass on the pavement. This is now a restaurant, but it reminds us

that this once was, and still is, a residential area – a fairly posh one, the local off licence is called Valhalla's Goat, for goodness sake. Dowanhill is to the left and Kelvinside to the right. A Kelvinside accent is often ridiculed in Glasgow as meaning that the possessor is irredeemably posh and their speech anglified. In Edinburgh, Morningside is the equivalent. A common joke is that, in Kelvinside and Morningside, sex is what you get your coal in. There are town-houses and flats here too, some very grand. Notable terraces along Great Western Road include Thomson's Great Western Terrace and the more delicate Grosvenor Terrace by John Thomas Rochead. The classic Venetian style is quite unlike a lot of the architect's other work which includes the phallic monolith of the Wallace Monument and the bulky monument to Duncan Ban McIntyre at Dalmally. There are substantial Victorian and Edwardian villas around here too very few of which are still individual residences. One of the best known is Stoneleigh built in the Elizabethan style for the stockbro-ker Joseph Turner in 1900 with a lavish art nouveau interior. I check it out. An apartment in the building would set you back about £700,000 smackers.

WAY OUT WEST

As you head past the top of Great Western the house numbers seem to accelerate into recent history: 1970, 1980, 1990... Continuing on would take to the fashionable suburbs of suburbs of Milngavie, Bearsden, but further on there are the precursors to the mountains, the Whangie and Craigmore where climbers tested their tackety boots before heading further afield: Ben Lomond, the Cobbler, Glencoe perhaps.

One saving grace of Glasgow, it has been said, is that it is very easy to get out off. From the twenties and thirties onwards, young people began to form cycling and rambling clubs and escaped from the dirt and grime of the industrial city to the hills and countryside. From the thirties onwards a club formed originally of workers from the shipyards and docks, the Creagh Dhu, developed an almost leg-endary reputation for not just their climbing but associated shenanagans.[13]

During the Depression, the hills were often a retreat from un-employment and poverty, but after the war, drinking and singing, as well as climbing, were said to be part of their stock in trade. Davy

Clark was a songwriter from Drymen just north of Glasgow. One of his songs remains eternally popular, *The Bar-room Mountaineers*:

> In Drymen town so fair and fine,
> There is a shop that sells good wine,
> It's full of wine and halves and beers,
> And so are the Bar-room mountaineers...
>
> We're the Bar-room mountaineers,
> We've never ever climbed a hill,
> And hope to Christ we never will,
> But we can always drink our fill,
> We're the Bar-room mountaineers.[14]

But is it one of Clark's songs? Other versions replace Drymen with Drummond or other names and the mountaineer Denis Gray insists it is an English production.

On the road to Drymen, the Carbeth Inn is an old coaching inn just north of Glasgow and in the woods and hills around lives a special community in a variety of green huts. These date back to just after the First World War, when the local landowner granted camping rights to returning soldiers. The huts, just about walkable from the city, were regarded as a healthy retreat from industrial Clydeside by generations of families. During the Second World War, they also served as a refuge from the blitz in Clydebank and it is possible to reach the huts from there by walking over the Kilpatrick Hills. The outdoor movement in Glasgow has always been associated with the socialist movement opposed to the landowners in the region and it has been necessary more than once for the people to fight for their right to these dwellings. In the recent past the owner of the area radically increased rents as, it was presumed, an attempt to chase the hutters away and release the land for property development. This developed into a small war, with some huts subject to arson attacks. In 2013, fortunately, a buy-out was arranged with the hutter's community paying £2m for the land. They are still there, enjoying their retreat from modern-day Glasgow.

Sadly, the climbing grounds of the Whangie and Craigmore nearby are mostly neglected these days in favour of (groan) indoor climbing walls. But many young Glaswegians still venture to the mountains, taking initial tentative steps out of the city then heading further afield.

Head for the Hills

Head for the hills:
sod-soaked heather and chossy crags,
leaking boots and frosted sleeping bags.
Howffs neath overhanging boulders,
rucksack-creased aching shoulders.

One day you will stand
on the sugar-cubed summit
of Schichallion and traverse
the saw-toothed band
of the Black Cuillin.

Head for the hills!

When I was eighteen, I wanted to be away from Glasgow, so I took a boat up to Shetland to get a job – first at the docks then in a fish processing factory. Many of my friends were there also, so there was a fair Glaswegian community in the far north of Scotland as there was, about the same time, on the west coast employed building oil rigs. Glaswegians have travelled all over the world and integrated with many different communities. I imagined a story, however, about one who didn't.

The End of the World

It wis 1972. Ah wis a right wee fly man. Ah wis on the broo an ah got the boat up tae Shetland tae try an get a job. It wis OK. Ah got a room up a close by the Queens Hotel – hingin right ower the water, it wis. An ah wis workin at the fish processing plant ower on Bressay. Ah ate fish every day. They'd gie you great big juicy mackerels fir nothing. The Shetlanders widnae eat it cause it wis a scavenger an a dirty fish – as faur as they were concerned.

Bressay wis a wee island opposite the harbour. They say that there were sae many steam trawlers in the auld days that you could walk right on tae the island ower the boats. You've gottae get on a wee motor boat noo but.

Ah wis workin on the fishmeal. Yid queue up in the mornin at the dock to see if yid be taken on like, an then, as lang as you wis, yid go ower tae the island an yid, like as no, hiv tae climb up the side o a big boat. Ower on the island there wis a sort o factory. It sed

QUALITY PROMOTES CONTINUITY

in big letters ower the door. Yid either hiv tae load the fishmeal or boxes o frozen fish on tae palettes tae be pit on the ship. You could go in the hold fir mair money if you wanted. But it wisnae worth it. You could get ban-jaxed wi one o the sacks if the sling broke. Pit the kibosh on yir paycheck that wid.

The fishmeal wis awfy stuff but. Wid get in yir eyes an up yir nose. An you couldnae wash it aff. You wir awways mingin. An the sacks wid tear wee holes in yir hauns an aw.

Every night, when you wir loused, yid hit the toon. Some o the places widnae let you in if you wir off the fish, like. I'd usually go tae the Marlax or the Thule Bar doon by the docks. Thule wis wit the Romans used tae caw the islands. Ultima Thule they'd say. It meant

THE END O THE WORLD

cause they thought it wis. Ah jist cawed it the Tooly.

The Tooly wisnae like an ordinary pub. It wis aw made o wood. Doonstairs wisnae up tae much. The seats wir aw cut open an bits o sodden foam rubber stuck oot. Auld men off the fishin boats hung aboot there, their faces hingin. An some foreign sailors. Ah couldnae folly the sailors at aw. Ah couldnae folly the locals either. Ah jist keeps masell tae masell. Geez, it wis a right fuckin dump, efter aw.

Anyway, there wis a upstairs bit an aw. You got tae it up an ootside staircase, like a fire escape. Ah went up there one night. Aw ah saw wis these wimmen, aw sittin roon one wall. An these wir seriously fuckin big lassies, set tae go a few roons wi Mick McManus, like as no. Aw done up tae the nines an reekin o mascara an lipstick. You didnae hiv tae be fuckin Albert Einstein tae see that they werenae there fir a fuckin sewin bee, if you know whit ah mean.

Ah went up tae the bar. There wir a whole load o boys aff the boats an the fish factory. Aw locals. They were staunin at the bar drinkin hauf an haufs, playin pocket billiards an eyeing up these lassies. Geez, ah ses tae one o them, ah know it's cauld up here, but yous must be fuckin desperate.

Then the one next tae me sed something tae me ah couldnae folly. They aw talk funny up there. Fir example, they used tae caw me

PEERIE MON

Come on, mate, ah ses, pointing oot one o the lassies that ah thought ah'd seen at the filleting or somewhere. Did ye haul her up frae the beach, eh. He looked at me a bit funny.

Ah had a slug o ma pint. Are those fuckin ears or fucking haunlebars or whit, ah sed.

Next thing, the biggest o the lot o them comes ower. Ah sees that she's aulder than the rest, massive, she wis, an stinkin o gin. Is this

THE SOOTH MOOTH

she ses tae her pal.

Well, ah collected ma pay when ah got oot the hospital an high tailed it back hame. Ah've nevir bin able tae lift onything heavy wi ma right haun since, but ah still like the mackerel, fried like, wi a wee bit o butter an pepper.

CITZ, THE CLUTHA, COINCIDENCES AND CONCLUSIONS

To walk is to lack a place
(Michel de Certeau)

You can never be lost if you don't care where you are
(Dennis the Menace)

I am coming to the end of my excursion around Glasgow and my page allocation for this book and I am well aware that I have only covered a fraction of this great, complex, puzzling and exhilarating city. I intend to end much were I started, on the banks of the Clyde. So, what are the lessons I have learned from my excursions?

Requiem

I took Glasgow for a stroll,
chewed it up, spat it out,
tried to lose it in a library,
introduced it to my friends,
knocked it around a bit,
gingerly took it to bed.

I reconstructed Glasgow from
the finger feel of old photos,
frothy patterns on a pint glass,
a rusty gramophone needle,
myths incarcerated in museums,
a book falling open at the same page.
Yet from a mince of memories,
the soles of well-worn shoes,
subway scents and tenement grit,
words of smoke and stone,
Glasgow, in fact,
reconstructed me.

When I was a lad, Glasgow Corporation ran the city and the titular head was the Lord Provost (the very same as eulogised by the Macdonald family). Glasgow Corporation was known for its buses, with their distinctive orange and green livery (now the multinational First runs the buses). In 1975, the Corporation became a Council and it is now Glasgow City Council – or, as Wikipedia would have it, Comhairle Bailie Ghlaschu, in Gaelic, or *Glasga Ceetie Cooncil* (honestly) in Scots.

Muscled up in the stern workhouses of Glasgow Victorian schools, starched libraries and invigorating public parks, municipality was a dubious gift, but at least its paternalist ideology was reasonably transparent. The current prevailing administration in Glasgow is a much more slippery customer. It even has various names. In 2007, Glasgow City Council set up a charitable trust called Culture and Sport Glasgow. In 2010, it was rebranded as Glasgow Life. Today, just about any enquiry regarding activities in Glasgow goes through a central hub

However, if there is one lesson that every citizen of Glasgow or visitor to the city must eventually learn about the powers-that-be, it is that there is no task, no matter how large or small – from unblocking a drain to demolishing a tower block, from running a library to a multi-million pound revamp of a museum – THAT THEY CANNOT FUCK UP.

Glasgow is undoubtedly a dysfunctional city, two-handed, caught between potent mythologies of destruction and regeneration. In the words of Miles Glendinning, '[a] city in its contradictory and often chaotic essence'[15] or according to Johnny Rodger,'[a] city seeking after 'boom' without any analysis of its relation to 'bust'.[16]

If the city were falling around their heads, the Glasgow people would endure and that is what – the city falling around the heads of the citizens – I am about to encounter shortly.

The Citizen's Theatre, or the Citz, stands pretty much alone now, having seen everything else in this area of the Gorbals demolished around it. Originally it was the Princess Royal Theatre but took its new name in 1945 from the company of actors, formed by the Scottish playwright James Bridie, that came to repertory there. It has a more impressive interior than exterior with a succession of quite gauche statues of elephants, muses and Shakespeare and Burns.

In the seventies, directed by Giles Havergal, it was determinedly international. Following an agenda that was specifically not Scottish; local or provincial. This attracted both praise and condemnation. It was also experimental and controversial. I was here constantly, precipitously perched in the cheap seats in the Gods, but I don't specifically remember the naked Hamlet or Dracula in drag. I do remember an experimental production of Macbeth for which the stage was painted in purple and yellow squares, the actors climbed over a wall to come on stage, and the head of Macbeth was revealed at the denouement, to the general hilarity of the audience, to be the head of a mop. And there was lots of Ibsen and Chekhov – Chekhov played in the traditional rather than the Stanislavskian manner with interminable chirping birds (and in which the gunshot off-stage was the highlight of the production). I remember the stage resplendent in corpses at the end of *The Duchess of Malfi*. And Brecht – great jazzy in-yer-face Brecht with Kurt Weill songs, twangy piano and giant alienating projected slides.

Tonight, however, is the premiere of the stage version of Alasdair Gray's *Lanark*[17] – an immense work in three acts that skips from 1950s Glasgow to the fictional dystopian city of Unthank, also recognisably a version of Glasgow. At the end of the play, as in the novel, the eponymous hero, Lanark, is left to die in the Necropolis, overlooking the cathedral and the Royal Infirmary, as Unthank/ Glasgow destroys itself in a great apocalyse.

In 1990, I was in taking part in a film for BBC Scotland based on my book about Glasgow, *Phantom Village*. It was a bitterly cold winter's day and the last scene was at night on the Necropolis re-enacting a part of the scene from *Lanark*. Glad to get out of the cold, I ran down to the Scotia and bumped into Alasdair Gray himself (I had corresponded with him but never met him in the flesh). That is one coincidence but leads to another, unfortunate, coincidence – for Alasdair is not at the opening of the play, he is, in fact, back overlooking the Necropolis, in the Royal Infirmary, recovering from a near fatal fall outside his flat. This, and other coincidences, connections and memories of Glasgow and Glasgow folk buzz through my head on this night.

A couple of days later, I'm just up the road at the Clutha again, for the launch of Stuart Murray's new book of drawings, *Glaswegians*. Well, I *am* there, eventually, but inconveniently late. Inconvenient because I actually have the books. But there has been a Scotland match at Hampden and a boy band at the Hydro, so I spent about three hours on the motorway.

Nevertheless, the launch goes as well as we can hope, especially since we have a heckler (at a book launch!). She is escorted from the premises by the bar staff, books are sold and we enjoy a quintessentially Glasgow night and raise some money for the Clutha Trust – and then over to the Scotia for a slow pint with some friends to finish where I started.

In Glasgow much is the same and much is different. The Duke of Wellington is still abroad, the iconography of Irn Bru, Big T and Tunnock's Teacakes is omnipresent, the ghosts of witches and businessmen still parade the Sarry Heid and the vaults of Central Station. The Sighthill Stone Circle pushes itself determinedly through the turf but the dust of Red Road has dispersed and settled. You can still order boquerones, sobrassada, pau vadu, bhel puri, marag dubh, Chakhokhbili, Tzimes and Stornoway black pudding (at least until the next restaurant trend). A whole constellation of allegorical figures – cherubs, goddesses, Mungos, Mercuries – look down on the goings-on of the citizens and, if you listen carefully, there is the satisfied murmuring of councillors (or artists) on the make. Listen even more carefully and you may hear Glasgow grandstanding – contemplating the next great magnificent project that will not work.

Things have changed, however. There has been reinventing, there has been repurposing. Buildings come and go. The Old College Bar is no longer the oldest pub in Glasgow, the whole block is to be demolished, following the Greyfriars Monastery on the same site and the University across the road some centuries ago. But Colin Beattie, the perennial entrepreneur, has promised to rebuild it 'bigger and better'. Sundry bars and shops I have recorded have changed their identity in one way or the other and, I realise, some of the photographs I have taken are now historical.

There are many ways to create a city: build it, burn it down, build it, demolish it, build it, regenerate it, build it… Glasgow has gone through these cycles many times and will probably continue to do so.

Yet there is a truism in the rather naff pink slogan now adorning buildings, bridges and bikes: 'People Make Glasgow'. The city has seen bad days, poverty, depression, unemployment and astonishing acts of corporate vandalism, but despite of (or because of) this the people of Glasgow are a happy bunch, with a coruscating sense of humour and a line in lively banter. They make Glasgow what it is.

In this city of contradictions, stability and change, a city obsessed with the superlative rather than the comparative, a city in which the predominant language is hyperbole, a city where regeneration is always on the agenda, it is sometimes the littlest things that deserve the most notice. One thing remains constant and it is to be found only a few yards away, amongst some stones on the banks of the Clyde, flowing through a culvert – the Molendinar. It trickles along steadily, taking no liberties but giving no quarter, poking its head into the open occasionally but always continuing, staunch in its purpose. It has done so for centuries and will not easily be diverted from its course, despite the busy thundering of the ever-shifting city around it. It is the perfect metaphor for the pure and enduring spirit of Glasgow and its people.[18]

Molendinar

Flow sweetly, little burn,
Hoping for some light on the way.
Let the city hug you tight,
For soon you will be free.

Notes

1. I have an unusual memory of this pub. I was amazingly leading the pub quiz when the last round turned out to be on ABBA songs. Well, I almost got one right (but the shepherd boy was *not* called Ivanhoe). We finished third.
2. Regarding Ord see Ian Spring, 'Robert Ford and John Ord: two Glasgow song collectors', in *Hamish Henderson and Scottish Folk Song* (Edinburgh: Hog's Back Press, 2014).
3. Frank Kuppner, *A Very Quiet Street* (Edinburgh: Polygon, 1989).
4. Brian Moore, *The Great Victorian Collection* (London Jonathan Cape, 1975).
5. BBC *Hairy Bikers' Best of British Series 2*: 5. Food and the Empire. First shown: 6.30pm 5 April 2013. Cited https://en.wikipedia.org/wiki/Chicken_tikka_masala#Origins
6. The Park features as a gay cruising ground in Louise Welsh, *The Cutting Room* (Edinburgh: Canongate, 2011).
7. Hugo Gifford (not Hugo Gifford the wizard who appears in Scott's *Marmion*) was the brother of Douglas Gifford, the noted Scottish academic. Andrew Cruikshank, the veteran Scottish actor, was also involved with the Strathclyde Theatre Group.
8. 'Museums in Britain: bouquets and brickbats', *The Burlington Magazine* (November 2007). See also Stephen Dawber, 'Blairism on the Walls at Kelvingrove' *Variant*, 27 (Winter, 2006) and David Bell, 'Tales From a River Bank: bullying, the Arts, and the production of museum space', *Variant*, 42 (Winter, 2011),
9. Amongst others, Alasdair Gray, who had been employed by Elspeth King as Glasgow artist/recorder, made an impassioned plea for her retention, but to no avail. This, and other useful material, can be found on the Workers City website http://www.workerscity.org.
10. William McIlvanney, *Laidlaw* (London: Hodder and Stoughton, 1977).
11. See Iain Crichton Smith, *Collected Poems* (Manchester: Carcanet, 1995).
12. See http://www.timorousbeasties.com. The name refers to a Burns poem.
13. See Ian Spring, 'Scottish Mountaineering Songs', in *Hamish Henderson and Scottish Folk Song* (Edinburgh: Hog's Back Press, 2014).
14. The noted climber and climbing historian, Dennis Gray, provided me with additional information regarding this song.
15. See Miles Glendinning, *Scottish Architecture* (London: Thames & Hudson, 2004).
16. See Johnny Rodger, *Contemporary Glasgow: the Architecture of the 1990s* (Edinburgh: The Rutland Press, 1999).
17. The play was written by one of Scotland's premier playwrights, David Greig.
18. A poem of 1832 titled 'Ode to the Molendinar' describes it thus: '...watch thine ever-changing hues/ And breathe the scents thy waves diffuse/ Roll on, with murky billows roll/ Juice of the mud-cart and the coal.' Quoted in John Moore, *Glasgow: Mapping the City* (Edinburgh: Birlinn, 2015).

WORKS CONSULTED

Freddy Anderson, *At Glasgow Cross and Other Poems* (Glasgow: Clydeside Press, 1987).

Thomas Annan, *Old Closes and Streets of Glasgow* (Glasgow: James MacLehose and Sons, 1900).

Nicola Balkind (ed.), *World Film Locations: Glasgow* (Bristol: Intellect Books, 2013).

William Barr, *Glaswegiana* (Glasgow: Vista, 1973).

W.G. Beaton, *Glasgow Our City: Yesterday, Today and Tomorrow* (Glasgow: Corporation of Glasgow Education Department, 1957).

Harry Bell, *Glasgow's Secret Geometry* (Glasgow: Leyline, 1993).

Norman M. Bett, *Civic Bronze* (Edinburgh: Scotland's Cultural Heritage, 1983).

Judith Bowers, *Lost Theatre: the Story of the Britannia Music Hall* (Edinburgh: Birlinn, 2014).

Allan Brown, *The Glasgow Smile* (Edinburgh: Birlinn, 2013).

Jenny Brownrigg, *Romantic Vanguard* (Glasgow: Royston Road Project, 2002).

Moira Burgess, *Imagining the City: Glasgow in Fiction* (Glendaruel: Argyll Publishers, 1998).

Helen Clark & Elizabeth Carnegie, *She Was Aye Workin': Memories of Tenement Women in Edinburgh and Glasgow* (Oxford: White Cockade, 2003).

James Cowan, *From Glasgow's Treasure Chest* (Glasgow: R.E. Robertson, 1951).

Anthony Cooke, *A History of Drinking: The Scottish Pub Since 1700* (Edinburgh: Edinburgh University Press, 2015).

Carol Craig, *The Tears that Built the Clyde* (Glendaruel: Argyll, 2010).

Tom F. Cunningham *The Diamond's Ace* (Edinburgh: Mainstream, 2001).

Carol Foreman, *Glasgow Street Names* (Edinburgh: John Donald, 1997).

Glasgow City Council, *Glasgow's Glasgow: the Words and the Stones* (Glasgow: The Words and the Stones, 1990).

John Gorevan, *Glasgow Pubs and Publicans* (Glasgow: Tempus, 2002).

Gerry Hassan, *Caledonian Dreaming* (Edinburgh: Luath, 2014).

Alison Irvine, *This Road is Red* (Edinburgh: Luath, 2011).

Alison Irvine, Mitch Miller & Chris Leslie, *Nothing is Lost* (Glasgow: Freight Books, 2015).

Peter Kearney, *The Glasgow Cludgie* (Glasgow: People's Publications, 1985).

G. Keelie, *The Wee Glasgow Facts Book* (Glasgow: Straight Line Publishing, 1989).

James Kelman, *Some Recent Attacks: Essays Cultural & Political* (Stirling: AK Press, 1992).

David Kemp, *Glasgow 1990: the True Story behind the Hype* (Glasgow: Famedram, 1990).

Rudolph Kenna & Anthony Mooney, *People's Palaces* (Edinburgh: Paul Harris, 1983).

Rudolph Kenna & Ian Sutherland, *The Bevvy* (Glasgow: Clutha Books, 2000).

Rudolph Kenna & Ian Sutherland, *They Belonged to Glasgow* (Glasgow: Clutha Books, 1996).

Sarah Lowndes, *Social Sculpture: the Rise of the Glasgow Arts Scene* (Glasgow: Stopstop, 2010).

Kevin McCarra & Hamish Whyte (ed.) *A Glasgow Collection: Essays in Honour of Joe Fisher* (Glasgow: Glasgow City Libraries, 1990).

Charles McKean, David Walker & Frank Walker, *Central Glasgow: an Illustrated Architectural Guide* (Edinburgh: Mainstream, 1989).

Ray McKenzie, *Public Sculpture of Glasgow* (Liverpool: Liverpool University Press, 2002).

Farquhar McLay, *The Reckoning* (Glasgow: Clydeside Press, 1990).

Nuala McNaughton, *Barrowland* (Edinburgh: Mainstream Publishing, 2013).

Michael Meaghan, *Glasgow Central* (Stroud: Amberley, 2013).

Mitchell Miller & Johnny Rodger, *The Red Cockatoo: James Kelman and the Art of Commitment* (Sandstone, 2011).

Kate Molleson et al, *Dear Green Sounds* (Glasgow: Waverley Books, 2015).

John Moore, *Glasgow: Mapping the City* (Edinburgh: Birlinn, 2015).

Michael Munro, *The Complete Patter* (Edinburgh: Birlinn, 2001).

Stuart Murray, *Glaswegians* (Edinburgh: Hog's Back Press, 2015).

Reuben Paris & Graham Fulton, *Pub Dogs of Glasgow* (Glasgow: Freight Books, 2014).

Eddie Perrett, *The Magic of the Gorbals* (privately published, 1990).

Brian Reilly, *Dennistoun Waverley FC* (Glasgow, privately printed, 2014).

Craig Richardson *Scottish Art since 1960: Historical Reflections and Contemporary Overviews* (Farnham: Ashgate, 2011).

John Robertson & Rachel Pateman, *Sauchiehall Street* (Glasgow: The Glasgow File, 1987).

Johnny Rodger, *Contemporary Glasgow: the Architecture of the 1990s* (Edinburgh: The Rutland Press, 1999).

Johnny Rodger, *The Hero Building: an Architecture of Scottish National*

Identity (London: Routledge, 2015).

Peter Ross, *Daunderlust* (Dingwall: Sandstone Press, 2014).

Adrian Searle & David Barbour, *Look Up Glasgow* (Glasgow: Freight Books, 2013).

Ronald Smith, *The Gorbals: Historical Guide and Heritage Walk* (Glasgow: Glasgow City Council, 1995).

Ian Spring, *Phantom Village: the Myth of the New Glasgow* (Edinburgh: Polygon, 1990).

Gavin Stamp, *Alexander 'Greek' Thomson* (Glasgow: Lawrence King Publishing, 1999).

Dan Sweeney, *Shadows of the City: Glasgow's Lost Mansions and Houses* (Windan Press, 2013).

Gordon Urquhart *Along Great Western Road: an Illustrated History of Glasgow's West End* (Ochiltree: Stenlake, 2000).

Visit Scotland, Set in Scotland: *a Film Fan's Odyssey* (Edinburgh: Visit Scotland, 2015).

Frank Worsdall, *The City that Disappeared* (Glasgow: Richard Drew, 1981).

Frank Worsdall, *The Glasgow Tenement: a Way of Life* (Glasgow: W.&R. Chambers, 1981).

Andrew McLaren Young & A.M. Doak (ed.), *Glasgow at a Glance* (Glasgow: Collins, 1965).

GLOSSARY

Aye	Aye, or Ay, means either yes or ever or always.
Batter	To be out on the batter means to seriously indulge in strong drink.
Bam	Or bampot. A nutcase.
Bawheid	A mild insult to someone suggesting they're not too smart.
Bell	To be on the bell means to buy a round of drinks.
Blooter	In football, a blooter is a big kick without much direction or objective.
Bluenose	A Rangers supporter.
Braw	Good.
Bunnet	Or Bunnit. A flat cap for a man.
Buroo	Or Broo. The labour exchange or social security office.
Cludgie	A toilet.
Crouse	Bold.
Daundle	To bounce a baby or child on the knee.
Dizzie	To give someone a dizzie is to stand them up on a date.
Droukit	Soaked.
Eskabibble	Or eskibibble. An expression that doesn't mean anything much.
Fan-dabbie-dozie	Excellent.
Fly	Clever (too clever).
Gaeltachd	Gaelic speaking part of Scotland.
Gallus	Someone who is gallus is confident or bold.
Ginger	Any lemonade or fizzy drink.
Glaikit	Stupid.
Haud the jaiket	To hold someone's jacket suggests they are going to fight.
Hauf n hauf	A half pint of heavy beer and a whisky.
Heehaw	Nothing.
Hingie	To have a hingie is to lean on a window sill in order to observe or talk to people on the street.
Howff	A small house, often used to refer to a pub.
Hun	A Rangers supporter.
Jigging	Dancing (in general).

Jimmy	A colloquial expression used to address a stranger.
Lannie	Colloquial name for Lanliq, a fortified wine.
Louse	To be loused is to be freed from work.
Lum	A chimney.
Ménage	Pronounced 'minodge'. A ménage was a local weekly saving scheme.
Messages	Shopping.
Minging	Smelly.
Papped oot	Thrown out.
Patter	Glasgow patois.
Poke	A bag.
Polis	Police. The expression 'murder polis' is used hyperbolically for a fuss.
Puggie	Fruit machine.
Schlammy	Muddy.
Scliff	To shuffle one's feet or to rub shoes on the ground.
Scunner	To take a scunner to something is to strongly dislike it.
Shop	Used colloquially for a public house.
Sook	Suck.
Stooshie	A fuss.
Swally	To have a swally is to have (usually more than one) drink.
Tawse	A belt for punishment in school.
Tickety-boo	Just fine.
Tim	A Celtic supporter or, more generally, a Roman Catholic.
Toe-ender	A shot at football with the toe of the boot.
Wean	A child.
Wee man	Men in Glasgow are often wee (small) but some of them are wee hard men. The expression of suprise or disbelief, 'in the name of the wee man', I take to be a folk reference to the devil.
Winch	Court in a romantic sense.
Wheesht	Be quiet.

THE PHOTOGRAPHS

ACKNOWLEDGEMENTS

Thanks to all those listed below who have accompanied me, physically and mentally, on my journey through this Glasgow, but special thanks to Stuart Murray who started the journey and with whom I have walked some mighty miles and to Willie Gallacher, whose walking legs have mostly deserted him these days but who remains a great source of Glasgow lore, and to John Cowan and Chris Wellington who were with me for my first Glasgow book and may yet make it to the next!

Peter Finch 'invented' this genre and I am grateful to him and all the staff at Seren for the opportunity to try my hand at it.

Dave Allan
Sylvia Allen
Gary Barton
Douglas Bennie
Graham Blaikie
Jenny Brownrigg
Tom Butler
John Cowan
Carol Craig
Donald Dalgleish
Malcolm Dickson
Fred Freeman
Peter Finch
Willie Gallacher
Alasdair Gray
Neil Gray
Margaret Guthrie
Mima Hart
Gerry Hassan
John Landsburgh
Michael McVeigh
Ranald MacColl
Colin McKay
Colin Macfarlane
Mitch Miller
Stuart Murray
Johnny Rodger
Calum Smith
May Miles Thomas
Stan Walsingham
Mike Wallace
Ciona Watson
Chris Wellington
Jean Rafferty
Chris Wellington
Mick West

THE AUTHOR

Ian Spring was born in Glasgow in 1955 and had a career in higher education in various institutions in the United Kingdom. He writes about Scottish cultural history, folk song and has also been responsible for some fiction, including detective stories under a pseudonym. He is currently working on a major cultural history of modern Scotland – *Scotland Seen and Imagined*.

INDEX